JUNIOR LEAGUE OF PASADENA, INC.

CALIFORNIA SIZZLES

Easy and Distinctive Recipes for a Vibrant Lifestyle

The Junior League of Pasadena, Inc., is an organization of women committed to promoting voluntarism and improving the community through the effective action and leadership of trained volunteers. Its purpose is exclusively educational and charitable.

The Junior League truly acts as a bridge to the community. In its 66 years, the League has provided effective volunteer service and financial support to the community through projects involving health, education, the arts and recreation, children's welfare, and women's issues. The Junior League of Pasadena is supported by thirteen hundred members, corporations, foundations, and community friends. Proceeds from *California Sizzles* will insure our continued support of vital community programs.

Photography by Andrew Taylor
Additional Photography by Benson Ng
Cover by Kerry Cervenka, Doris Jew, and Bryce Reynolds
Design by Doris Jew and Bryce Reynolds
Additional Design by Evelyn Esaki and Yvette Harris
Map Illustration by Frances Tann
Written Text by Marilyn Langsdorf
Copyright © 1992 by The Junior League of Pasadena, Inc.
    and Art Center College of Design,
First Edition
First Printing: October 1992
Printed in the United States of America by Wimmer Brothers
    Memphis, Tennessee
The Junior League of Pasadena, Inc.
149 South Madison Avenue
Pasadena, California 91101
Library of Congress Catalog Card Number: 91-078331
ISBN: 0-9632089-1-8

Introduction

From the fireworks exploding across the summer skies at the Hollywood Bowl to the sun sparkling on the blue-green waters of Malibu, Southern California sizzles with energy and excitement. Known throughout the world for its carefree outdoor lifestyle, Southern California is a land of refreshing contrasts, of distinguished art museums and roller blading at Venice Beach, of Hollywood glitz, Rodeo Drive glamour, and mountain biking in the clear air of the San Gabriels.

Join us for a taste of the distinctive flavors of trend-setting Southern California. Whether uptown and elegant or designed for picnic basket or poolside barbecue, these carefully selected recipes are as fresh and original as the regions they represent. The emphasis is on ease of preparation and simple, yet imaginative dishes in keeping with an active, healthy lifestyle.

Colorful photographs of favorite getaway locations enhance the California Lifestyles section, which provides a close-up look at that charming, off-beat California spirit. Designed for locals and visitors alike, this section includes menus to suit the highlighted location or event, such as the Tournament of Roses Parade, a mountain picnic on a starry night, or a winter outing to Palm Springs.

Take a flavorful trip to one of the sunniest places on earth. Discover for yourself how Southern California sizzles!

Contents

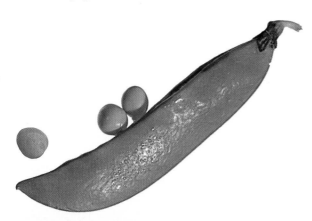

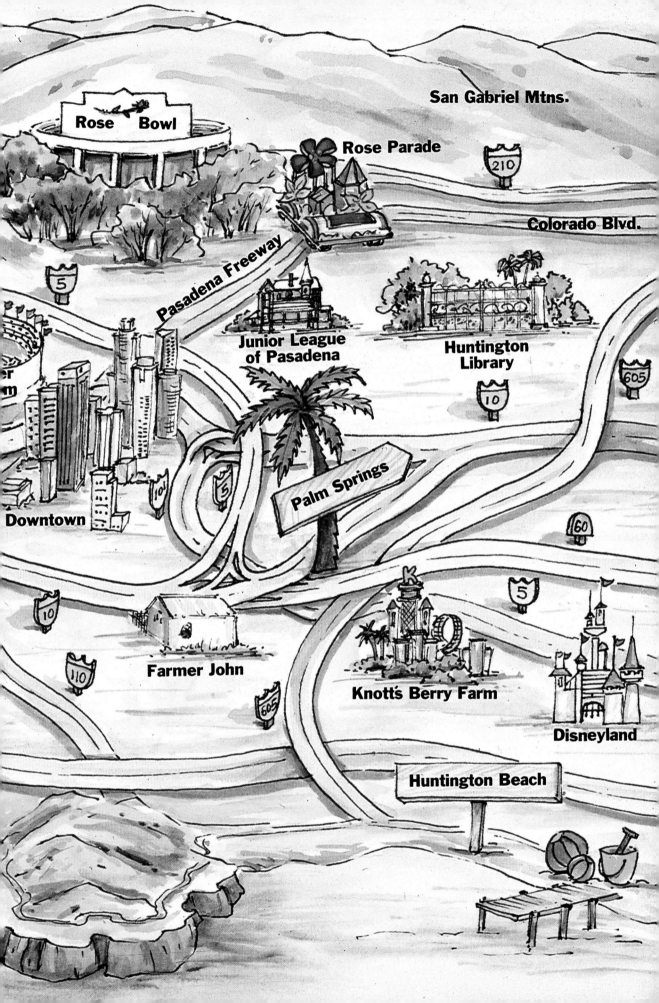

The Junior League of Pasadena, Inc. gratefully acknowledges the generous support of the following businesses and organizations.

Farmers Market

The Los Angeles Dodgers

Farmer John Meats

Bristol Farms Cook 'N' Things

Acknowledgements

The Junior League of Pasadena wishes to thank these friends who contributed to *California Sizzles*.

Harriet Aberle
Susan Aberle
Sheri Syler Adams
Cindy Albrecht
Rebecca Alescardeo
Rebecca Alexander
Tali Brockmiller Arnold
Roberta Arnott
Lynne Ashley
Chris Atkinson
Diane Bach
Janet Bachman
Jill Baran Scott
Janice Bea
Sherry Behrle
Marilyn Belmont
Stephanie Bender
Tricia Berry
Caroline Snyder Blakeslee
Anne Blomstrom
Sally Boynton
Kitty Bridges
Sharon Briffet
Betsy Brown
Laurie Brumeister
Valerie P. Carli
Debbie Carrico
Suki Carson
Joyce Cassel
Joan Cavenah
Julie Coleman
Kerry Cervenka
Susan Chandler
Loretta Clougherty-Dodd
Nancy Cole
Sharon Collins
Amy Colton
Terri Connelly
Susan Coogan
Georgette Cooper
Kathe Cordova
Lyndsey Cotter
Greg Custer
Nadine Danz
Cynthia Dickerson
Susan Hamlin Dixon
Elizabeth S. Downs
Brenda Eberle
Betsy Edwards
Sabrina Espinosa
Joan Fauvre
Jennifer Fedde
Kathy Feely
Doris Ferguson
Zemula Fleming
Jim Folsom
Kandi Franks
Ruth Fuller
Margaret Gagliano
Priscilla Gamb
Robin Garber
DeeAnne Gibbons

Cindy Gilbert
Marcia Good
Helen Gredig
Katy Grey
Mary Grace Gudis
Cari Hall
Nancy Hammond
Mary Hampton
Barbara Harrill
Michael Harter
Helen Harter
Janet Hayward
Tiffany Hegarty
Marguerite Hennacy
Susan Holbrook
Nancy Hornberger
Jill Hotvet
Terry Hynes
Joanne Ibach
Phillis Itjelte
Jennifer Izbicki
Cameron Joy
Bill Garrett Jurgensens
Joan Kennedy
Nancy Kennedy
Shirley Kerins
Sherry Kirchheimer
Catherine Krell
John Lamb
Lisa Laudeman
SueLin Lee
Donna Hoffman Lehmas
Mary Lou Linstedt
Susan Long
Debbie Longenecker
Margie Lowe
Gayle Lowrey
Diane Ma
Sandy Mallory
Robin Maloof
Wendy Hayward Marshall
Kathryn Mayer
Georganne McAdams
Julie McCarthy
Jan McDonnell
Jan McEachern
Mary Ann McGovern
Nancy McGowan
Joan McPherson
Catherine Meek
Linda Mennis
Candice Merrill-Hole
Sharon Molihan
Heidrun Mumper-Drumm
Allen Neelley
Muriel Newell
Marianne Nouskajian
Jane Nyman
Connie Page
Ann Palmer
Nancy Payne
Sara Pelton

Marcia Penido
Andrea Phelps
Patricia Plunkett
Ann Rogers Quadrini
Sharon Ramsey
Sheila Rawlins
Myrna Rea
Eileen White Read
Joy Redmond
Christine Reeder
Suzanne Riepe
Holly Robinson
Pam Rockwell
Pat Romero
Nancy Sapozink
Susanne Schiff
Melissa Schiller
Robin Schlinger
Diane Scott
Susan Scurlock-Weinberger
Nancy Sechrest
Chrisine Shapp
Inez Sharp
Kit Shenk
Teresa Sherman
Peggy Simpson
Loretta Smith
Gerry Soderberg
Betty Southam
Karen Spalding
Candi Sperling
Jayne Staley
Randy Stanislawski
Lindsay Steinblock
Beth Stevens
Karen Stracka
Kathleen Swaidan
Amy Sykes
Andy Taylor
Cathy Taylor
Jasmina Theodore
JoAnn Thompson
Don Tutich
Linda Van der Touw
Katie Verhovek
Andrea Walker
Linda Weber
Betty Wells
Francy Welty
Mary Wheeler
Maureen Wheeler
Phyllis Wilburn
Rita Wilkins
Barbara Williams
Brenda Williams
Julie Wofford
Jan Wolf
Victoria Wray-Greening
Josephine Wrobel
LaVonne Young
Eileen Zimmerman

The Cookbook Committee

Chairman	Terry Clougherty
Marketing Chairman	Susan Reitnouer
Recipe Chairman	Ann Miller
Advisor	Kathleen LeRoy
Recipe Advisor	Chris Benter
Marketing Advisor	Joan Cathcart

Recipe Committee

Recipe Coordinator	Pauline Baerveldt
Menu Coordinator	Linnea Warren
Bread and Breakfast	Bonnie McCreery
Hot and Cold Appetizers	Karen Johnston
Soups, Chilis and Stews	Martha Bowman
Salads	Martha Bowman
Pastas	Sandra Awad and Adrienne Renwick
Poultry	Christy Bakaly
Seafood	Laura Lugar-Beiler
Beef, Lamb and Pork	Beth Fishbein
Vegetables and Rice	Sharon Grosshans
Desserts	Kathleen Bertch and Judy Waldo
Editing/Testing	Marianne Lynch

Marketing Committee

A.B.A. Coordinator	Maureen Nelson
Advertising	Beatrice Hamlin
Art Coordinator	Ann Bussard
Book Production	Tammy Fredrickson
Corporate Sponsors	Susan Fleming
Computer Coordinator	Rita Whitney
Mail Order Coordinator	Joan Thomas
Operations Manager	Lynn Conrad
Promotions	Sue Edmonston
Public Relations	Brooke Larsen Garlock
Sales Materials	Amelia Lamb
Support Materials	Jennifer Hendrix
Treasurer	Kim Daswick
Writer	Marilyn Langsdorf

The Junior League of Pasadena gratefully acknowledges the 1990-1991 Ways and Means Committee:

Jennifer Walston Johnson, Chairman
Kelly Brown
Christl Drewry
Katy Hedrick
C.J. Hole
Cynthia Ison
Pallie Jones
Jeanne Randol
Theresa Sinclair
Their careful research led to the development of this cookbook.

Chapter 1

START
YOUR
ENGINES

Bread and Breakfast Dishes

How do our days start?

By starting our engines,

of course. Here are

bread and breakfast

ideas certain to start your day

off right, California style.

Honey Baked Granola

Much better than the store-bought variety and sure to be a family favorite.

Makes 10-12 cups

½ cup oil
⅔ cup honey
6 cups rolled oats
½ cup sesame seeds
½ cup sunflower seeds
½ cup crushed wheat germ
1 cup sliced almonds
1½ cups natural
  unsweetened coconut
1 tablespoon vanilla
  extract
1 teaspoon ground nutmeg
2 teaspoons ground
  cinnamon
1 cup raisins

1. Preheat oven to 350°. Combine oil and honey. Set aside.

2. Mix all other ingredients, except raisins.

3. Pour honey mixture over and stir. Pour into 9x13-inch pan.

4. Bake for 30 minutes. Stir 3 times. Cool.

5. Add raisins.

Wholesome Banana-Oat Pancakes

The subtle flavor of bananas and buttermilk will keep them coming back for more.

Serves 4-6

¾ cup quick-cooking
  rolled oats
⅔ cup whole wheat flour
½ teaspoon salt
1 teaspoon baking powder
½ teaspoon baking soda
½ teaspoon ground
  nutmeg
1 large egg
¾ cup mashed ripe
  bananas
¾ cup buttermilk
2 tablespoons vegetable oil
½ teaspoon vanilla extract

1. Combine oats, flour, salt, baking powder, baking soda and nutmeg.

2. Beat egg with mashed bananas until blended. Add buttermilk, oil and vanilla. Mix until smooth.

3. Add the dry ingredients to the banana mixture and stir until blended.

4. Heat griddle. Brush griddle lightly with oil. Spoon about ¼ cup of batter, per pancake, onto griddle. Cook until top of pancake is set, about 2 minutes, and flip. Cook until medium brown, about 1½ minutes more.

Note: Serve plain or sprinkle with cinnamon and drizzle with warm maple syrup.

Rose Parade Pancakes

Light as a feather and scrumptious with our homemade Cinnamon Syrup.

Serves 4

1 egg, beaten
1 cup milk
2 tablespoons vegetable oil
1 cup all purpose flour,
    sifted
½ teaspoon salt
2 tablespoons baking
    powder
2 tablespoons sugar

1. Combine egg, milk and oil.

2. Add dry ingredients and beat until smooth. Batter should be thick.

3. Heat griddle. Brush griddle lightly with oil. Spoon about ¼ cup of batter, per pancake, onto griddle. Cook until top of pancake is set and flip. Cook until golden brown.

Cinnamon Syrup

A must with your favorite pancakes.

Makes 2 cups

1 cup sugar
½ cup light corn syrup
¼ cup water
¾ teaspoon cinnamon
½ cup evaporated milk

1. Combine sugar, syrup, water and cinnamon in a saucepan.

2. Bring to a boil and cook 2 minutes, stirring constantly.

3. Cool 15 minutes and add evaporated milk.

Company French Toast

Serves 4

6 eggs, well beaten
⅔ cup orange juice
⅓ cup Grand Marnier
⅓ cup milk
3 tablespoons sugar
¼ teaspoon vanilla extract
¼ teaspoon salt
8 ¾-inch thick slices
    French bread
Melted butter
Powdered sugar

1. Mix eggs, orange juice, Grand Marnier, milk, sugar, vanilla and salt in a bowl.

2. Dip bread into the mix. Coat both sides.

3. Refrigerate overnight. Turn if possible.

4. Cook slowly in melted butter in frying pan, approximately 8 minutes on each side.

5. Sprinkle with powdered sugar and serve.

Crispy French Toast

The cornflakes give this fabulous French toast extra crunch.

Serves 2-4

1 cup milk
4 eggs
1 teaspoon vanilla extract
⅛ teaspoon nutmeg
3 tablespoons sugar
6 1-inch slices sourdough
   or French bread
Cornflakes
Melted butter

1. Combine milk, eggs, vanilla, nutmeg and sugar.

2. Dip bread slices in milk mixture and roll in crushed cornflakes.

3. Put in buttered skillet over low heat and brown 5 minutes on each side.

Note: To serve, butter and sprinkle toast with cinnamon and top with maple syrup.

Baked French Toast with Berries

A make-ahead French toast dressed up with berries.

Serves 8

1 small 8-9 ounce day-old
   loaf of French bread
3 eggs
3 tablespoons sugar
1 teaspoon vanilla extract
2¼ cups milk
½ cup all purpose flour
6 tablespoons dark brown
   sugar, packed
½ teaspoon ground
   cinnamon
¼ cup butter or margarine
1 cup blueberries, fresh or
   frozen
1 cup strawberries, fresh or
   frozen

1. Diagonally cut bread into 1-inch slices and place in a well-greased 9x13-inch baking dish.

2. In a medium bowl, lightly beat eggs, sugar and vanilla. Stir in the milk until well blended. Pour over bread, turning pieces to coat well. Cover and refrigerate overnight.

3. Preheat oven to 375°.

4. In a small bowl, combine the flour, brown sugar and cinnamon. Cut in butter until mixture resembles coarse crumbs.

5. Turn bread over in baking dish. Scatter blueberries over bread. Sprinkle evenly with crumb mixture. Bake about 40 minutes until golden brown.

6. Cut into squares. Top with strawberries or serve them on the side.

Spinach and Cheese Soufflé Roll

A little more effort, but a spectacular result.

Serves 8

7 eggs, separated
⅓ cup butter or margarine
6 tablespoons all purpose
   flour
Dash of cayenne pepper
¾ teaspoon salt, divided
1¼ cups milk
½ cup grated Parmesan
   cheese
½ cup coarsely grated
   sharp Cheddar cheese
¼ teaspoon cream of tartar

Spinach Filling:
20 ounces chopped frozen
   spinach
2 tablespoons butter or
   margarine
¼ pound mushrooms,
   chopped
½ cup finely chopped
   onion
¼ teaspoon salt
½ teaspoon nutmeg
¼ cup grated sharp
   Cheddar cheese
½ cup sour cream
Additional grated
   Parmesan cheese
¼ pound Cheddar cheese,
   sliced

1. Preheat oven to 350°. Place egg whites and yolks in separate bowls. Let whites warm to room temperature, about 1 hour. Grease bottom of 15x10½x1-inch jellyroll pan. Line bottom with waxed paper and then grease with butter.

2. Melt butter in saucepan. With a wire whisk, stir in flour, cayenne and ½ teaspoon salt and cook over low heat, stirring until smooth. Gradually stir in milk. Bring to a boil, stirring. Reduce heat and simmer, stirring, until thick and mixture leaves bottom of pan. Beat in ½ cup Parmesan and ½ cup Cheddar.

3. With a whisk, beat yolks. Beat in cheese mixture. With mixer at high speed, beat whites with ¼ teaspoon salt and cream of tartar until stiff peaks form when beater is slowly raised. With under-over motion, fold ⅓ of the whites into the cheese mixture.

4. Carefully fold in remaining whites to combine. Turn into the jellyroll pan. Bake 15 minutes or until surface is puffed and firm when pressed with finger tip. Prepare Spinach Filling: Cook spinach to package directions. Turn into sieve and press well to remove water.

5. Melt butter in a medium skillet. Sauté mushrooms and onion until golden. Add spinach, salt, nutmeg, Cheddar and sour cream, mixing well. With metal spatula, loosen edges of soufflé. Invert on waxed paper sprinkled lightly with Parmesan. Peel off waxed paper.

6. Spread surface evenly with Spinach Filling. From the long side, roll up and place seam-side down on a greased cookie sheet. Arrange cheese slices over top. Broil about 4 inches from heat until cheese melts. Use a large spatula to remove to a serving dish or board.

Phyllo-Cheese Casserole

½ pound Monterey Jack cheese, grated

2 cups cottage cheese

½ cup grated Parmesan cheese

½ bunch fresh spinach, chopped

1 teaspoon salt

½ onion, chopped

¼ teaspoon dried mint

¼ cup chopped fresh parsley

4 ounces mushrooms, sliced

1 egg

1 pound prepared phyllo dough

½ pound unsalted butter, melted and cooled slightly

1. Preheat oven to 350°.

2. Combine Monterey Jack cheese, cottage cheese, Parmesan cheese, spinach, salt, onion, mint, parsley, mushrooms and egg in a large bowl and blend well.

3. Cut a 1 pound package of phyllo dough in half. Freeze the other half. Keep the rest of the dough covered with a damp paper towel while you are working, as it dries quickly.

4. Butter a 9x13-inch pan. Take 1 sheet of phyllo and fold in half and lay in the pan. Brush with melted butter. Place 3 more sheets on top of first sheet, brushing every sheet with butter. Fold edges of sheets to fit pan.

5. Spread ½ of cheese mixture over the phyllo. Place 4 more sheets of phyllo on top of cheese, brushing with butter every second sheet. Spread remaining ½ of cheese mixture. Place 2 more sheets on top, brushing with butter after second sheet of phyllo. Place 3 more sheets of phyllo on top, brushing last sheet with butter.

6. Cut into 10 serving pieces before baking. Casserole may be covered with foil and frozen at this point.

7. Bake uncovered for 45 minutes or until golden brown.

Note: If you have frozen the casserole, defrost it completely prior to baking.

Chicken Kisses

Each little dough-wrapped packet looks like a chocolate kiss.

Serves 4

4 breasts of chicken, boned
4 ounces cream cheese
2 tablespoons milk
4 green onions, sliced
½ teaspoon lemon pepper
4 ounces sliced almonds,
   blanched
1 can refrigerated crescent
   roll dough
4 tablespoons butter,
   melted
4 tablespoons bread
   crumbs

1. Preheat oven to 350°. Poach chicken breasts in water until just tender. Cool and cut into small cubes.

2. Beat together cream cheese, milk, green onions and lemon pepper. Add chicken cubes and almonds.

3. Separate crescent rolls into 4 sections. Press 2 triangles together to form 4 squares.

4. Put ¼ chicken mixture in the center of each square. Pick up the 4 corners and twist at the top to seal. Dip into the melted butter, then bread crumbs.

5. Place on cookie sheet and bake for 15-20 minutes.

Note: May be made several hours ahead, covered tightly with plastic wrap and refrigerated.

Fiesta Tortilla Quiche

For that special luncheon when you care more about flavor and presentation than cholesterol count, these individual quiches set in fluted tortilla cups are sensational.

12 medium flour tortillas
18 eggs
9 cups grated Monterey
   Jack cheese
1 cup evaporated milk
⅓ cup dry onion
4 ounces diced green chiles
¼ cup diced red bell
   pepper
½ teaspoon seasoned salt
¼ teaspoon garlic powder
⅛ teaspoon pepper
Garnish with salsa, sour
   cream and chopped
   olives

1. Preheat oven to 325°.

2. Line 12 4-inch pie pans with the 12 tortillas, folding to fit.

3. In a large bowl, mix eggs, cheese, evaporated milk, onion, chiles, red pepper, seasoned salt, garlic powder and pepper.

4. Fill each pan with ¾ cup of the egg mixture.

5. Bake 30-40 minutes until inserted knife comes out clean.

6. Serve with salsa, sour cream and chopped olives.

Asparagus-Ricotta Tart

An elegant tart for a spring luncheon.

Crust:
2 cups all purpose flour
¼ teaspoon salt
½ cup chilled unsalted
   butter, cut into pieces
¼ cup solid vegetable
   shortening
8 tablespoons cold water

Filling:
¼ pound bacon
1 pound asparagus,
   trimmed and cut into ½-
   inch pieces, saving 6
   spears for garnish
4 large eggs
15 ounces ricotta cheese
1 teaspoon salt
1 teaspoon pepper
¼ teaspoon nutmeg
3 green onions, chopped

1. Preheat oven to 400°. Prepare Crust: Combine flour and salt in the bowl of a food processor. Add butter and shortening and process until mix resembles coarse crumbs. Add 4 tablespoons water. Blend in enough of remaining water to form dough that just holds together and pulls away from sides of bowl. Flatten into a circle and refrigerate for 30 minutes.

2. Roll out on floured surface to 14-inch round. Transfer to an 11-inch quiche pan with 1-inch high side. Pierce bottom and sides of crust with fork to prevent shrinkage.

3. Put on preheated cookie sheet and bake for 10-12 minutes or until light brown. Cool. Reduce oven temperature to 375°.

4. Prepare Filling: Fry bacon until crisp. Drain and crumble.

5. Cook asparagus in boiling water until crisp, about 3 minutes. Drain and dry.

6. Whisk eggs, ricotta cheese, salt, pepper and nutmeg in a bowl. Stir in onions, bacon and asparagus. Spoon Filling into crust, arranging 6 whole spears on top.

7. Bake until Filling is firm, about 35 minutes. Serve warm or at room temperature.

Bacon and Onion Quiche

4 eggs
¾ pint milk
½ cup all purpose flour
2 onions, sautéed in butter
½ pound Swiss cheese,
   grated
¾ pound bacon, fried crisp

1. Preheat oven to 400°.

2. Mix all ingredients together in a bowl.

3. Pour into a buttered 9-inch pan.

4. Bake for 25 minutes.

Note: This easy, crustless quiche can be frozen after baking.

Smoked Salmon Dill Quiche

The hint of dill adds so much.

Serves 6

7 frozen phyllo pastry
  sheets, thawed according
  to package directions
3 tablespoons unsalted
  butter, melted
4 large eggs
1 tablespoon plus 1
  teaspoon Dijon mustard
2 cups half and half
6 ounces smoked salmon,
  chopped
6 green onions, chopped
¼ cup chopped fresh dill or
  1 tablespoon dried
  dillweed
Salt and Pepper to taste
Dill sprigs

1. Generously butter a 9-inch deep-dish pie plate.

2. Prepare crust: Place 1 phyllo sheet on work surface. Cover remaining pieces with plastic wrap and then with a damp towel. Brush phyllo sheet with butter and fold in half lengthwise. Brush folded surface with butter. Cut in half crosswise.

3. Place 1 phyllo rectangle, buttered side down, in prepared pie plate, covering bottom and letting 1 end of rectangle overhang edge of pie plate. Brush top of phyllo in pie plate with butter. Prepare second phyllo sheet as described in step 2 above and then set into pie plate, covering bottom and letting sheet overhang another section of edge by ½-inch. Brush with butter. Repeat process with remaining 5 phyllo sheets, making certain entire surface of plate is covered to form crust. Fold overhang under to form crust edge flush with edge of pie plate. Brush crust edges with butter. This can be prepared 4 hours ahead. Cover and refrigerate.

4. Preheat oven to 350°.

5. Prepare filling: Whisk eggs and mustard in medium bowl to blend. Add half and half, salmon, onions and chopped dill. Season with salt and pepper.

6. Pour into prepared crust. Bake until center is set, about 50 minutes. Transfer to wire rack. Cool. Garnish with dill sprigs and serve slightly warm or at room temperature.

Ham and Spinach Quiche

A winning combination of flavors graces this effortless brunch or supper dish.

Serves 4-6

10 ounces frozen chopped
   spinach, thawed and
   squeezed dry
10 ounces Cheddar cheese,
   grated
2 eggs, beaten
2 cups ham pieces
3 green onions, chopped
1 9-inch prepared pie
   shell, unbaked

1. Preheat oven to 350°.

2. Mix spinach, cheese, eggs, ham and green onions and pour into pie shell.

3. Bake for 30-40 minutes or until top is golden brown.

Herb-Baked Eggs

Serves 4

4 pieces ham, thinly sliced
3 large eggs
1 teaspoon prepared
   mustard
¼ cup plain yogurt
¾ cup shredded Cheddar
   cheese
2½ teaspoons chopped
   fresh chives
2½ teaspoons chopped
   fresh parsley
Sprigs of herbs to garnish

1. Preheat oven to 375°. Grease 4 ramekins.

2. Line ramekins with ham slices.

3. In a medium bowl, beat eggs, mustard and yogurt. Stir ¼ cup of cheese into egg mixture.

4. In a small bowl, mix chives and parsley and add ½ of these mixed herbs to egg mixture. Stir well and then spoon into prepared ramekins and sprinkle with remaining cheese and herbs.

5. Bake 25-30 minutes until golden and set. Turn out onto serving plates.

Overnight Ham and Cheese Bake

Perfect for your overnight guests.

6 slices bread

2 tablespoons butter

2 cups grated Cheddar
cheese

¾ pound ham, thinly
sliced

½ pound mushrooms,
sliced and sautéed in
butter

1 7-ounce can diced green
chiles

2 cups grated Monterey
Jack cheese

6 eggs

2 cups milk

2 teaspoons salt

½ teaspoon paprika

½ teaspoon basil

¼ teaspoon onion salt

½ teaspoon pepper

½ teaspoon dry mustard

1. Butter 6 slices of bread and place buttered side down in a 9x13-inch baking dish.

2. Sprinkle with 2 cups Cheddar cheese.

3. Place ham on top of cheese and then layer with mushrooms and chiles. Top with Monterey Jack cheese.

4. In a bowl, beat eggs and add milk, salt, paprika, basil, onion salt, pepper and dry mustard. Pour over ingredients in dish. Cover with plastic wrap and refrigerate overnight.

5. Preheat oven to 325°. Uncover casserole and bake 50 minutes. Let stand 10 minutes to set before serving.

Make-Ahead Sausage Soufflé

The croutons give this dish extra flavor. Try using garlic or herb cheese croutons as a variation.

Serves 6-8

1 package Cheddar cheese
  or herbed croutons (2-3
  cups)
4 eggs
2½ cups milk
1 can cream of mushroom
  soup
2 cups shredded Cheddar
  cheese
1 pound bulk spicy
  sausage, browned and
  drained
1 pound mushrooms,
  sliced and sautéed

1. Place croutons in a greased 7x11-inch glass baking dish.

2. Mix eggs, milk and soup together and pour over croutons.

3. Sprinkle with cheese and sausage and top with mushrooms.

4. Prepare the soufflé up to this point the night before. Cover and refrigerate.

5. Take out 1 hour before baking. Bake at 325° for 45 minutes.

Cinnamon Fruit Compote

A tasty winter side dish.

1 8-ounce can apricots,
  unpeeled and pureed
2 teaspoons sugar
2 teaspoons lemon juice
1 cinnamon stick
Dash of nutmeg
2 medium oranges, peeled
  and sectioned
1 8-ounce can pineapple
  chunks, drained
1 tablespoon apricot
  brandy or Grand
  Marnier
1 cup halved strawberries
  (optional)

1. Combine apricot puree, sugar, lemon juice, cinnamon stick and nutmeg and bring to a boil. Simmer 10 minutes.

2. Add oranges and pineapple to mixture and refrigerate overnight.

3. Add liqueur and strawberries before serving.

Braided Sausage Strudel

Elegant and delicious.

Serves 6-8

½ (17¼-ounce) package
  frozen puff pastry
10 ounces pork sausage
1 egg, beaten
1 onion, finely chopped
2 apples, finely chopped
¼ teaspoon nutmeg
1 egg, beaten for glaze
2 tablespoons chopped
  fresh parsley or 1
  tablespoon dried parsley
1 tablespoon dried basil
¾ cup dried herb stuffing
  mix
½ cup chopped almonds,
  blanched
2 tablespoons sesame seeds
Apple slices and sage leaves
  to garnish

1. Preheat oven to 400°. Roll out pastry to an 18x14-inch rectangle. Transfer pastry to a large cookie sheet, long sides at top and bottom. Let stand.

2. In a large bowl, mix sausage, egg, onion, apples, nutmeg, parsley, basil and stuffing mix.

3. Spoon sausage filling down center of pastry leaving about 4 inches of pastry at top and bottom and 2 inches on each side of filling.

4. Make 3-inch cuts at 2-inch intervals down each long side of pastry. Brush pastry with beaten egg. Fold 1 strip over filling from alternate sides until filling is completely enclosed. Tuck pastry end under. Sprinkle almonds and sesame seeds evenly over surface.

5. Bake for 30 minutes or until golden.

Note: Makes a wonderful side dish. Garnish with apple slices and sage leaves. Serve hot or cold.

Lemon Fruit Sauce

Serve as a sauce over fresh summer fruit or use as a fruit dip.

Serves 4-6

½ cup powdered sugar
1 teaspoon minced lemon
  peel
1 teaspoon lemon juice
¼ teaspoon vanilla extract
1 cup sour cream

1. Mix all ingredients together.

2. Refrigerate overnight.

Grilled Citrus Cups

Attractive for a brunch buffet.

Serves 4

2 pink grapefruit
1 white grapefruit
3 oranges
1 lime
3 tablespoons sherry
4 tablespoons light brown
  sugar
2 tablespoons butter
Sprigs of lemon balm for
  garnish
Mint leaves for garnish

1. Cut grapefruits in half. Remove pulp and cut in sections. Reserve grapefruit shells.

2. Cut away top and bottom from oranges and lime and then remove skin and pith. Cut in sections, reserving juices.

3. In a baking dish, mix grapefruit, orange and lime sections. Sprinkle with sherry and marinate 1 hour.

4. Put fruit in reserved grapefruit shells. Sprinkle with brown sugar and dot with butter. Broil until brown sugar melts.

5. Top with reserved juices and garnish with mint.

Swiss Cheese Potato Pie

Just as good as it sounds!

Serves 8

6 large eggs
1 cup chopped green
  onions
½ teaspoon salt
½ teaspoon pepper
3 cups diced, peeled and
  cooked potatoes, or
  frozen diced hash
  browns, thawed
6 ounces grated Swiss
  cheese
4 ounces bacon or ham,
  diced
½ cup diced green bell
  pepper
½ cup milk

1. Preheat oven to 350°. Generously butter a 9-inch pie dish.

2. Whisk eggs, onions, salt and pepper in a large bowl. Add potatoes, cheese, ham or bacon, bell pepper and milk, stirring to blend.

3. Pour into prepared dish. Bake until set, about 1 hour and 20 minutes. Cut into wedges.

Caramel-Pecan Pull Aparts

Incredibly easy and guaranteed to be a favorite.

Serves 6-8

1 cup brown sugar
½ cup butter
2 tablespoons water
½ cup chopped pecans
⅓ cup currants
2 cans refrigerated crescent
    roll dough
¼ cup sugar
1 teaspoon cinnamon

1. Preheat oven to 350°. Combine brown sugar, butter and water in saucepan. Bring to a slow boil and remove from heat.

2. Add nuts and currants to caramel mixture.

3. Remove dough from packages, retaining their log shapes. Cut each log into 10 equal slices.

4. Combine sugar and cinnamon. Toss with roll slices.

5. Place half the slices in greased bundt pan. Pour half the caramel sauce over them. Repeat with remaining slices and sauce.

6. Bake for 30-35 minutes. Invert onto warm platter to serve.

Chocolate Chip Sour Cream Coffeecake

This is especially good served warm. A chocolate lover's delight!

1 cup butter
2 cups sugar
2 eggs, beaten
2 cups sour cream
1 tablespoon vanilla
    extract
2 cups all purpose flour
1 tablespoon baking
    powder
2 cups chocolate chips

1. Preheat oven to 350°. Grease a 10-inch bundt pan and lightly dust with flour.

2. Cream together the butter and sugar. Add eggs, blending well, then the sour cream and vanilla.

3. Sift together the flour and baking powder.

4. Fold the dry ingredients into the creamed mixture and beat just until blended. Do not overbeat.

5. Stir in chocolate chips and pour into prepared pan.

6. Set on the middle rack of the oven and bake for about 60 minutes or until cake tester, when inserted in the center, comes out clean.

Easy Cheese Danish

A sure winner!

Serves 8

16 ounces cream cheese, softened
1½ teaspoons vanilla extract
½ cup sugar
2 packages refrigerated crescent roll dough
½ cup raspberry or apricot jam
1 egg, beaten
4 ounces sliced almonds (optional)

1. Preheat oven to 350°. Mix cream cheese, vanilla and sugar in a bowl.

2. Unroll 1 can crescent roll dough on a cookie sheet, sealing perforations. Spread filling on dough, leaving ¼-inch edges. Top with jam.

3. Unroll second can of crescent roll dough and lay on top of first layer. Seal edges with edge of fork. Brush with beaten egg. Sprinkle with sliced almonds.

4. Bake for 30 minutes.

Apple Streusel Coffeecake

Nothing else makes the house smell so good.

4 eggs
2 cups sugar
1 cup vegetable oil
3 teaspoons vanilla extract
3 cups all purpose flour
3 teaspoons baking powder
1 teaspoon salt
½ cup orange juice
3 teaspoons ground cinnamon
½ cup sugar
5-6 tart cooking apples, peeled and sliced

1. Preheat oven to 325°. Mix eggs, sugar, oil and vanilla.

2. Mix flour, baking powder and salt and add to egg mixture alternately with orange juice.

3. Combine cinnamon with sugar.

4. Layer in greased bundt pan as follows: ⅓ egg mixture, ⅓ sliced apples and ⅓ cinnamon mixture. Repeat 3 times.

5. Bake for 1½ to 2 hours.

Cranberry Tart

How can something this good be so easy to make? An unusually delicious coffeecake that may also be served with vanilla ice cream for dessert.

2 eggs, beaten
1½ cups sugar
½ cup butter, melted
1 cup all purpose flour,
    sifted
½ cup chopped nuts
2 cups whole cranberries

1. Preheat oven to 325°.

2. Combine all ingredients in the order listed.

3. Pour into greased 10-inch pie pan.

4. Bake for 50-60 minutes until done.

5. Serve warm.

Harvest Pumpkin Bread with Orange Butter

The delicious orange butter makes this moist bread a standout.

Makes 2 loaves

Pumpkin Bread:
1 teaspoon baking soda
½ cup hot water
¾ cup vegetable oil
3 cups sugar
2 cups canned pumpkin
4 eggs
1 teaspoon ground
    cinnamon
½ teaspoon ground cloves
1 teaspoon salt
3½ cups all purpose flour

Orange Butter:
½ pound butter, softened
½ box powdered sugar
Grated rind of 2 oranges
2 tablespoons orange juice
    concentrate

1. Preheat oven to 350°. Prepare Pumpkin Bread: Dissolve soda in hot water.

2. Mix together oil, sugar and pumpkin and add to soda mixture.

3. Add eggs, cinnamon, cloves, salt and flour and mix until moistened.

4. Pour batter into 2 greased and floured loaf pans. Bake for 1 hour. Remove from loaf pans and cool on wire racks.

5. Prepare Orange Butter: Beat butter and sugar together.

6. Add orange rind and juice concentrate and mix well. Place into decorative crock and serve with Pumpkin Bread.

Cream Cheese Apricot Bread

Makes 1 loaf

Batter:
1 cup dried apricots, cut
  into thin strips
½ cup raisins
4 tablespoons butter, room
  temperature
½ cup sugar
½ cup packed light brown
  sugar
1 large egg, room
  temperature
2 cups all purpose flour
2 teaspoons baking powder
½ teaspoon baking soda
½ teaspoon salt
¾ cup orange juice
½ cup chopped walnuts

Filling:
6 ounces cream cheese,
  room temperature
1 large egg, room
  temperature
1 tablespoon grated orange
  zest

1. Preheat oven to 350°. Prepare Batter: Combine apricots and raisins in a small bowl. Add boiling water to cover. Let stand 30 minutes, then drain.

2. In a bowl, beat butter and sugars until creamy. Beat in egg.

3. In a separate bowl, sift together flour, baking powder, baking soda and salt. Add flour mixture alternately with orange juice to butter mixture. Stir in apricots, raisins and walnuts.

4. Prepare Filling: Place all ingredients in a food processor and process until smooth.

5. Pour ⅔ of Batter into greased and floured 9x5-inch loaf pan. Top with Filling, then Batter. Insert a knife and swirl to marbleize.

6. Bake for 55-60 minutes, or until golden. Cool 10 minutes, then turn out onto wire rack.

Note: Can refrigerate for 1 week or freeze up to 2 months.

Glazed Cranberry Orange Bread

A treat for Christmas morning . The orange flavor gives it a delicious California touch.

Batter:
2 cups all purpose flour
1 cup sugar
1 teaspoon salt
1 tablespoon grated orange
　rind
1½ teaspoons baking
　powder
½ teaspoon baking soda
2 tablespoons vegetable oil
¾ cup orange juice
1 egg, well beaten
2 cups cranberries
1 cup chopped walnuts

Orange Glaze:
¾ cup powdered sugar
½ cup orange juice

1. Preheat oven to 350°. Prepare Batter: Mix flour, sugar, salt, orange rind, baking powder and baking soda.

2. Add oil, orange juice and egg and mix to moisten. Fold in cranberries and walnuts.

3. Pour Batter into greased and floured 9x5-inch loaf pan.

4. Bake for 1 hour.

5. Prepare Orange Glaze: Combine sugar and orange juice in a small saucepan.

6. Bring to a boil and remove from heat.

7. Remove bread from oven when done and cool slightly. While bread is still warm, prick with a fork and drizzle with Orange Glaze.

Note: Bread tastes best when made 24 hours ahead.

Country Pecan Morsels

These morsels, which are more confection than muffin, literally melt in your mouth.

½ cup all purpose flour
1½ cups dark brown sugar,
　firmly packed
1½ cups chopped pecans
Pinch of salt
3 large eggs, lightly beaten
½ teaspoon vanilla extract

1. Heavily grease 3 miniature muffin tins.

2. Combine flour, brown sugar, nuts and salt.

3. By hand, stir in eggs and vanilla. Batter will be lumpy.

4. Spoon batter into prepared tins, filling about ⅔ full.

5. Place muffins in cold oven, turn thermostat to 300° and bake for 25 minutes.

6. Remove from oven. Cool 1 minute, then run a knife gently around the edge of tin to loosen muffins.

7. Cool partially before turning out onto wire rack to cool.

Raspberry Muffins

The raspberries make these muffins a delectable change of pace.

Makes 12 muffins

4 tablespoons margarine (not butter), at room temperature
1 cup sugar
1 cup milk
1 egg, beaten
1⅓ cups all purpose flour, divided
2 teaspoons baking powder
¾ teaspoon cinnamon
2 teaspoons grated nutmeg
¼ teaspoon salt
4 teaspoons vanilla extract
1 cup fresh or frozen raspberries, thawed

1. Preheat oven to 375°. Grease a 12 muffin tin heavily and set aside.

2. Cream together margarine and sugar with an electric mixer on low speed until light and fluffy.

3. Add the milk, egg, ⅔ cup flour, baking powder, cinnamon, nutmeg, salt and vanilla. Beat until blended.

4. By hand, fold in the remaining ⅔ cup flour. The batter should still be lumpy.

5. Fill muffin tins ¾ full and carefully place a few raspberries on top of each muffin.

6. Bake for 20-30 minutes, until the muffins are golden brown. Let cool in the pan for 5 to 10 minutes. Remove and let cool on a rack.

Note: These muffins are sticky, so loosen around the edges before turning out. Serve warm.

Gorgonzola Popovers

Makes 8

4 eggs
1 cup finely crumbled Gorgonzola cheese, chilled
2 cups milk
2 tablespoons butter, melted
2 cups all purpose flour
½ teaspoon salt

1. Preheat oven to 450°.

2. Beat eggs and Gorgonzola cheese with electric mixer.

3. Add milk, butter, flour and salt and beat just until batter is smooth.

4. Pour into well-greased ¾ cup capacity popover pans, filling each about ¾ full.

5. Bake for 25 minutes. Reduce heat to 350° and bake 20 minutes longer until puffed and browned.

Note: Glass custard cups may be used instead of popover pans.

Double Orange Scones with Orange Butter

Unique and delicious!

Serves 8

Batter:
2 cups all purpose flour
2½ teaspoons baking
  powder
3 tablespoons sugar
1 tablespoon grated orange
  rind
⅓ cup butter
11 ounces canned
  Mandarin oranges,
  drained
¼ cup milk
1 egg, beaten
1 tablespoon sugar

Orange Butter:
¼ cup butter, softened
2 tablespoons orange
  marmalade

1. Preheat oven to 400°. Prepare Batter: Mix flour, baking powder, sugar and orange rind. Cut in butter to form coarse crumbs.

2. Add oranges, milk and egg and then stir until mix leaves sides of bowl and forms sticky dough. Flour hands and knead lightly 10 times.

3. Place on a greased cookie sheet and pat into 6-inch circle ¾-inch thick. Cut into 8 wedges and separate slightly. You may roll out dough on a floured board and cut with a floured biscuit cutter into smaller rounds. You may also sprinkle with 1 tablespoon sugar.

4. Bake for 15-20 minutes or 10-12 minutes if dough was cut into smaller pieces.

5. Prepare Orange Butter: Mix softened butter and marmalade and place in decorative crock. Serve with warm scones.

Potato Rolls

1 package yeast
2 cups water
½ cup sugar
1½ teaspoons salt
½ cup butter, melted and
  cooled
1 egg
¼ cup instant potatoes
5½-6 cups all purpose
  flour

1. Dissolve yeast in warm water (90-105°). Add sugar and stir until dissolved.

2. Add salt, butter, egg, instant potatoes and flour and mix together until smooth dough forms.

3. Put in greased bowl, turning over to grease top. Cover and let rise in a warm place until doubled, approximately 1½ hours.

4. Punch dough down and form into 24 balls. Place on cookie sheets, cover and let rise until doubled again, approximately 1½ hours.

5. Bake in a preheated 425° oven for 10 minutes.

Note: Make these delicious rolls in a larger size for sandwiches.

Bountiful Breakfast Muffins

You couldn't ask for more flavor than you'll find in these moist, hearty muffins.

Makes 21 muffins

2¼ cups all purpose flour
1¼ cups sugar
1 tablespoon ground
   cinnamon
2 teaspoons baking soda
½ teaspoon salt
½ cup shredded coconut
½ cup raisins
2 cups grated carrots
1 Granny Smith apple,
   peeled and grated
8 ounces canned
   pineapple, crushed and
   drained
½ cup chopped pecans or
   walnuts
3 eggs
1 cup vegetable oil
1 teaspoon vanilla extract

1. Preheat oven to 350°. Grease muffin tins and set aside.

2. Sift flour, sugar, cinnamon, soda and salt into a large bowl.

3. Stir in coconut, raisins, carrots, apple, pineapple and nuts.

4. Mix together eggs, oil and vanilla and add to dry ingredients and fruits. Stir until just combined.

5. Spoon into muffin tins, filling each cup ¾ full. Fill empty muffin cups with water to prevent burning.

6. Bake for 25-30 minutes. Remove to wire racks and serve warm.

Old Fashioned Brown Bread

Makes 1 loaf

2 cups whole wheat flour
1 cup unbleached flour
1 teaspoon baking soda
1 teaspoon salt
⅔ cup molasses
1 cup buttermilk
¾ cup milk

1. Preheat oven to 350°. Mix flours, baking soda and salt together.

2. Add molasses, buttermilk and milk to dry ingredients and mix until moistened.

3. Pour into greased 9x5-inch loaf pan.

4. Bake for 60-70 minutes or until done.

Blue Cornbread Madeleines

These are particularly good with a Mexican brunch or dinner. They can also be made in miniature muffin tins.

Makes 24-30

1 cup all purpose flour
1 cup blue cornmeal
 (yellow may be
 substituted)
1 tablespoon baking
 powder
¼ teaspoon salt
2 eggs
1 cup milk
6 tablespoons butter,
 melted
¼ cup honey
¼ cup corn kernels,
 canned, drained
¼ cup chopped fresh
 cilantro

1. Preheat oven to 425°. Stir together flour, cornmeal, baking powder and salt.

2. In a small bowl, beat the eggs. Whisk in the milk, butter and honey. Gently stir in corn and cilantro.

3. Make a well in the dry ingredients and pour in the egg-milk mixture. Stir just until well blended. Spoon batter into well buttered and floured madeleine pans, filling each shell ¾ full.

4. Bake for about 6 minutes. Invert pan over wire rack and tap to release madeleines. Serve warm.

Overnight Crescent Rolls

These very special yeast rolls are a snap to make.

Makes 3 dozen

½ cup butter, softened
½ cup vegetable
 shortening
1 cup sugar
1¾ teaspoons salt
1 cup boiling water
2 packages dry yeast
2 eggs, beaten
1 cup cold water
6 cups all purpose flour

1. Place butter, shortening, sugar and salt in a large bowl. Add boiling water, stirring until dissolved. Cool slightly.

2. Dissolve yeast in lukewarm mixture. Add eggs, cold water and flour. Stir and refrigerate for at least 4 hours or overnight.

3. Three hours before serving, roll dough into 3 circles on a floured board. Cut each circle into 12 segments as for a pie. Starting at wide end, roll up each segment and place tip down on an ungreased baking sheet, far enough apart so that they will not touch during rising or baking. Let rise in a moderately warm place for 3 hours.

4. Preheat oven to 400°. Bake 12-15 minutes until golden brown.

Rosemary Buttermilk Biscuits

Makes 12 Biscuits

2¼ cups all purpose flour
4 teaspoons ground fresh
  rosemary or 1 teaspoon
  dried rosemary
2 tablespoons sugar
¾ teaspoon salt
2 tablespoons baking
  powder
½ cup plus 1 tablespoon
  solid vegetable
  shortening or butter
¾ cup buttermilk
3 tablespoons butter,
  melted
½ cup dried currants
  (optional)

1. Preheat oven to 400°. Combine flour, rosemary, sugar, salt and baking powder. Mix well.

2. Cut in shortening until mixture is crumbly.

3. Add buttermilk and currants, if desired, and mix until just moistened.

4. Scoop into 12 greased muffin tins and brush with melted butter.

5. Bake for 10-15 minutes or until golden brown.

Pan Con Tomato

A traditional Catalan dish for a brunch or an outdoor grilled dinner.

1 large loaf of crusty
  peasant bread
Olive oil
2 very ripe tomatoes
Garlic salt

1. Cut thick slices from loaf of bread and toast both sides lightly under the broiler.

2. Drizzle 1 side of bread slices generously with olive oil.

3. Cut a very ripe tomato in half. Rub it over the toasted bread, squeezing gently and leaving juice and pulp.

4. Sprinkle generously with garlic salt.

5. Reheat gently under broiler and serve.

Bohemian Beer Bread

Serves 6

4 cups all purpose flour
2 tablespoons butter or
    margarine
2 packages fast-acting dry
    yeast
1 teaspoon caraway seeds
1 teaspoon salt
½ teaspoon garlic powder
¾ cup beer
2 tablespoons honey or
    sugar
½ cup warm water
1 egg, beaten

1. Preheat oven to 375°. Place flour, butter, yeast, caraway seeds, salt and garlic powder in bowl of food processor. Use dough blade and pulse several times until well mixed and butter is cut in.

2. Heat beer, honey and water until warm (about 130°). With machine running, slowly add warm liquid mixture through feed tube. Process until dough is smooth and leaves sides of the bowl.

3. Remove dough and shape into smooth ball. Place in greased 1½ -2 quart casserole dish, turning once to grease top. Flatten gently to edges. Cover loosely with plastic wrap and let rise in a warm place until doubled, about 20-25 minutes.

4. Brush top of loaf with a beaten egg. Place in oven for 25-30 minutes. Loaf is done when it sounds hollow when tapped. Remove from pan and cool on wire rack.

Note: For the most authentic Bohemian bread, substitute 1¼ cups rye or wheat flour for the same quantity of white flour.

Brown Bag Herb Bread

A different twist on an old favorite.

½ cup butter, softened
2 tablespoons chopped
    fresh parsley
2 tablespoons chopped
    green onion tops
1 tablespoon chopped
    celery tops
1 teaspoon dried sweet
    basil
½ teaspoon lemon juice
1 loaf white bread,
    unsliced

1. Mix butter, parsley, onions, celery, basil and lemon juice until smooth and soft.

2. Trim off ends of bread and top crust. Slice bread part of the way through loaf, leaving slices attached at the bottom.

3. Spread butter mixture between bread slices. Wrap loaf in a brown paper bag and tie up with a string. Let sit overnight.

4. Preheat oven to 350°.

5. Bake in bag for 30 minutes. Serve warm.

Herb-Bread Sticks

Serves 6

2 tablespoons butter,
  softened
¼ cup grated Parmesan
  cheese
4 cloves garlic, crushed
Garlic powder
Pinch of tarragon
Pinch of dried parsley
Pinch of Italian seasoning
Pinch of celery seed
1 large round loaf
  sourdough bread
¼ cup grated Parmesan
  cheese

1. Preheat oven to 375°.

2. Mix first 8 ingredients together.

3. Cut loaf of bread into slices, then turn loaf a quarter-turn and slice again. (The result will be like breadsticks standing on end.)

4. Butter inside of bread with mixture on all sides.

5. Sprinkle top with Parmesan cheese.

6. Wrap in foil and bake for 20 minutes.

Cheese Spread

1 pound Cheddar cheese,
  grated
2 ounces Romano cheese,
  grated
1½ pounds butter or
  margarine
½ teaspoon garlic powder
1 teaspoon paprika
4 drops hot pepper sauce
2 tablespoons
  Worcestershire sauce
French or sourdough bread

1. Mix all ingredients in a food processor and refrigerate for at least 2 hours before using.

2. Spread mixture on bread and broil until bubbly.

Chapter 2

Sneak
Previews

Hot and Cold Appetizers

Whether you're planning

a glittering evening at the

Academy Awards or simply

hosting a casual get-together in

front of the TV on Oscar

night, these tasty appetizers

will start your evening off with

style and ease.

Palisades Iced Tea

The best iced tea we've ever tasted!

Makes 8 cups

½ cup sugar
Juice of 2 lemons
4 cups boiling water
3 tablespoons Earl Grey
   loose tea or 4 teabags
Handful of mint leaves
4 cups cold water

1. Combine sugar, lemon juice and 2 cups of boiling water and steep for 15 minutes.

2. In another container, combine tea, mint and 2 cups of boiling water and steep for 15 minutes.

3. Remove mint and strain both mixtures. Add 4 cups of cold water.

Note: The amount of tea and water may be adjusted for a stronger or weaker taste.

Frozen Banana Cooler

Frosty and delicious on a warm summer day.

1½ cups sugar
6 cups water
1 12-ounce can frozen
   orange juice concentrate,
   thawed
3 cups pineapple juice
3 cups grapefruit juice
5 bananas
1 32-ounce bottle
   carbonated lemon-lime
   soda or 1 28-ounce
   bottle club soda, chilled

1. Dissolve sugar in water. Add orange, pineapple and grapefruit juices.

2. Puree bananas in a blender and stir into mixture. Combine well.

3. Pour into 2½ gallon freezer containers and freeze overnight or up to 6 months.

4. Remove containers from freezer 1-2 hours before serving (until slushlike). Break up large chunks with a spoon.

5. Add lemon-lime soda or club soda and stir well. Serve in a punch bowl.

California Sunset

A simple, refreshing punch that is easy to make for a crowd.

Serves 4

3 cups cranberry juice
¾ cup lemon-lime soda
¾ cup orange juice

1. Mix all ingredients well. Serve chilled.

Fruit Smoothie

Healthy and refreshing.

Serves 2

½ cup plain yogurt
½ cup orange juice
1 banana
5 strawberries (fresh or
   frozen)

1. Mix the ingredients in a blender on high speed until well blended and smooth.

2. Serve immediately over ice.

Solano Sunrise

The perfect addition to a festive beach picnic.

Serves 6

1 12-ounce can pink
   lemonade concentrate,
   thawed
12 ounces gin
12 ounces milk

1. Mix all ingredients and serve over ice.

Mulled Wine

A holiday tradition to be savored year after year.

2 bottles red wine
4 cups water
¼ cup sugar
½ teaspoon bitters
½ teaspoon allspice
2 cinnamon sticks
4 whole cloves
Rind of 1 orange, pared
Rind of 1 lemon, pared

1. Pour wine and water into a large saucepan. Add the sugar and bitters. Wrap the remaining ingredients in a piece of cheesecloth and add to the pan. Simmer for 30 minutes. Do not boil.

2. Serve in mugs.

Coffee with all the Fixings

The grand finale to a wonderful brunch, dessert party or dinner party.

Choose from the following ingredients:
Orange peel
Lemon peel
Whipped cream
Heavy cream
Colored sugar
Light brown sugar
Sugar cubes
White sugar
Ground cinnamon
Cinnamon sticks
Chocolate sprinkles
Shaved chocolate
Powdered chocolate
Freshly grated nutmeg
Grand Marnier
Irish cream
Amaretto
Cognac
Coffee-flavored liqueur

1. Select a variety of ingredients from the list and serve with a pot of your favorite coffee.

Note: Display ingredients elegantly in decorative bowls on a silver tray, or for an informal gathering, in baskets.

Mexican Coffee

A wonderful hostess or teacher gift.

½ cup unsweetened cocoa
1 cup brown sugar, firmly
    packed
4 teaspoons cinnamon
1 cup instant coffee
Brandy
Whipped cream

1. In a food processor, mix all ingredients to a smooth consistency.

2. To serve, place 2 rounded teaspoons of mixture in a cup. Add boiling water and stir. Add a shot of brandy and top with whipped cream.

Note: Place dry coffee mixture in a pretty jar and place in a basket with a small bottle of brandy. Label with instructions listed under number 2 above.

Crown City Cordials

For the irresistible flavor of Irish cream.

Makes 1 quart

3 fresh eggs, well beaten
¼ teaspoon coconut extract
½ cup genuine chocolate
   syrup
½ cup heavy cream
14 ounces sweetened
   condensed milk
1 cup whiskey

1. Blend all ingredients together. Refrigerate in a covered container until ready to serve.

Note: Try serving this cordial after dinner in a goblet with 1 scoop of vanilla ice cream and fresh raspberries. Fabulous!

Almond-Flavored Liqueur

Makes 1 quart

1½ cups brown sugar
1 cup sugar
2 cups water
2 teaspoons vanilla extract
1 tablespoon almond
   extract
1¾ cups vodka

1. In a saucepan, combine brown sugar, sugar and water. Bring the liquid to a boil, reduce the heat and continue to slow boil for 15 minutes. Set aside and let the mixture cool.

2. When the sugar mixture has completely cooled, add the vanilla, almond extract and vodka. Mix well.

3. Store in a covered container.

Coffee Liqueur

For an exotic after-dinner drink, blend with cream or add to coffee.

Makes 1 quart

2 cups sugar
1½ cups water
1 tablespoon vanilla extract
¼ cup instant coffee
½ cup boiling water
2 cups vodka

1. In a saucepan, combine sugar and water. Bring to a boil, reduce heat and continue to slow boil for 20 minutes. Remove from heat and add the vanilla. Let the mixture cool.

2. In a small bowl, combine the instant coffee and boiling water. Mix well and set aside to let the mixture cool.

3. Combine both mixtures and add the vodka.

4. Store in a covered container.

Vegetable Medley Pizza

Create your own masterpiece of flavors and colors.

2 8-ounce packages refrigerator crescent dinner roll dough
2 8-ounce packages cream cheese, softened
1 cup mayonnaise
1 package ranch dressing mix

Variation I
1 cup broccoli, flowerets
1 cup cauliflower, cut into small pieces
1 large carrot, shredded
4 green onions, chopped
1 large tomato, seeded and chopped
1 cup shredded Cheddar cheese
½ cup grated Parmesan cheese

Variation II
1 cup broccoli, flowerets
⅓ cup chopped red bell pepper
⅓ cup chopped green bell pepper
½ cup thinly sliced mushrooms
½ cup chopped onion
1 large carrot, shredded
1 large tomato, seeded and chopped
½ cup shredded Cheddar cheese
½ cup shredded Monterey Jack cheese
½ cup grated Parmesan cheese

1. Preheat oven to 350°.

2. Press dough on a cookie sheet, making a raised edge. Bake for 10 minutes. Cool.

3. Combine cream cheese, mayonnaise and ranch dressing mix, mixing well. Spread the mixture evenly on the crust.

4. Decorate the crust with an assortment of raw vegetables. See Variations I and II for suggested vegetable toppings or select your choice of seasonal vegetables. Gently press the vegetables into the cream cheese mixture. Sprinkle with cheeses.

5. Refrigerate at least 1 hour. Cut into 1½-inch squares or triangles and arrange on a platter.

Poolside Pineapple Cheese Ball

A refreshing start to a warm summer's eve.

1 8-ounce package cream
    cheese, softened
¼ cup finely chopped
    green bell pepper
2 tablespoons chopped
    onion
1 8-ounce can crushed
    pineapple, drained very
    well
½ teaspoon seasoned salt
1 cup chopped walnuts

1. Cream together cream cheese, green pepper, onion, pineapple and seasoned salt.

2. Form a ball and roll it in the chopped walnuts. Chill well.

Note: Serve with crackers.

Hot Clam Dip

Serves 6-8

¼ pound Mozzarella cheese
3 tablespoons butter
1 small onion, chopped
½ green bell pepper,
    chopped
1 4-ounce can minced
    clams, drained
4 tablespoons catsup
1 tablespoon
    Worcestershire sauce
¼ teaspoon cayenne
    pepper
1 tablespoon sherry

1. Melt cheese in a double boiler.

2. In a small frying pan, melt butter and sauté onion and green pepper. Add to cheese in double boiler.

3. Add clams and other ingredients. Mix together and cook slowly until heated thoroughly.

Note: Serve from a chafing dish with crackers. Can be made ahead.

Artichoke-Caviar Dip

An elegant first course.

Serves 10

14¾ ounces marinated
  artichoke hearts, drained
  and chopped
4 eggs, hard boiled and
  finely chopped
1 cup mayonnaise
6 green onions, chopped
3½ ounces black caviar,
  rinsed and drained

1. Layer ingredients in the order listed in a 10-inch round dish.
    Refrigerate overnight.

Note: Must be prepared 1 day in advance. Serve with crackers.

La Jolla Salmon with Capers and Green Onions

6 ounces fresh salmon,
  poached (may substitute
  1 6½-ounce can salmon
  plus 2 tablespoons
  liquid)
1 tablespoon capers
4 green onions, diced, with
  tops discarded
1 tablespoon mayonnaise
1 tablespoon Dijon
  mustard
1 teaspoon lemon juice

1. Flake salmon into pieces in a medium mixing bowl.

2. Gently add remaining ingredients and stir until just blended.

Note: Serve with crackers.

Smoked Salmon with Belgian Endive Dippers

Beautiful presentation.

Serves 8-10

8-10 heads Belgian endive and/or small toasted French bread rounds
8 ounces light cream cheese, softened
¼ cup light sour cream
8 ounces smoked salmon, minced
1-2 tablespoons minced onion
1 tablespoon lime juice
3 tablespoons fresh chopped dill or 2 teaspoons dry dill weed

1. Wash endive in cold water. Separate into leaves and break into small pieces for dipping. Wrap in paper towels and store in plastic bag in refrigerator for 1 hour, or up to 3 days.

2. Beat cream cheese until fluffy; add sour cream and beat until combined. Add smoked salmon, onion, lime juice and dill, mixing well. Refrigerate for 2 hours, or up to 3 days.

3. Before serving, bring dip to room temperature and beat briefly to a fluffy consistency.

4. To serve, place dip in a small bowl on a platter. Surround with endive in a sunburst pattern. May also use thinly sliced toasted French bread rounds.

Marinated Goat Cheese and Garlic

For added flavor, rub a marinated garlic clove onto the French bread before spreading the cheese.

Serves 8

2 large heads garlic
16 ounces olive oil
11 ounce log Montrachet goat cheese
1½ tablespoons dried rosemary
2 bay leaves
1 tablespoon black peppercorns
French bread

1. Carefully separate garlic into cloves. Peel, leaving cloves whole. Place peeled garlic in a small saucepan and add just enough olive oil to cover well. Cook very slowly over low heat until garlic cloves soften. (If garlic cooks too quickly or browns, it will be bitter.) Remove from heat and cool.

2. Meanwhile, slice goat cheese in 1-inch rounds and place in a crock or jar with a tight-fitting lid. Add remaining olive oil, herbs, pepper and cooled garlic with its cooking oil.

3. Cover and leave at room temperature for 24 hours. Store in refrigerator for up to 2 weeks. Serve at room temperature with lightly toasted French bread.

Hot Chile-Spinach Dip in a Bread Round

1 large round loaf unsliced
  Shepherd's bread or
  French bread
2-3 jalapeño chiles, minced
1 7-ounce can diced green
  chiles
1 small onion, chopped
2 tablespoons vegetable oil
2 tomatoes, chopped
1 10-ounce package frozen
  chopped spinach,
  thawed, drained and
  squeezed dry
1 tablespoon red wine
  vinegar
8 ounces cream cheese,
  softened
2 cups grated Monterey
  Jack cheese
1 cup half and half
1 teaspoon cumin
Salt and Pepper to taste
Tortilla chips

1. Preheat oven to 325°. Cut the top off the bread ¼ of the way down. Carefully scoop out the inside, leaving a 1-inch shell. Reserve the top.

2. In a medium skillet over medium heat, cook the chiles and onions in the oil, stirring, for 4 minutes, or until the onions are softened. Add the tomatoes, and cook the mixture, stirring, for 2 more minutes. Stir in the spinach, vinegar, cream cheese, Monterey Jack cheese, half and half, cumin, salt and pepper and heat gently.

3. Pour the sauce into the bread round, replace top and wrap in heavy foil.

4. Place in a baking pan and bake for 1½ hours.

5. To serve, place the bread round on a platter and surround with tortilla chips for dipping. The dip may also be served in a chafing dish.

Wonton Chips

Crunchy and addictive, these can be made ahead of time and stored in an airtight container.

1 package square wonton
  skins
½ cup butter or margarine,
  melted
1 cup coarsely grated
  Parmesan cheese

1. Preheat oven to 450°.

2. Cut wonton skins in half. Brush bottom of cookie sheet with melted butter. Lay wonton skins on cookie sheet with edges touching until entire pan is covered with skins.

3. Brush remaining butter on top side of skins.

4. Sprinkle heavily with Parmesan cheese.

5. Bake for 6 minutes or until brown. Watch closely, as they burn easily.

Crab Stuffed Mushrooms

1¼ pounds small
   mushrooms (about 25)
¼ cup butter or margarine,
   melted
1 6-ounce can of crab
   meat, liquid reserved
8 ounces light whipped
   cream cheese
½ pound grated Monterey
   Jack cheese
6 green onions, finely
   chopped
1 tablespoon
   Worcestershire sauce
Grated Parmesan cheese

1. Preheat oven to 325°.

2. Rinse mushrooms well and remove stems. Pat dry. Dip each
   mushroom in melted butter. Set on a cookie sheet.

3. Drain liquid from crabmeat and set aside. Mix crabmeat, cream
   cheese, Monterey Jack cheese, green onions, Worcestershire sauce
   and ¼ cup of the reserved liquid from the crabmeat. The mixture
   should not be runny.

4. Stuff mushrooms with the crabmeat mixture and top with
   Parmesan cheese. Can be made several hours ahead of time and
   refrigerated.

5. Bake for 30 minutes.

Shrimp Spread

Serves 6-8

8 ounces bay shrimp,
   cleaned and coarsely
   chopped
1 5-ounce can water
   chestnuts, drained and
   chopped
4-5 green onions, chopped
Juice of ½ lemon
2 teaspoons curry powder
¼ cup light mayonnaise

1. In a bowl, gently combine shrimp, water chestnuts and green
   onions.

2. Combine lemon juice, curry powder and mayonnaise in a small
   bowl. Add to shrimp mixture.

Note: Serve on crackers or sliced baguettes.

Shrimp and Roquefort

Start a holiday tradition with this intriguing blend of flavors.

New Orleans Shrimp Boil:
6 cups water
2 bay leaves
1 teaspoon dried basil
1 teaspoon dried thyme
2 teaspoons minced garlic
1 teaspoon salt
1 teaspoon dried mustard
½ teaspoon cayenne
   pepper
½ teaspoon pepper
1 pound large shrimp or 2
   pounds medium shrimp,
   unpeeled

Shrimp and Roquefort:
3 ounces cream cheese,
   softened
1 ounce crumbled
   Roquefort cheese
1 clove garlic, minced
½ teaspoon sugar
1 teaspoon grainy mustard
1-2 tablespoons Madeira
   wine
Fresh parsley, chopped
1 lemon, thinly sliced

Shrimp Cocktail Sauce:
1 cup prepared chili sauce
1 tablespoon fresh lemon
   juice
1 teaspoon creamed
   horseradish

1. Prepare New Orleans Shrimp Boil: Place the water and spices in a large pot and bring to a boil. Reduce heat and simmer 5 minutes.

2. Return water to boiling and add shrimp.

3. Cook shrimp uncovered over high heat 3-5 minutes or until pink. Drain shrimp and cool.

4. Prepare Shrimp and Roquefort: Shell and devein the cooked shrimp. Carefully slit each shrimp along the outside lengthwise. Set aside.

5. Blend the cream cheese and Roquefort cheese. Add garlic, sugar, mustard and wine.

6. Stuff the cheese mixture into the slits of the shrimp. Chill.

7. Just before serving, roll the shrimp's stuffed side in chopped parsley. Arrange on a platter garnished with lemon slices and serve with Shrimp Cocktail Sauce.

8. Prepare Shrimp Cocktail Sauce: Combine all ingredients in a small bowl and mix well. Serve at room temperature.

Note: After boiling the shrimp, you can stuff it with the Shrimp and Roquefort mixture, or serve the shrimp alone with the Shrimp Cocktail Sauce.

Veal Balls with Mustard Sauce

A hearty appetizer that is a flavorful addition to a party buffet.

1 pound ground veal
1 egg, beaten
¼ cup fresh bread crumbs
1 garlic clove, minced
2 tablespoons chopped
   parsley
¼ teaspoon salt
½ teaspoon ground sage
⅛ teaspoon white pepper
⅛ teaspoon fresh ground
   nutmeg

Mustard Sauce:
1 cup lowfat sour cream
¼ cup coarse-grain
   mustard

1. Preheat oven to 350°.

2. In a large bowl, combine veal, egg, bread crumbs, garlic, parsley, salt, sage, pepper and nutmeg. Using your hands, mix thoroughly.

3. Shape into small balls and place on a cookie sheet with sides. Bake the meatballs approximately 25-30 minutes, turning them occasionally, to brown the entire ball.

4. Transfer balls to a plate and keep warm.

5. Prepare Mustard Sauce: In a skillet, combine the sour cream and mustard. Cook sauce over medium heat, stirring frequently, until the sauce has thickened.

6. To serve, transfer to a chafing dish and gently stir the balls to coat with the Mustard Sauce.

Melton Chicken Paté

A fabulous combination of flavors.

Serves 4-6

2 chicken breasts, boned,
   skinned and cooked
¼ cup mayonnaise
¼ cup sour cream
1 tablespoon dried
   rosemary
½ cup fresh chopped
   parsley
Salt and Pepper to taste
3 tablespoons dried
   currants or finely
   chopped raisins
   (optional)
Rosemary sprigs to garnish

1. Cut chicken into pieces. In a food processor, using the steel blade to grind, mix the chicken, mayonnaise, sour cream, rosemary, parsley, salt and pepper to a creamy consistency.

2. Stir in currants or raisins.

3. Garnish with rosemary sprigs.

Note: For a creamier consistency, add more mayonnaise and sour cream in equal amounts. Serve with crackers.

Spicy Bread Round

Great with margaritas.

8 ounces cream cheese,
   softened
½ cup sour cream
½ cup salsa
2 cups shredded Cheddar
   cheese
1 round loaf pumpernickel
   or sourdough, with the
   top sliced off and
   reserved, and the loaf
   hollowed out

1. Preheat oven to 400°.

2. Mix all ingredients except bread.

3. Place mixture in bread and replace bread lid. Wrap in foil and
   bake for 1½ hours.

Note: Serve warm with sliced, raw vegetables and toasted pumpernickel or sourdough chunks. Particularly good with red, green and
   yellow bell peppers.

Spinach and Feta Cheese in Phyllo Pastry

Makes 5 dozen

2 eggs
1 medium onion,
   quartered
8 ounces crumbled Feta
   cheese
8 ounces cream cheese,
   softened
10 ounces frozen chopped
   spinach, thawed and
   drained
2 tablespoons fresh
   chopped parsley
1 tablespoon fresh
   chopped dill
Dash of pepper
1 pound phyllo dough,
   thawed according to
   directions
1 cup butter, melted

1. Preheat oven to 375°. Combine eggs, onion and Feta in a blender
   or food processor. Blend until smooth, add cream cheese and
   blend again.

2. Squeeze all the water out of the spinach and add to the cheese
   mixture. Mix in parsley, dill and pepper. Refrigerate at least 1
   hour.

3. Cut phyllo into lengthwise strips, 2 inches wide, keeping uncut
   phyllo sheets covered with a damp towel. Brush with melted
   butter. Place a rounded teaspoon of spinach filling on one end and
   fold like a flag to the other end.

4. Arrange triangles of filled pastry on ungreased jellyroll pan. Brush
   with remaining butter.

5. Can be frozen at this point, up to 1 month but do not thaw
   pastries prior to baking.

6. Bake for 20 minutes or until golden brown. Serve hot.

Mushroom-Walnut Turnovers

Well worth the extra effort.

Dough:
½ cup butter, softened
4 ounces cream cheese, softened
1 tablespoon milk
1¼ cups flour, sifted
¼ teaspoon salt

Mushroom Filling:
1 large green onion, minced
3 tablespoons butter
½ pound finely chopped mushrooms
½ teaspoon fresh lemon juice
¼ cup walnuts, finely chopped
½ teaspoon hot pepper sauce
Salt and Pepper to taste
¼ cup sour cream
1 egg, beaten

1. Prepare Dough: With an electric mixer, cream together butter and cream cheese. Add the milk to thin the mixture. Sift in flour and salt, mixing until it is well combined and soft dough forms. Wrap the dough in waxed paper and chill at least 2 hours.

2. Prepare Mushroom Filling: Over medium heat, cook green onion in butter for 10 seconds. Add mushrooms and cook over low heat until tender and the liquid has evaporated.

3. Remove from heat and stir in lemon juice, walnuts, hot pepper sauce, sour cream, salt and pepper. Cool filling.

4. Preheat oven to 400°.

5. Prepare Turnovers: Using a floured rolling pin on a well-floured surface, roll out ½ the Dough to ⅛-inch thickness. Cut into rounds with a 2½ to 3-inch cookie cutter.

6. Put 1 teaspoon of Mushroom Filling mixture in the center of round. Moisten edges of rounds with beaten egg. Fold the rounds in half and press the edges together with a fork to seal.

7. Turnovers may be frozen at this point.

8. Place turnovers on a greased cookie sheet and brush with a beaten egg.

9. Bake for fifteen minutes until golden brown. Serve hot.

Artwalk Paté

Makes 3 cups

½ cup walnuts, shelled
2 large green onions
2 large garlic cloves, peeled
1 medium onion, peeled
    and quartered
4 tablespoons butter
1 Granny Smith apple,
    peeled, cored and
    quartered
½ pound chicken livers,
    trimmed
4 ounces pork sausage,
    casings removed
2 tablespoons cognac
4 ounces cream cheese,
    softened
Dash of salt
⅛ teaspoon pepper
¼ teaspoon dried tarragon
⅛ teaspoon thyme
⅛ teaspoon allspice
¼ cup finely chopped
    walnuts
Walnut halves for garnish

1. In a food processor with a metal blade, process the walnuts for 5 seconds, set aside. With machine running, drop green onions and garlic through the feed tube and process until finely minced. Add the onion and turn the machine on and off 7 to 8 times to chop it. In a 9-inch skillet, melt 2 tablespoons of the butter. Add green onions, garlic and onion. Set aside.

2. Put the apple in the processor and turn machine on and off 8 to 10 times to chop them. Add apple to the onion mixture and cook, stirring occasionally until the mixture is soft and transparent. Return the mixture to the processor.

3. Melt the remaining butter in the skillet and sauté the livers and sausage until cooked through, about 10 minutes. Meanwhile, gently warm the cognac in a small saucepan. When the meats are done, ignite the cognac and pour it over them. Let the mixture cool slightly. Add it to the processor and process for about 30 seconds, stopping once to scrape down the bowl. Add the cream cheese and seasonings and process until smooth. Add the walnuts and turn the machine on and off 3 to 4 times to mix them in. Transfer the mixture to a 9-inch mold. Top with walnuts. Cover with plastic wrap and chill.

Note: The paté will turn dark if it comes into contact with metal. Be sure to line the 9-inch mold, if aluminum, with plastic wrap before pouring in the paté.

South of the Border Shrimp

Serves 6-8

2 pounds large uncooked
  shrimp, peeled, deveined
  with tails left intact
¾ cup olive oil
½ cup fresh finely chopped
  cilantro
¼ cup white wine vinegar
2-3 tablespoons fresh
  lemon juice
2 jalapeño peppers, seeded
  and minced
2 large cloves garlic,
  minced
½ teaspoon cayenne
  pepper
½ teaspoon red pepper
  flakes
Salt and Pepper to taste
1 large lemon, sliced
1 large red onion, sliced

1. Bring a large pot of water to boil. Add the shrimp and cook until
   pink, about 3 minutes. Transfer to a large bowl of ice water.
   Drain. Place shrimp in a large bowl.

2. In a medium-sized bowl, whisk together the next 9 ingredients.
   Pour marinade over shrimp, gently tossing to coat.

3. In a large shallow dish, layer shrimp, lemon slices and onion. Pour
   remaining marinade over shrimp. Cover and refrigerate at least 6
   hours.

Avocado Dip

Makes 2 cups

1 avocado
1 small clove of garlic,
  minced
¼ cup fresh chopped
  cilantro
1 tablespoon lime juice
9 ounces tomatillos
2-4 tablespoons diced
  green chiles
2 tablespoons minced
  onions
¼ teaspoon cumin

1. In a food processor, puree the avocado. Add the remaining
   ingredients and puree until the mixture is smooth.

Note: Serve the dip with tortilla chips.

Roasted Herbed Nuts

Tasty with drinks and an ideal hostess gift.

1 egg white
8 ounces pecan halves
8 ounces almonds, whole
8 ounces cashews, whole
¼ cup sesame seeds
1 tablespoon crumbled
   thyme
½ teaspoon pepper
Salt (optional)

1. Preheat oven to 325°. Lightly oil a baking sheet.

2. In a large bowl, whisk the egg white until frothy and it begins to hold soft peaks. Add the pecans, almonds, cashews, sesame seeds, thyme and pepper. Toss the mixture until the nuts are evenly coated.

3. Place coated nuts in a single layer on the baking sheet, making sure nuts are separated.

4. Bake, stirring and turning, approximately 40 minutes until crispy. Sprinkle with salt, if desired. Allow to cool completely before serving. Store in an airtight container.

Salsa Cheesecake

A flavorful starter for a large dinner party.

2 tablespoons butter,
   melted
½ cup bread crumbs
12 ounces cream cheese,
   softened
4 ounces Roquefort cheese
1 cup sour cream
2 tablespoons flour
1 cup grated Parmesan
   cheese
½ cup salsa
4 large eggs
1 tablespoon dried parsley
1 bunch fresh cilantro
   leaves, of which 1
   tablespoon is minced

1. Preheat oven to 350°.

2. Brush sides and bottom of a 9-inch springform pan with the melted butter and carefully coat with ¼ cup bread crumbs. Tap out excess.

3. In a mixer, combine cream cheese and Roquefort. Add sour cream, flour, Parmesan and salsa, beating well between additions. Scrape bowl, turn motor to high and add eggs one at a time. Beat well to make certain all is blended properly.

4. Pour batter into the prepared pan. Sprinkle with remaining bread crumbs, parsley and minced cilantro.

5. Bake approximately 1 hour and 15 minutes until top is lightly browned. Turn off oven and cool in oven with door ajar for 1 hour.

6. To serve, arrange cilantro around perimeter of plate and place cheesecake in center. Cut into wedges. This may also be served as a first course.

Spicy Cayenne Toasts with Sun-Dried Tomato Spread

Sensational, yet so simple.

Serves 8-10

Sun-Dried Tomato
  Spread:
1½ ounces sun-dried
  tomatoes
¼ cup olive oil
2 cloves garlic, minced
2 tablespoons minced
  parsley
5 basil leaves, chopped
1 green onion, chopped
1 teaspoon pepper
½ teaspoon salt
Pinch of sugar
4 ounces goat cheese

Cayenne Toasts:
1 loaf French bread
  baguette, sliced into
  ¼-inch slices
½ cup olive oil
2 teaspoons cayenne
  pepper
1 teaspoon salt
1 teaspoon sugar
½ teaspoon black pepper
1 teaspoon paprika
1½ teaspoons garlic
  powder

1. Prepare Sun-Dried Tomato Spread: To rehydrate sun-dried tomatoes, place them in boiling water for 5 minutes. Drain.

2. Place tomatoes and remaining ingredients, except goat cheese, in a container and refrigerate for 4 hours.

3. Process in a food processor until smooth.

4. Prepare Cayenne Toasts: Preheat oven to 200°.

5. Combine ingredients, other than bread, in food processor, mixing well.

6. Lay bread slices on a cookie sheet. Brush one side lightly with spread.

7. Cook 1 hour until crisp. Cool. May be frozen.

8. To serve, place Sun-Dried Tomato Spread on Cayenne Toasts and top with a sprinkle of goat cheese.

Vegetable Herb Dip

Serves 6-8

10 ounces frozen chopped
   spinach, drained
1 cup fresh chopped
   parsley
1 teaspoon dill
Juice of ½ lemon
½ cup finely chopped
   yellow onion
4 green onions, chopped
1 cup sour cream
1 cup mayonnaise
Salt and Pepper to taste

1. Combine all ingredients in a bowl and mix well. Chill at least 1 hour before serving.

Note: Mound the dip in the center of a platter and serve with an assortment of seasonal vegetables.

Rye Bread Snacks

8 ounces grated sharp
   Cheddar cheese
1 fresh green chile, diced
   or 4 ounce can diced
   green chiles
½ cup mayonnaise
2 tablespoons white wine
   vinegar
1 teaspoon Worcestershire
   sauce
Dash of hot pepper sauce
8 ounces tomato sauce
4½ ounces black olives,
   chopped
2 garlic cloves, minced
2 tablespoons chopped
   onion
1 teaspoon pepper
1 loaf party rye bread,
   sliced

1. Preheat oven to 350°.

2. Mix all ingredients together, except bread.

3. Place a teaspoon of the mixture on a slice of bread.

4. Bake for 15-20 minutes until the cheese has melted.

Broccoli Bake

Makes 3 cups

1 envelope vegetable soup
  mix
2 cups light sour cream
10 ounces frozen broccoli,
  chopped, thawed and
  squeezed dry
1 cup shredded Cheddar
  cheese

1. Preheat oven to 350°.

2. In a 1-quart casserole dish, combine soup mix, sour cream,
   broccoli and ¾ cup cheese until smooth. Top with remaining ¼
   cup cheese.

3. Bake for 30 minutes.

Note: Serve with crackers.

Fat Pretzels

Fun to make and a real crowd pleaser.

¼ ounce active dry yeast
1½ cups warm water
1 teaspoon salt
1 tablespoon sugar
4 cups flour
1 large egg, well beaten
Coarse salt

1. Preheat oven to 425°.

2. Dissolve yeast in warm water. Add salt and sugar. Blend in flour
   and knead dough until smooth.

3. As soon as dough is kneaded, cut into small pieces and roll into ½-
   inch ropes. Twist ropes into pretzel shapes. Place on foil-lined
   cookie sheets.

4. Brush pretzels with beaten egg and sprinkle with coarse salt.

5. Bake for 12-15 minutes until brown.

Snow Peas with Lemon Dijon Sauce

Don't let the anchovies scare you away, for they add a wonderful element.

Makes 1 cup

1¼ pounds snow peas or 2
  pounds small sugar peas

Lemon Dijon Sauce:
2 tablespoons whipping
  cream
2 ounces anchovies,
  undrained (optional)
Juice of ½ lemon
3-4 tablespoons Dijon
  mustard
½ cup sour cream
3 ounces cream cheese,
  softened
2 green onions, chopped
  (white parts only)
Pepper to taste
1 tablespoon capers, rinsed
  and drained (optional)

1. Clean and string snow peas.

2. In a food processor, mix the Lemon Dijon Sauce ingredients, except capers, and process to a smooth consistency. Refrigerate.

3. To serve, bring the sauce to room temperature and garnish with capers. Arrange snow peas on a platter. Put sauce in a bowl and place in the center of the platter.

Note: Blanched asparagus, green beans or cucumbers are also good choices as accompaniments.

Peanut Dip

Makes 1½ cups

1 cup dry roasted peanuts
¼ cup brown sugar, firmly
  packed
8 ounces cream cheese,
  softened
½ teaspoon vanilla extract
Apple slices
Celery slices

1. In a food processor, blend the peanuts, brown sugar, cream cheese and vanilla until smooth.

2. Serve peanut dip at room temperature with apple and celery slices.

Note: To prevent apple from turning brown, mix 2 cups of water and 2 tablespoons lemon juice and dip apple slices in liquid before serving.

Asparagus Canapés

24 slices extra thin white
bread, crusts removed
4 ounces crumbled Bleu
cheese
8 ounces cream cheese,
softened
1 tablespoon mayonnaise
1 egg, beaten
24 fresh asparagus spears,
blanched
½ cup butter, melted
Red leaf lettuce

1. Preheat oven to 400°.

2. Roll each piece of bread flat.

3. Mix Bleu cheese, cream cheese, mayonnaise and egg in a small bowl.

4. Spread each piece of bread with approximately 1 tablespoon of the cheese mixture. Center asparagus spear on the edge of the bread and roll tightly. Cut in half or thirds and secure with a toothpick.

5. Lightly dip each piece in melted butter. Place on an ungreased cookie sheet.

6. Bake for 15-20 minutes until lightly browned.

7. To serve, shred red leaf lettuce into ½-inch pieces. Place shredded lettuce on a platter and arrange canapés on top.

Note: May be prepared 1 day in advance. Bake just before serving.

Brie with Sun-Dried Tomatoes

1 pound Brie cheese, well
chilled
3 tablespoons minced
Italian parsley
3 tablespoons fresh basil,
cut into strips
3 cloves garlic, minced
2 tablespoons chopped
pine nuts
8 sun-dried tomatoes,
minced
3 tablespoons grated
Parmesan cheese

1. Remove rind from top of Brie and place on a serving platter.

2. Combine remaining ingredients in a small bowl and spread on top of the cheese.

Note: For optimum flavor, refrigerate 2-3 hours prior to serving, warm to room temperature and serve with Lahvosh crackers.

Roasted Eggplant Spread

Makes 2½ cups

1½ pounds eggplant
3 Italian tomatoes
1 medium onion,
    quartered
4 large cloves garlic, peeled
2 tablespoons olive oil
2 teaspoons dried thyme
1 teaspoon salt
¼ cup Italian parsley
Lemon juice (optional)

1. Preheat oven to 400°. Cut eggplant and tomatoes in half, lengthwise. Place eggplant, tomatoes, onion and garlic in a roasting pan and drizzle with the oil and thyme. Bake approximately 50-55 minutes until the eggplant is very tender. Cool slightly and peel eggplant.

2. Place eggplant, tomatoes, onion, garlic, salt and parsley in a food processor and process until smooth. Season with lemon juice, if desired.

3. Chill before serving.

Note: Serve with water crackers or pita toasts. Eggplant does not store well and may become bitter after 2-3 days.

Sesame Chicken Bites

3 tablespoons butter
1½ pounds chicken
    breasts, boned and cut
    into 1-inch pieces
1 egg, beaten
⅓ cup milk
¼ cup flour
½ teaspoon baking powder
1 teaspoon salt
1 tablespoon paprika
½ teaspoon pepper
½ cup chopped macadamia
    nuts
¼ cup sesame seeds
Apricot jam
Spicy grained mustard

1. Preheat oven to 400°.

2. Melt butter in a 9x9-inch baking dish in the oven. Set aside.

3. Thoroughly clean and dry chicken pieces.

4. Combine egg and milk in a small bowl.

5. Combine flour, baking powder, salt, paprika, pepper, macadamia nuts and sesame seeds in another bowl. Mix well.

6. Dip the chicken pieces in the egg mixture first, and then in the dry mixture. Coat chicken pieces well. Place chicken in the baking dish, turning to coat with butter.

7. Bake chicken skin side down for 15 minutes. Remove from oven and turn each piece. Bake another 15 minutes until lightly browned and tender.

8. Serve with heated apricot jam and a spicy grained mustard.

Sizzling Beef

This hearty appetizer may be grilled for an outdoor party or broiled for an indoor party.

2 pounds flank steak, trimmed and thinly sliced on the bias
5 green onions, chopped
4 cloves garlic, minced
½ cup plus 2 tablespoons soy sauce
¼ cup sugar
¼ cup sesame oil
¼ cup sherry
1 teaspoon fresh minced ginger
½ teaspoon pepper

1. Score each piece of meat with an "X."

2. Combine the remaining ingredients in a bowl. Add the meat to the marinade and refrigerate overnight.

3. Grill or broil the meat for 3 minutes. Turn the meat and continue grilling or broiling another 3 minutes. Baste the meat with marinade as needed.

4. To serve, cut strips of beef in halves or thirds. Serve on toothpicks.

Berry Baked Brie

1 pound wheel of Brie or 2 wedges placed to form a triangle
17½ ounce package frozen puff pastry, thawed according to package directions
1 cup whole berry cranberry sauce
1 egg, beaten
1 teaspoon water

1. Preheat oven to 400°.

2. Remove rind from top of Brie.

3. Lightly roll puff pastry, being sure to seal the cracks where the pastry was folded.

4. Place Brie on the pastry and spread cranberry sauce on top of Brie. Bring edges of pastry up around Brie and twist to form a pretty top knot.

5. Whisk egg and water together and brush over entire pastry.

6. Bake for 25 minutes on an ungreased cookie sheet. Let cool for at least 30 minutes before serving.

Note: Your favorite preserves may be substituted for the cranberry sauce. For another blend of flavors, try ½ cup crumbled Bleu cheese and 1 cup apricot preserves. Layer on Brie in the order listed.

Salami Puffs

A crowd-pleaser prepared with minimum effort.

Makes 30 pieces

1 sheet puff pastry (½ of a
  17½ ounce package),
  thawed according to
  package directions
1 egg, beaten
3 cups shredded Longhorn
  Colby cheese
2 teaspoons Italian herb
  seasoning
2 cups diced salami
1 cup sliced green onions

1. Preheat oven to 450°.

2. On a lightly floured board, roll pastry into an 11x16-inch triangle. Transfer to an ungreased 10x15-inch jellyroll pan, pushing edges up the sides. Brush surface of pastry with beaten egg. Prick pastry with a fork.

3. Bake pastry for 10-15 minutes, until brown and puffy. Remove from oven and cool.

4. Sprinkle the pastry with the following ingredients in the order listed: cheese, herb seasoning, salami and onions.

5. Bake for 5 minutes until the cheese is melted. Remove from oven and cool slightly.

6. To serve, transfer to a cutting board and cut into 2-inch squares. Arrange on a serving tray around fresh cut flowers or greens from the garden.

Note: May be prepared in advance but change the final baking time to 8-10 minutes. The remaining pastry may be refrozen.

Artichoke Spread

Serves 6-8

14¾ ounces water packed
  artichoke hearts, drained
  and finely chopped
2 cloves garlic, pressed
1 cup shredded Mozzarella
  cheese
½ cup grated Parmesan
  cheese
2-3 drops hot pepper sauce
½ cup mayonnaise

1. Preheat oven to 350°.

2. Combine all ingredients and blend well.

3. Spread into an ovenproof serving dish. At this point spread may be refrigerated up to 1 day in advance.

4. Bake for 25-30 minutes or until golden and bubbly.

Note: Serve with assorted crackers.

3-Cheese Pizza with Eggplant

A wonderful appetizer that could also be served as a luncheon entree.

Makes 16 slices

3 medium Japanese
eggplants, thinly sliced
lengthwise
1 tablespoon olive oil
Salt and Pepper to taste
2 cups grated Mozzarella
cheese
1 16-ounce ready made
pizza crust
1 pound Italian tomatoes,
seeded and chopped
4 ounces crumbled
Montrachet goat cheese
5-6 garlic cloves, minced
8 fresh basil leaves, thinly
sliced
½ cup grated Parmesan
cheese

1. Preheat broiler. Arrange eggplant slices on a large baking sheet and brush both sides with olive oil. Season with salt and pepper. Broil eggplant approximately 8 minutes until tender and brown, turning frequently.

2. Preheat oven to 500°.

3. Sprinkle 1 cup Mozzarella cheese on pizza crust. Place eggplant slices, tomatoes, goat cheese, garlic and basil on crust. Add remaining Mozzarella cheese and Parmesan cheese to pizza.

4. Bake approximately 12-15 minutes until cheese melts and pizza edges are brown. Cut into wedges and serve on a platter.

Note: Ingredients may be prepared in advance and refrigerated in separate containers. Assemble pizza just prior to baking.

Cheddar Log

Delicious with a cold cocktail.

Serves 6

2 cups grated Cheddar
cheese, firmly packed
4 ounces cream cheese,
softened
2 tablespoons mayonnaise
½ teaspoon hot pepper
sauce
¼ teaspoon Worcestershire
sauce
3 green onions, sliced
6 slices of bacon, fried and
crumbled
½ cup chopped pecans

1. In a food processor, blend Cheddar cheese, cream cheese, mayonnaise, pepper sauce, Worcestershire and green onions until smooth. Add crumbled bacon and process briefly.

2. Drop mixture onto waxed paper forming an 8-inch log. Freeze 30 minutes until firm.

3. Remove the log from waxed paper. Roll log in pecans to coat. Wrap in plastic and refrigerate.

Note: Serve with crackers. May be prepared 1 week in advance.

Sun-Dried Tomato Torte

An interesting combination of taste and texture for that special party.

Serves 8-10

8 ounces cream cheese, softened

4 tablespoons butter, softened

1 cup grated Parmesan cheese

8 ounces sun-dried tomatoes packed in oil, drained, with 1 tablespoon oil reserved

4 pocket bread rounds

3-4 tablespoons butter, melted

Garlic salt to taste

1 bunch fresh basil leaves, julienned

1. In a food processor, mix cream cheese, butter and Parmesan cheese until smoothly blended. Set aside ½ of the cheese mixture in a bowl.

2. Add tomatoes and oil to ½ of the cheese mixture in the food processor. Process until tomatoes are smoothly pureed. Add pureed mixture to cheese mixture. With a mixer, gently beat to blend. Cover and refrigerate until mixture is firm enough to shape.

3. Preheat oven to 350°. Cut around edge of pita to make 2 halves, then cut each pocket bread round into 8 triangles. Place triangles in a single layer on a cookie sheet. Brush with melted butter and sprinkle with garlic salt. Bake triangles approximately 8-10 minutes or until lightly toasted.

4. Mound cheese on a platter. Arrange basil and pocket bread toast triangles around cheese torte. Serve cheese at room temperature on triangles topped with basil.

Rounds of Pesto

Makes 36

¾ cup slivered fresh basil leaves

1 cup grated Parmesan cheese

1 clove garlic, pressed

½ cup mayonnaise

French bread baguette, 36 slices cut ¼-inch thick

1. Stir together basil, Parmesan cheese, garlic and mayonnaise until well blended.

2. Spread each piece of French bread with a generous amount of mayonnaise mixture. Arrange bread slices in a single layer on a cookie sheet.

3. Broil bread slices approximately 3-4 minutes until bubbly and lightly browned.

4. Arrange bread slices on a decorative platter.

Cheese Tarts

Be prepared for rave reviews.

Makes 24

¼ cup plus 1 tablespoon
  mayonnaise
¼ cup plus 1 tablespoon
  sour cream
6 tablespoons butter,
  softened
4 ounces cream cheese,
  softened
1 cup flour
½ cup shredded Monterey
  Jack cheese
½ cup shredded Cheddar
  cheese
Paprika

1. Combine mayonnaise and sour cream in a small bowl. Set aside.

2. In a food processor, prepare the crust by creaming together the butter and cream cheese. Gradually add the flour and process until the mixture is thoroughly combined. Form a ball with the dough and wrap in waxed paper. Refrigerate until the dough is chilled enough to handle.

3. Preheat oven to 350°.

4. Divide the dough into 24 pieces. Press each piece into a mini-cup muffin tin, covering the bottom and sides of the cups. Sprinkle a small amount of each shredded cheese in the bottom of each pastry shell. Spoon 1 teaspoon of mayonnaise mixture over the cheese. Sprinkle with paprika.

5. Bake for 30 minutes until lightly browned. Allow tarts to cool slightly before removing from muffin tin. Serve warm.

Black Bean Torte

Unusual and delicious.

2 cups dried black beans
2 14½-ounce cans chicken broth
1 large chicken bouillon cube
2 cups water
1½ teaspoons ground cumin
1 large tomato, seeded and chopped with excess juice pressed out
½ cup thinly chopped red onion
4 ounces crumbled Feta cheese
½ cup sour cream
Cilantro leaves for garnish

Cilantro Pesto:
2 bunches fresh cilantro leaves
2 tablespoons olive oil
1 teaspoon pressed garlic
½ cup pine nuts

1. Rinse black beans. Place beans in a large pan. Add chicken broth, bouillon cube, water and cumin. Bring to a boil. Cover and simmer approximately 2½ hours until beans are tender. Stir mixture occasionally. Drain liquid.

2. Mash 1 cup of beans. Gently hand mix remaining whole beans with mashed beans. Let cool.

3. Prepare Cilantro Pesto: In a food processor or blender, puree all the ingredients.

4. Line a 4x8-inch loaf pan with plastic wrap, with edges overlapping rim.

5. Gently press ⅓ bean mixture in pan making the layer smooth. Spread Cilantro Pesto over the bean mixture. Press another ⅓ of bean mixture over the Cilantro Pesto, making the bean layer smooth. On top of beans, make an even layer of chopped tomatoes and onions. Sprinkle crumbled Feta cheese on top of mixture. Top cheese with remaining beans, pressing gently to make a smooth loaf.

6. Cover tightly with plastic wrap and refrigerate until loaf is firm.

7. To serve, invert loaf onto a platter and remove plastic wrap. Spoon sour cream down the center and garnish with cilantro leaves.

Note: Serve with crackers or tortilla chips or loaf may be sliced into ½-inch pieces and served as a first course.

Chapter 3

BOWL
ME
OVER

Soups, Chilis and Stews

For a summer picnic

before an evening concert

or a winter supper by

the fire, the following

soups and stews are sure

to bowl you over with

their hearty goodness.

Red and Green Soup

Don't let the name of this soup limit it to the holidays. The colors and flavors are wonderful any time of the year.

Serves 4

¼ cup butter
1 medium onion, finely
   chopped
2 28-ounce cans tomato
   puree
1 teaspoon sugar
¼ teaspoon dried
   crumbled oregano
½ cup half and half
1 10-ounce package frozen
   chopped spinach,
   thawed and well-drained
¼ cup fresh chopped basil
   or 1 tablespoon dried,
   crumbled
Salt and Pepper to taste
½ cup milk
½ cup grated Parmesan
   cheese

1. Melt butter in heavy large saucepan over medium-low heat. Add onion and sauté until very tender, about 5 minutes.

2. Stir in tomatoes, sugar and oregano. Simmer 10 minutes.

3. Mix in half and half, spinach and basil. Simmer 3 minutes longer. Season with salt and pepper. Thin soup with milk if necessary. Garnish with Parmesan cheese.

Carrot Ginger Soup

A perfect first course for an autumn party, this soup is worth its weight in gold. It can be prepared through step 3 a day ahead and refrigerated.

Serves 10

¼ cup butter
2 pounds carrots, peeled
  and thinly sliced
2 large onions, chopped
1½ teaspoons ground
  ginger
3 teaspoons grated orange
  peel
½ teaspoon ground
  coriander
5 cups chicken broth
½ cup milk
½ cup half and half
Salt and Pepper to taste
½ cup grated Parmesan
  cheese
½ cup fresh minced parsley

1. Melt butter in heavy saucepan over medium heat. Add carrots and onions. Cover saucepan and cook until vegetables begin to soften, stirring occasionally, about 15 minutes.

2. Mix in ginger, orange peel and coriander. Add 2 cups broth. Reduce heat to medium-low. Cover pan and simmer soup until carrots are very tender, about 30 minutes.

3. Puree soup in batches in processor or blender. Return puree to saucepan and stir in remaining 3 cups broth, milk and half and half. Season with salt and pepper.

4. Cook over medium heat until warm. Ladle into bowls and garnish with Parmesan cheese and parsley.

Cold Avocado Soup

A California classic.

Serves 4

1 large avocado
1 tablespoon lemon juice
⅛ teaspoon salt
1½ teaspoons minced
  instant onions
5 drops hot pepper sauce
1 cup sour cream
1 can chicken broth
Parsley, chopped for
  garnish
2 strips bacon, cooked and
  crumbled for garnish

1. Combine avocado, lemon juice, salt, onions and pepper sauce in blender. Add sour cream and blend again. Add chicken broth and blend again.

2. Chill well and garnish with chopped parsley and crumbled bacon.

Cold Cream of Green Chile Soup

A show-stopper for a picnic dinner at the Hollywood Bowl.

Serves 8

1½ cups chicken broth
⅓ cup minced onion
1 large garlic clove
½ pound green chiles
8 ounces cream cheese,
    softened
1 cup sour cream
¼ teaspoon ground cumin
1 cup milk
Salt and White Pepper to
    taste
Red, yellow and green bell
    peppers, julienned
Additional sour cream for
    garnish

1. In a saucepan, bring chicken broth to a boil with onion. Boil mixture for 5 minutes and let cool.

2. In a food processor, finely chop the garlic and chiles. Add the cream cheese, sour cream and cumin and blend mixture until it is well combined.

3. With motor running, add the broth mixture in a stream. Blend the mixture until well combined and transfer to a large bowl.

4. Stir in milk, salt and white pepper. Chill the soup well. Garnish with pepper slices and a dollop of sour cream.

Sherry Tomato Bisque

Almost shamefully easy, this soup has been a well-guarded secret for years.

1 10-ounce can cream of
    tomato soup
⅓ cup sour cream
¼ cup dry sherry
1 10-ounce can beef
    consommé
¼ cup grated onion
½ teaspoon celery salt

1. Mix all ingredients together and heat thoroughly.

Garden Gazpacho

Fresh and colorful, this is the best gazpacho we've ever tasted. Cooked scallops or shrimp could be added to make a wonderful summer main dish.

Serves 6-8

2¾ cups vegetable juice
   cocktail
1 medium cucumber, cut
   into chunks
3 medium tomatoes, cut
   into chunks
1 tablespoon sugar
¼ cup red wine vinegar
¼ cup olive oil
1 small red onion, finely
   chopped
2 celery stalks, diced
2 green onions, chopped
   (green parts only)
1 zucchini, chopped
1 small green bell pepper,
   finely chopped
½ cup cilantro, chopped
   and additional sprigs for
   garnish
7-8 drops hot pepper sauce
Salt and Pepper to taste
Croutons and sour cream
   for garnish

1. In a blender or food processor, combine 1¼ cups vegetable juice cocktail, ½ the cucumber, 1 tomato, sugar, vinegar and olive oil. Blend until smooth.

2. Pour mixture into a large bowl and add remaining tomatoes, remaining cucumber, red onion, celery, green onions, zucchini, green pepper, cilantro, pepper sauce, salt and pepper. Stir to blend.

3. Serve well chilled with croutons, a dollop of sour cream and cilantro sprigs.

Butternut Squash Soup

The beautiful golden color of this soup makes it a perfect selection for an autumn party. It would also be ideal as a light luncheon entree served with a green salad or Tomatoes Vinaigrette.

Serves 6

3 tablespoons butter or margarine
2 medium onions, chopped
2 cups diced butternut squash
1 Granny Smith or Pippin apple, peeled and chopped
2 cloves garlic, minced
3 tablespoons flour
1-2 teaspoons curry powder
Pinch of nutmeg
3 cups chicken broth
1½ cups milk
Grated rind and juice of 1 orange
Salt and Pepper to taste
Chopped parsley

1. In a large frying pan melt butter and sauté onions over medium heat until soft. Add squash, apple and garlic. Sauté for 3-5 minutes, stirring occasionally.

2. Add flour, curry powder and nutmeg, stirring constantly to blend. Slowly add chicken broth, milk and orange rind, stirring constantly to combine. Simmer 20-30 minutes until vegetables are very soft.

3. Puree in batches in blender or food processor. Season with salt and pepper. Serve hot and garnish with parsley.

Corona Corn Chowder

A wonderful, zesty soup sure to please a crowd on a wintry evening.

Serves 8-10

1 pound fresh chorizo or
hot Italian sausage,
casings removed and
sausage meat crumbled
2 cloves garlic, minced
1 cup chopped onion
½ cup chopped celery
1 red bell pepper, chopped
1 green bell pepper,
chopped
4 cups corn, fresh or frozen
1 bay leaf
1 teaspoon dried thyme,
crumbled
6 cups chicken broth
2 boiling potatoes, peeled
and cut into ½-inch
cubes
¾ cup half and half
Salt and Pepper to taste
2 tablespoons cilantro

1. In a kettle, brown the sausage over moderate heat, stirring occasionally. Add the garlic, onion, celery and bell peppers. Cook the mixture, stirring occasionally, until the vegetables are softened.

2. Add the corn, bay leaf, thyme and chicken broth. Cook the mixture, stirring for 1 minute.

3. Refrigerate prepared sausage and vegetables in kettle for 30 minutes or up to 1 day. Remove from refrigerator and skim off all congealed fat.

4. Add potatoes and half and half and simmer mixture, stirring occasionally, for 25 minutes, or until potatoes are tender.

5. Discard the bay leaf, season chowder with salt and pepper, and garnish with cilantro.

Effortless Spinach Potato Soup

Guests will think you slaved over this delicious soup, but it couldn't be easier to make. Also great chilled.

Serves 2-4

1 10-ounce package frozen
   spinach souffle, thawed
1 10½-ounce can cream of
   potato soup
1½ cups lowfat milk
¼ cup lowfat yogurt
2 green onions, chopped
1 teaspoon lemon juice
¼ teaspoon dried thyme
Pepper to taste

1. Place all ingredients in blender and blend until smooth.

2. Transfer to large saucepan. Bring soup to boil over medium-high heat, stirring frequently.

Newport Clam Chowder

Serves 6-8

1 medium onion, chopped
3 tablespoons butter or
   margarine
1 bottle clam juice
12 ounces clams, minced
   with liquid reserved
6 ounces whole clams, with
   liquid reserved
4 large raw potatoes, pared
   and diced
4 cups milk
2 cups half and half
Salt and White Pepper to
   taste

1. Sauté onion in butter or margarine in a deep kettle until transparent. Add the bottled clam juice plus the liquid from the clams. Add potatoes and cook until the potatoes are just tender.

2. Add remaining ingredients and bring to a boil. Refrigerate overnight. Remove excess fat. Heat before serving.

Bonfire Soup

There is nothing more cheering on a wintry day than coming home to a piping hot bowl of this flavorful soup.

1 pound spicy sausage, ground with casings removed
1 onion, chopped
1 green bell pepper, chopped
1 large potato, diced
2 cloves garlic, minced
6 cups beef stock
1 cup canned kidney beans, drained
1 cup canned chopped tomatoes in juice
1 bay leaf
1 teaspoon salt
½ teaspoon thyme
½ teaspoon dried basil
½ teaspoon dried rosemary
¼ teaspoon black pepper
⅛ teaspoon cayenne pepper
¼ cup red wine
Parsley

1. In a large sauce pan, sauté sausage. Remove and pat dry.

2. Sauté the onion, green pepper, potatoes and garlic. Add the sausage, beef stock, kidney beans, tomatoes and spices. Simmer for ½ hour.

3. Skim off any fat that has risen to the surface. Add red wine. Garnish with chopped parsley.

Tortellini Soup with Chicken

Substantial and satisfying.

Serves 10-12

4½ quarts chicken broth
18 ounces fresh cheese-
   filled spinach tortellini
¾ pound spinach leaves,
   stemmed and julienned
1 pound chicken breasts,
   skinned, boned and cut
   into ½-inch chunks
½ pound mushrooms,
   sliced
1 medium red bell pepper,
   diced
2 teaspoons dry tarragon
   or sage
Grated Parmesan cheese

1. In a large stock pot, bring chicken broth to a boil over high heat. Add tortellini and cook until al dente, about 5-8 minutes.

2. Add spinach, chicken, mushrooms, bell pepper and tarragon or sage. Return to boil over high heat and cook about 5 minutes more or until chicken is no longer pink. Cut to test.

3. Ladle into bowls and garnish with Parmesan cheese.

Onion Soup with Roquefort Croutons

A traditional favorite dramatically enhanced by the tasty Roquefort croutons.

Serves 6

¼ cup butter or margarine
3 onions, thinly sliced
½ cup minced green
   onions
¼ cup flour
1½ teaspoons paprika
6 cups chicken broth
1 cup dark beer
1 French bread baguette,
   sliced
Olive oil
8 ounces Swiss cheese,
   grated
8 ounces Roquefort cheese,
   crumbled

1. Melt butter or margarine in a large saucepan. Add both onions and cook over medium heat until soft but not brown, 5-7 minutes.

2. Add flour and cook for 2 minutes, stirring constantly. Blend in the paprika, chicken broth and beer. Bring to a boil. Reduce heat and simmer for 1 hour, uncovered.

3. Preheat oven to 350°. Brush bread slices with oil and toast for 12-15 minutes, until golden. Combine cheeses and spread thickly on the toasts. Broil until melted and bubbling. Place 1 to 2 in each bowl and pour hot soup over toasts. Serve immediately.

Tortilla Soup

Serve with warm buttered tortillas and a fresh fruit salad.

Serves 10

1 large onion, sliced

8 garlic cloves, minced

6 tablespoons vegetable oil, plus additional for frying tortillas

7 green chiles, stemmed and seeded

4 cups water

5 tomatoes, seeded and chopped

8 cups chicken broth

Salt and Pepper to taste

12 corn tortillas, cut into strips

1½ cups shredded Monterey Jack cheese

2 avocados

1. In a stock pot, cook onion and garlic in 4 tablespoons oil over medium heat, stirring until soft. Increase heat and add chiles, stirring to avoid burning. Cook for 1 minute or until soft. Remove 1 chile and cut into 10 strips, reserve for garnish.

2. To the pot, add 4 cups water and tomatoes and bring the liquid to a boil. Simmer mixture for 30 minutes.

3. In a blender, puree the mixture in batches.

4. In pot, heat 2 tablespoons of remaining oil over medium heat until hot, but not smoking. Return the puree and cook, stirring, for 5 minutes. Stir in the broth, salt and pepper. Simmer soup for 15 minutes.

5. In a large skillet, heat ½-inch of additional oil over high heat until hot, but not smoking. Fry the tortilla strips in batches, stirring for 30 seconds until crisp. Transfer to paper towels to drain.

6. Divide fried tortillas among 10 heated bowls. Pour the soup over them and top each one with 1 strip of the reserved chile. Sprinkle each serving with some shredded cheese and top soup with sliced avocado wedges.

Sicilian Calamari Soup with Anchovies and Basil

Serves 4

1 pound squid, cleaned
   (body and tubes only)
¼ cup olive oil
1 medium onion, cut into
   eighths and layers
   separated
2-3 cloves garlic, minced
4 cups chicken broth
½ teaspoon pepper
1 2-ounce can flat anchovy
   fillets, in oil
¼ cup coarsely chopped
   fresh basil leaves
¼ cup lemon juice
½ cup dry white wine
   mixed with 2
   tablespoons cornstarch
Pepper to garnish
Whole basil leaves for
   garnish

1. Rinse squid under cold running water and drain on paper towels. Slice the bodies crosswise into ¼-inch rings. Heat the oil in a 4-quart saucepan over medium heat until hot, but not smoking.

2. Add the onions and garlic, stirring frequently until wilted. Add the chicken broth and bring to a boil.

3. Add the squid, pepper, anchovies and basil. Simmer gently, uncovered, for 15 minutes. Stirring gently, add the lemon juice and the wine mixed with cornstarch. Cook for 2 minutes longer.

4. Garnish with pepper and whole basil leaves.

Note: Serve as a main course with a green salad and crusty Italian bread or cheese Boboli.

Lawman Chili

The high quality meats really make the difference in this prize-winning chili.

4 large garlic cloves,
  minced
1 brown onion, finely
  chopped
1 red onion, finely
  chopped
1 green bell pepper, finely
  chopped
2 tablespoons vegetable oil
2 pounds beef sirloin,
  ¼-inch cubes
1 pound pork tenderloin,
  ¼-inch cubes
Salt to taste
2 tablespoons chili powder
½ teaspoon cayenne
  pepper
½ teaspoon paprika
½ teaspoon ground cumin
3 cups water
1 6-ounce can tomato
  paste
3 medium tomatoes,
  coarsely chopped
1 green chile, finely
  chopped
1 jalapeño pepper, finely
  chopped
Cheddar and Monterey
  Jack cheese for garnish
Sour cream for garnish

1. Sauté garlic, onions and bell pepper in vegetable oil in a large saucepan over medium heat, until translucent.

2. Remove onion and pepper mixture from pan, leaving liquid. Add beef and pork cubes and brown over medium heat, stirring occasionally and adding salt to taste. Cook meat at least 15-20 minutes or until tender.

3. Add onion and pepper mixture to meat. Stir and let cook together another 5 minutes. Add dry seasonings and again stir mixture. Add water, tomato paste, tomatoes, fresh chile and jalapeño pepper. Let entire mixture simmer for at least 2 hours, stirring occasionally. Serve with cheeses and sour cream.

Black Bean Turkey Chili

Excellent.

Serves 8-10

2 tablespoons olive oil
2 medium onions, chopped
1 red bell pepper, chopped
1 pound Italian turkey
  sausage
2 pounds ground turkey
6 cloves garlic, minced
8 ounces diced green chiles
½ teaspoon pepper
1 teaspoon salt
3 tablespoons chili powder
1 tablespoon dried oregano
1 tablespoon dried basil
1 12-ounce can tomato
  paste
1 28-ounce can Italian
  plum tomatoes
1 16-ounce can Italian
  plum tomatoes
1 cup beer
1 32-ounce can black
  beans, rinsed and well
  drained
¼ cup chopped fresh
  cilantro

1. In a large skillet or Dutch oven, heat oil over low heat. Sauté the onions and red pepper for about 10 minutes or until tender but not browned.

2. Add the sausage and turkey and brown over medium heat. Drain any excess fat from pan.

3. Add the garlic, chiles, pepper, salt, chili powder, oregano, basil and tomato paste.

4. Stir in the tomatoes, beer and beans.

5. Simmer over low heat for 20-30 minutes. Taste to adjust seasonings. Stir in cilantro before serving. May be made ahead and reheated.

Ragout of Lamb

A foolproof party dish, easily prepared in the morning and then heated 1½ hours before serving.

Serves 4-6

**3 pounds leg of lamb, cut
 in 1-inch cubes**
¼ cup flour
½ teaspoon salt
**⅛ teaspoon freshly ground
 pepper**
¼ cup olive oil
1½ cups chicken broth
½ cup California sherry
2 cloves garlic, minced
**2 tablespoons fresh lemon
 juice**
**2 tablespoons finely
 chopped parsley**

1. Preheat oven to 350°.

2. Dredge lamb cubes with flour that has been mixed with salt and pepper.

3. Heat an 8-inch heavy frying pan and sauté the lamb in olive oil until lightly browned. Do not put too many pieces in the pan at once. Pour chicken broth and sherry over lamb.

4. Add garlic and heat until bubbling, then cover and transfer to oven.

5. Bake until lamb is very tender, about 1½ hours. There should be no more than 1 cup gravy. If there is, return pan to stove, uncovered, and boil quickly until gravy is reduced. If the meat is very well done, then remove it before boiling liquid down.

6. Add lemon juice and chopped parsley to gravy. Return the meat. Stir until boiling and serve. Can make ahead and refrigerate.

Spicy Mahi Mahi with Ragout

Serves 4

4 cups chicken or fish
   broth
½ pound carrots, cut into
   1-inch by ⅛-inch
   julienne strips
½ teaspoon red pepper
   flakes
Salt and Pepper to taste
2 large cloves garlic,
   minced
1 bay leaf
1 medium onion, cut into
   eighths, layers separated
½ pound firm red
   tomatoes, seeded and
   diced
½ pound cucumber, cut
   into ¼-inch thick slices
2 pounds mahi mahi,
   skinless and boneless, cut
   into 1½-inch cubes
½ cup fresh shredded basil
¼ cup dry vermouth
4 tablespoons cornstarch

1. Put the broth in a large 4-quart kettle and bring to a boil. Add the carrots, red pepper flakes, salt and pepper, garlic and bay leaf. Let simmer for 4-5 minutes, until carrots are crisp, yet tender. Add the onion, tomatoes, cucumbers, fish and basil.

2. Cover and let cook over high heat about 4-5 minutes more. Do not stir as this will break up vegetables. Reduce heat to simmer. Add the vermouth mixed with the cornstarch, stirring very gently for about 1 minute.

Note: May be served hot, chilled or at room temperature in large bowls over rice or with crusty sourdough garlic bread.

Italian Sausage Ragout

Serves 6

½ cup fresh parsley,
  packed
2 large garlic cloves,
  chopped
¼ cup olive oil
2 medium onions,
  chopped
1 pound Italian sweet
  sausage, cut into 1-inch
  pieces
1 pound Italian hot
  sausage, cut into 1-inch
  pieces
4 red bell peppers, cut into
  ¼-inch strips
2 large tomatoes, peeled,
  seeded and chopped
1¼ teaspoons fresh
  rosemary
¼ pound prosciutto, diced
1 small head green
  cabbage, cut into
  1½-inch strips

1. Chop parsley and garlic together and set aside.

2. Heat the oil in a large flameproof casserole over medium heat. Sauté the onions in the oil until slightly browned.

3. Add the sausages to the onions and cook for 20 minutes, stirring frequently.

4. Add the parsley mixture, peppers, tomatoes, rosemary and prosciutto and continue cooking for 10 minutes.

5. At serving time, steam the cabbage until tender, about 7 minutes. Stir into the sausage mixture and cook an additional 10 minutes to heat through.

Greek Beef Stew

A magnificent stew. The Feta cheese makes it distinctively different.

Serves 6-8

3 pounds of beef, cut into
  pieces
4 tablespoons butter or oil
1 tablespoon salt
Pepper to taste
3 ounces tomato paste
1 clove garlic
Bay leaf
1½ cups condensed beef
  broth
1 cup red wine
2 pounds small white
  onions, peeled
2 tablespoons chopped
  parsley
¼ teaspoon oregano
1 cup walnuts
½ pound Feta cheese, cut
  into small cubes

1. Brown the beef in butter or oil.

2. Add salt, pepper, tomato paste, garlic, bay leaf, broth and wine.

3. Add cold water if necessary to cover meat. Simmer for 1½ hours.

4. Add onions and continue cooking until tender. Bring to a boil and thicken sauce. Add parsley, oregano and walnuts.

5. Just before serving, top with Feta cheese.

Chapter 4

Botanical Gardens

Salads

These salads are as fresh

and bountiful as the regions

they represent.

Tomatoes Vinaigrette

A zesty salad that begs for an outdoor dinner on a summer evening.

Serves 4-6

2 medium tomatoes, sliced
1 medium cucumber,
   thinly sliced
½ onion, sliced
¼ teaspoon each, ground
   savory, ground tarragon,
   crumbled bay leaf and
   celery salt
⅛ teaspoon pepper
¼ teaspoon salt
½ cup oil
⅓ cup red wine vinegar
1 head lettuce, shredded
2 tablespoons fresh
   chopped parsley

1. Alternate layers of tomatoes, cucumber and onions in a shallow glass dish.

2. Beat together all spices with oil and vinegar in a small bowl.

3. Pour over vegetables and chill, covered, for several hours.

4. Drain and serve on shredded lettuce. Sprinkle with parsley.

Greek Shrimp Salad

A hearty salad full of robust flavor and texture. This can be made one day in advance and kept covered in the refrigerator.

Serves 6

1½ pounds small shrimp,
   cooked
2 tablespoons lemon juice
¼ cup red wine vinegar
1 teaspoon dried crumbled
   oregano leaves
Salt and Pepper to taste
4 tablespoons olive oil
6 ounces coarsely
   crumbled Feta cheese
2 medium tomatoes,
   seeded and chopped
1 cup thinly sliced celery
1 cup sliced black olives

1. Rinse cooked shrimp and place in a large bowl.

2. In a small bowl, combine lemon juice, vinegar, oregano, salt and pepper. Whisk in olive oil until dressing emulsifies.

3. Toss the shrimp with dressing, Feta cheese, tomatoes, celery and olives until well combined.

Indian Niçoise

An impressive luncheon dish. The secret is in the unusual dressing.

Serves 6-8

Dressing:
¾ cup olive oil
½ cup red wine vinegar
3 tablespoons peanut
  butter
2 tablespoons chutney
2 tablespoons half and half
1½ teaspoons
  Worcestershire sauce

2 bunches spinach, washed
  with stems removed
2 cups fresh green beans,
  blanched
1 8¾-ounce can garbanzo
  beans, drained
1 8¾-ounce can red kidney
  beans, drained
1 cup sliced red potatoes,
  cooked
1 cup thinly sliced red
  onions
¾ cup pitted black olives
1½ cups marinated
  artichoke hearts,
  quartered
2 medium tomatoes,
  seeded and cut into large
  chunks
2 7½-ounce cans tuna
  packed in water, drained
8 hard-boiled eggs,
  quartered
1 bunch watercress,
  snipped

1. Whisk all dressing ingredients in a small bowl and set aside.

2. Line large salad bowl with spinach leaves.

3. In a separate bowl, toss together green beans, garbanzo beans, kidney beans, potatoes, red onions, olives and artichoke hearts.

4. Add half of the dressing to vegetables and toss again. Place vegetables in spinach-lined bowl.

5. Arrange tomatoes, tuna, eggs and watercress over vegetable mixture. Chill until serving time. Serve remaining dressing with salad.

Summer Garden Salad

A beautiful, brilliantly colored salad that showcases summer's produce.

Serves 8-10

1 head Romaine lettuce, torn into small pieces

1 head Butter or Bibb lettuce, torn into small pieces

2 small yellow squash, sliced ¼-inch thick

1 small red onion, quartered and thinly sliced

16 cherry tomatoes, cut in half

1 small red bell pepper, cut into strips

1 small yellow bell pepper, cut into strips

4 large red radishes, thinly sliced

1 jicama, peeled and cut into ½-inch slices

1 large avocado, peeled and sliced

2 cucumbers, peeled, seeded and sliced

1 bunch green onions, chopped

½ pound string beans or snow peas, blanched

½ pound thinly sliced mushrooms

1 cup crumbled Bleu cheese

½ cup fresh chopped cilantro

1. Combine all the salad ingredients together in a large salad bowl.

2. Combine all the Lemon-Lime Vinaigrette ingredients and mix well.

3. Toss the salad with the Lemon-Lime Vinaigrette dressing.

Continued on next page

Summer Garden Salad

Continued

Lemon-Lime Vinaigrette:
1 lemon, juiced
1 teaspoon grated lemon
     peel
2 limes, juiced
1 teaspoon grated lime
     peel
1 tablespoon white wine
     vinegar
2 tablespoons chopped
     cilantro
¼ teaspoon ground cumin
2 cloves garlic, finely
     chopped
½ teaspoon salt
6 tablespoons olive oil

Balboa Broccoli

So easy and so delicious. An added plus is that it must be made ahead!

Serves 4-6

2 bunches fresh broccoli,
     broken into flowerets
1 pound bacon, cooked
     and crumbled
1 cup raisins
1 large chopped red onion
1½ cups grated Cheddar
     cheese

Dressing:
1 cup mayonnaise
¼ cup red wine vinegar
3 tablespoons sugar

1. Cook broccoli until crisp, yet tender, then drain well.

2. Toss all ingredients together, including dressing, and refrigerate for 24 hours.

Jicama Carrot Salad

Almost a relish, this salad is delightfully crunchy and refreshing. Serve small portions on a lettuce leaf.

Serves 10-12

2 carrots, grated
3 cups peeled and grated
  jicama (about 1¼
  pounds)
1 red bell pepper, diced
¼ cup chopped onion

Dressing:
½ cup rice wine vinegar
3 tablespoons chopped
  cilantro
1 jalapeño chile, seeded
  and minced
2 teaspoons minced garlic
½ teaspoon red pepper
  flakes
¼ teaspoon salt

1. Combine salad ingredients in a large bowl.

2. Whisk dressing ingredients in a small bowl or food processor.

3. Toss the vegetables with the dressing and refrigerate for 2 hours to combine flavors.

Cornucopia Salad

An original combination of great flavors.

Serves 6

Candied Almonds:
½ cup sliced almonds
3 tablespoons sugar

½ head green leaf lettuce,
   torn into bite size pieces
½ head Romaine lettuce,
   torn into bite size pieces
1 cup chopped celery
4 green onions, chopped
1 11-ounce can Mandarin
   oranges
1 avocado, cut into chunks
1 apple, diced
¼ cup dried currants
½ cup crumbled Bleu
   cheese
3 chicken breast halves,
   cooked and shredded

Dressing:
½ teaspoon salt
½ teaspoon pepper
¼ cup oil
1 tablespoon chopped
   parsley
2 tablespoons sugar
2 tablespoons white wine
   vinegar

1. Prepare Candied Almonds: Melt 3 tablespoons sugar in large frying pan with sliced almonds, stirring continuously until almonds are coated. Don't let sugar burn. Spread out on foil to cool.

2. Mix all salad ingredients and Candied Almonds. Toss with dressing.

Island Chicken Salad

Beautiful for a special luncheon.

Serves 4

4 boneless chicken breasts,
  grilled
¼ cup olive oil
3 tablespoons red wine
  vinegar
1 teaspoon Dijon mustard
¼ teaspoon dried sage
6 cups salad greens,
  assorted
1 papaya, peeled, seeded
  and chopped
1 cup pineapple chunks
1 6-ounce basket
  raspberries
½ cup toasted chopped
  almonds

1. Cut chicken into bite size pieces.

2. Whisk olive oil, vinegar, mustard and sage to blend in a small bowl or food processor.

3. Combine chicken, salad greens, papaya, pineapple and raspberries in a large bowl. Add dressing and toss well.

4. Serve on plates and garnish with almonds.

Black Bean Salad with Vinaigrette Dressing

This salad may be made a day in advance, kept chilled and covered. Great with chicken or pork.

Serves 8-10

1 pound dried black beans,
  picked over, soaked
  overnight in cold water
  to cover, and drained
2 cups frozen corn, thawed
2 cups canned chopped
  tomatoes
¾ cup thinly sliced green
  onions
½ cup chopped cilantro

Dressing:
½ cup olive oil
½ cup lime juice
2 teaspoons salt

1. In a large saucepan, combine the black beans and enough cold water to cover them by 2 inches. Bring the water to a boil and simmer for 45 minutes to 1 hour, or until tender, but not too soft.

2. Drain the beans and put in a bowl. Combine beans with corn, tomatoes, green onions and cilantro.

3. In a small bowl, whisk together oil, lime juice and salt.

4. Pour dressing over vegetables while the beans are still warm. Let the salad cool, stirring occasionally until the beans are room temperature. Serve at room temperature or slightly chilled.

Baja Salad

Great for a festive luncheon on the patio.

Serves 8

1 16-ounce package dried
  black beans, picked over,
  soaked overnight in cold
  water to cover, and
  drained
1 red bell pepper, diced
1 green bell pepper, diced
⅓ cup chopped green
  onions
1 10-ounce package frozen
  corn, thawed
⅓ cup chopped cilantro
8 chicken breast halves,
  skinned and grilled

Cumin-Lime Dressing:
½ cup lime or lemon juice
1 tablespoon Dijon
  mustard
2 tablespoons ground
  cumin
1 teaspoon minced garlic
1 teaspoon pepper
½ teaspoon salt
¾ cup olive oil
¾ cup vegetable oil

Garnish:
1-2 avocados, sliced
1 cup salsa
½ cup sour cream
Chopped cilantro

1. In a large saucepan, combine the black beans and enough cold water to cover them by 2 inches. Bring the water to a boil and simmer for 45 minutes to 1 hour, or until tender, but not too soft.

2. Mix together dressing ingredients and let stand 1 hour or more.

3. Drain the black beans and mix with vegetables in a large mixing bowl. Toss with Cumin-Lime Dressing.

4. Place vegetables with dressing on large round platter. Cut chicken into strips and arrange on top with sliced avocado.

5. Drizzle salsa on top. Put extra salsa and sour cream in bowls.

Note: This can also be made with grilled shrimp instead of chicken.

Chutney Chicken Salad

A fresh interpretation of a luncheon classic.

Serves 8

5 cups diced cooked
   chicken
1 cup chopped celery
3 green onions, chopped
1 8-ounce can sliced water
   chestnuts
2 cups halved seedless red
   grapes
1 cup raisins
½ cup slivered almonds
1 cup shredded coconut
3 bananas, sliced or 2 cups
   pineapple chunks
1 3-ounce can Chinese
   noodles

Dressing:
1 cup mayonnaise
1 cup sour cream or plain
   yogurt
1 teaspoon curry powder
1 tablespoon soy sauce
4 tablespoons chutney

1. Blend dressing ingredients and chill for at least one hour.

2. Combine salad ingredients in large bowl. Toss lightly with dressing. Serve immediately.

Note: If made ahead, reserve almonds and Chinese noodles for last minute addition.

Chinatown Chicken Salad

Great for a luncheon served with sliced sweet bread and melon wedges.

Serves 4-6

½ package wonton
  wrappers
Vegetable oil
1 medium head lettuce,
  shredded
6 boneless chicken breasts,
  cooked and cut into bite
  size pieces
1 cup roasted peanuts
3 tablespoons sesame seeds
2 tablespoons chopped
  cilantro

Sesame Dressing:
1 teaspoon dry mustard
½ teaspoon powdered
  ginger
2 teaspoons soy sauce
2 tablespoons sugar
1 tablespoon sesame oil
⅓ cup vegetable oil
⅓ cup rice wine vinegar

1. Slice wontons into ½ inch strips and deep fry in vegetable oil until lightly browned. Drain and set aside.

2. Combine lettuce, chicken pieces, peanuts, sesame seeds and cilantro. Toss with Sesame Dressing.

3. Add fried wontons immediately before serving. Toss again.

Bengal Salad

Serves 6

1 cup crab meat
1 cup shrimp
1 cup chopped celery
½ cup sliced water
  chestnuts
¼ cup sliced green onions
1 small can pineapple
  chunks
½ cup pine nuts or toasted
  almonds
4 tablespoons chutney
2 tablespoons raisins
  (optional)
1 head lettuce, torn into
  bite size pieces

Dressing:
¼ cup sour cream
½ cup mayonnaise
½ teaspoon curry

1. Combine all salad ingredients together and toss with dressing.

Note: May be made with chicken instead of seafood.

Wild West Rice Salad

An excellent choice for a large group.

Serves 8

¾ cup wild rice
3 cups water
1½ cups white rice
1 cup chicken broth
½ cup olive oil
½ pound mushrooms, quartered
½ cup chopped green onions
1 large red bell pepper, chopped
1 large green bell pepper, chopped
½ cup rice wine vinegar
1 teaspoon salt
1 tablespoon sugar
¼ teaspoon pepper
⅓ cup chopped parsley

1. Rinse wild rice. Measure water into saucepan and add wild rice. Bring to a boil, reduce heat, cover and cook gently for 25 minutes.

2. After 25 minutes, stir in white rice and chicken broth. Return to a boil, reduce heat, cover and cook gently for 15-20 minutes or until rice is tender and all liquid has been absorbed.

3. Heat 2 tablespoons of oil in a large skillet and sauté mushrooms until golden. Remove from heat. Stir in remaining oil, green onions, peppers, vinegar, salt, sugar and pepper. Immediately pour over rice. Stir to combine well.

4. Cool to room temperature and add parsley. Put into large bowl and refrigerate overnight.

Curried Rice and Shrimp Salad

An unusual main dish salad.

Serves 4-6

1 package rice and
    vermicelli mix, cooked as
    directed (should be fairly
    dry)
4 medium green onions,
    chopped
½ red bell pepper, chopped
½ cup sliced stuffed green
    olives
½ cup chopped celery
1 6-ounce jar marinated
    artichoke hearts,
    quartered and marinade
    reserved
1 cup sliced mushrooms
1 pound shrimp, cooked
Salt and Pepper to taste

Dressing:
Marinade from artichoke
    hearts
⅓ cup mayonnaise
2 teaspoons curry powder

1. Cook rice and cool. Put in a large bowl and add onions, pepper, olives, celery and artichoke hearts.

2. Mix dressing together and add to rice mixture.

3. Cover and refrigerate overnight.

4. Before serving, add mushrooms and shrimp.

Santa Rosa Valley Salad

Serves 6-8

1 box long grain and wild
rice mix, cooked with
seasonings
Juice of 1 lemon
3 chicken breast halves,
cooked and diced
4 green onions, chopped
1 red bell pepper, diced
3 ounces Chinese peapods,
ends removed
2 medium avocados, diced
1 cup chopped pecans,
toasted
Lettuce leaves for garnish

Dressing:
2 cloves garlic, minced
1 tablespoon Dijon
mustard
½ teaspoon salt
¼ teaspoon sugar
¼ teaspoon pepper
⅓ cup seasoned rice wine
vinegar
⅓ cup vegetable oil

1. Combine dressing ingredients in blender. Cover and refrigerate.

2. Mix all salad ingredients except avocados and pecans. Combine with dressing and refrigerate 2-4 hours. Before serving, add avocados and pecans and garnish with lettuce leaves.

Note: May be made a day ahead.

Sweet and Sour Spinach Salad

This warm sweet and sour dressing is wonderful.

Serves 4

1 bunch spinach, torn into
   bite size pieces
1 can sliced water
   chestnuts
1 cup bean sprouts
½ pound bacon, cooked
   and crumbled
2 eggs, hard boiled and
   diced
¼ pound mushrooms,
   sliced
4 green onions, sliced

Dressing:
½ cup oil
¼ cup sugar
2 tablespoons vinegar
3 tablespoons catsup or
   chili sauce
1 medium onion, grated
Salt and Pepper to taste

1. Combine all salad ingredients, except bacon.

2. In a small sauce pan, heat dressing ingredients until warm.

3. Combine dressing with salad and serve with bacon crumbled on top.

Very Berry Spinach Salad

The strawberries are a beautiful contrast to the dark green leaves. An inspired combination!

Serves 4-6

1 bunch fresh spinach,
    torn into bite size pieces
1 pint strawberries, sliced

Dressing:
⅓ cup vegetable oil
⅓ cup cider vinegar
½ cup sugar
2 tablespoons sesame seeds
1 tablespoon minced onion
¼ teaspoon Worcestershire
    sauce
¼ teaspoon paprika

1. Mix spinach and strawberries in a bowl.

2. Combine dressing ingredients in a pint size jar and shake well. (Dressing makes enough for two salads.)

3. Drizzle dressing over salad and toss. Serve immediately.

Honey and Nut Salad

A very flavorful side salad with a secret ingredient: roasted garlic.

Serves 4-6

1 head Butter lettuce, torn
    into bite size pieces
½ pound bacon, cooked
    and crumbled
⅓ cup pine nuts, toasted

Dressing:
1 head garlic, roasted
3 tablespoons olive oil
1 tablespoon Dijon
    mustard
1 tablespoon whipping
    cream
¼ cup balsamic vinegar
2-3 tablespoons honey

1. Preheat oven to 350°.

2. To roast garlic: Place entire head of garlic in a small casserole dish. Pour about 3 tablespoons olive oil over the garlic and cook in oven for an hour. Let cool completely, squeeze out cloves and mash.

3. Combine torn lettuce, crumbled bacon and pine nuts in a large bowl.

4. Combine all dressing ingredients and garlic. Let sit to blend flavors for at least 2 hours in refrigerator.

5. Add dressing to salad ingredients. Serve immediately.

Romaine and Walnut Salad

A nice garlic-flavored salad with crunch and personality.

Serves 4-6

1 head Romaine lettuce,
   torn into bite size pieces
2 red Delicious apples, cut
   into chunks
4 ounces Gorgonzola
   cheese, crumbled (or
   Bleu cheese)
½ cup coarsely chopped
   walnuts, lightly toasted

Dressing:
2 teaspoons Dijon mustard
2 cloves garlic, minced
¼ cup white wine vinegar
¼ teaspoon salt
¼ teaspoon pepper
⅓ cup olive oil

1. Combine salad ingredients in a large bowl.

2. Whisk together dressing ingredients in a small bowl and add to salad ingredients.

Mushroom, Currant and Green Onion Salad

This is a terrific side salad. The currants and almonds really add pizzazz.

Serves 4

½ head red leaf lettuce,
   torn into bite size pieces
1 pound mushrooms,
   sliced
4 green onions, thinly
   sliced
½ cup dried currants
3 tablespoons sliced
   almonds

1. Combine all ingredients together in a large bowl. Toss with your favorite dressing. Our Rose Queen Dressing is highly recommended.

Simply Caesar Salad

Caesar Salad doesn't have to be difficult anymore. Save leftover dressing to spark up plain lettuce the next day.

Serves 4

1 head Romaine lettuce
2 tablespoons olive oil
1 cup French bread, cubed
  into ½-inch pieces
1 clove garlic, minced

Dressing:
½ cup freshly grated
  Parmesan cheese (about
  2 ounces)
¼ cup olive oil
¼ cup vegetable oil
¼ cup lemon juice
2 cloves garlic
1 teaspoon Worcestershire
  sauce

1. Combine all dressing ingredients in blender or food processor. Blend until smooth. Cover and refrigerate until ready to use, up to 2 days ahead.

2. Rinse and tear lettuce into bite size pieces. Place in a bowl and chill.

3. Sauté bread in the oil and garlic until golden brown.

4. When ready to serve, combine lettuce and desired amount of dressing. Top with garlic croutons.

Capistrano Pasta Salad

Quick, easy and colorful.

Serves 4

2 6-ounce jars marinated
    artichoke hearts
1-2 tablespoons
    mayonnaise
Lemon pepper to taste
8 ounce package small
    pasta shells, cooked,
    drained and chilled
1½ cups fresh chopped
    tomatoes or cherry
    tomatoes, cut in quarters
1 bunch green onions,
    thinly sliced
1 6-ounce can black olives,
    sliced
3 slices prosciutto, cut into
    strips (optional)
¾ cup grated Parmesan
    cheese

1. Drain artichoke hearts, reserving marinade. Cut artichokes into quarters.

2. Mix reserved marinade with mayonnaise and lemon pepper.

3. Combine pasta, artichokes, tomatoes, onions, olives and prosciutto in bowl and toss with dressing. Before serving, mix in cheese.

Linguine and Salmon Salad

Try this as a summer dinner served with toasted cheese bread.

Serves 6

1 pound linguine
1½ cups frozen peas,
    thawed
¼ cup mayonnaise
½ cup plain lowfat yogurt
¼ cup fresh minced dill
¼ cup finely chopped
    green onions
½ cup chopped red onion
2 tablespoons capers
3 tablespoons lemon juice
4 7½-ounce cans salmon,
    drained and flaked into
    large pieces
1 cup finely chopped celery
Salt and Pepper to taste

1. In a large saucepan of boiling salted water, cook the linguine al dente. Add the peas and cook the mixture until the pasta is just tender.

2. Drain the mixture in a colander, then rinse under cold water and drain well.

3. In a small bowl, whisk together mayonnaise, yogurt, dill, onions, capers, lemon juice, salt and pepper.

4. Combine pasta and pea mixture with the salmon, celery and dressing mix. Stir until all is combined.

Bleu Cheese Slaw

Bleu cheese lovers will line up for this one.

Serves 6-8

1 head cabbage, shredded
½ pound crumbled Bleu
    cheese

Dressing:
⅓ cup cider vinegar
¼ teaspoon dry mustard
1 teaspoon celery seed
2 tablespoons sugar
2 cloves garlic, minced
¼ cup minced onion
Salt and Pepper to taste
¾ cup oil

1. Mix cabbage and Bleu cheese in a large bowl.

2. Whisk dressing ingredients in a small bowl and then add to salad.

Oriental Sesame Noodle Salad

You'll feel like an accomplished Chinese chef when you serve this impressive noodle dish.

Serves 4

8 ounces vermicelli
4 ounces snow peas
4 ounces smoked ham, cut
   into thin strips
1 bunch green onions,
   chopped
½ cup chopped peanuts
2 tablespoons sesame seeds
Cilantro leaves for garnish

Dressing:
2 tablespoons rice wine
   vinegar
2 tablespoons soy sauce
2 tablespoons smooth
   peanut butter
1 teaspoon ground ginger
   or 1 tablespoon minced
   fresh ginger root
2 cloves garlic, minced
2 teaspoons sugar
1 teaspoon red pepper
   flakes
4 tablespoons vegetable oil
2 teaspoons sesame oil

1. Prepare Dressing: Whisk together vinegar, soy sauce, peanut butter, ginger, garlic, sugar and red pepper flakes. Whisk in both oils until well blended. (Can be prepared several hours in advance.)

2. Bring saucepan of salted water to boil. Break pasta into 4 inch lengths. Cook vermicelli in boiling water until al dente. Add snow peas to pan for the last 30 seconds. Drain pasta and peas in colander, then run under cold water to stop cooking.

3. In mixing bowl, combine pasta, snow peas, ham and green onions. Add dressing and toss until coated. Cover and chill at least one hour or up to 8 hours.

4. When ready to serve, add peanuts and toss. Place on large platter and sprinkle with sesame seeds, cilantro leaves and more red pepper flakes, if desired.

Peas and Peanuts Slaw

Crunchy and colorful.

Serves 6-8

½ head red cabbage,
  shredded
½ head green cabbage,
  shredded
1½ cups thinly sliced celery
½ cup thinly sliced green
  onions
½ cup diced green bell
  pepper
1 10-ounce package petite
  peas, thawed
1 cup chopped dry roasted
  peanuts

Dressing:
¾ cup sour cream
¾ cup mayonnaise
2 tablespoons lemon juice
2 tablespoons prepared
  horseradish (or more to
  taste)
1 tablespoon Dijon
  mustard
½ teaspoon salt
¼ teaspoon pepper

1. Mix cabbages and celery in a large bowl. Cover and chill until ready to serve.

2. Meanwhile, combine all other ingredients except peanuts.

3. Just before serving, toss cabbage mixture with dressing mixture. Stir in peanuts.

Ritzy Ramen Salad

Everyone will ask you what gives this terrific salad its extra crunch. Then they'll ask for the recipe.

Serves 8

1 head cabbage, shredded
6 green onions, sliced
2 packages ramen soup
  mix, oriental flavor
½ cup slivered almonds,
  lightly toasted
½ cup sunflower seeds
1 bunch cilantro, chopped
6 chicken breast halves,
  cooked, cut into bite size
  pieces

Dressing:
¾ cup vegetable oil
½ teaspoon salt
6 tablespoons rice wine
  vinegar
½ teaspoon pepper
4 teaspoons sugar
1 seasoning packet from
  one of the above ramen
  packages

1. Combine cabbage and green onions in large bowl and set aside. Can be done the night before and covered.

2. Mix dressing ingredients and refrigerate.

3. Just before serving, crumble uncooked soup noodles. Toss cabbage and onions with the dressing and add almonds, sunflower seeds, cilantro, chicken and noodles.

Toasted Walnut Slaw

A great accompaniment to roasted chicken and parsley potatoes.

Serves 6

Dressing:
½ cup salad oil
1 cup walnut pieces
1 teaspoon salt
¼ teaspoon pepper
⅓ cup red wine vinegar
1 teaspoon salt

1 small head Savoy
  cabbage, shredded
3 medium cucumbers,
  diced
1 10-ounce package frozen
  peas, thawed
2 medium carrots,
  shredded

1. In large skillet, heat oil over medium-high heat. Add walnuts and sauté 3 minutes, or until lightly browned, being careful not to burn. Line plate with paper towels and with slotted spoon, remove walnuts to prepared plate to drain.

2. Remove skillet from heat and cool oil.

3. Pour oil into jar with tight fitting lid. Add remaining dressing ingredients, including walnuts, and shake to blend.

4. In a large bowl, combine salad ingredients. Add dressing and toss to coat. Cover bowl and refrigerate at least 2 hours to blend flavors.

Southern California Bread Salad

Bread Salad? Yes, it sounds a bit strange, but this trendy salad just may replace your family's favorite potato salad.

Serves 6-8

½ pound day old
  sourdough bread, crust
  removed and sliced
2 large tomatoes, peeled,
  seeded and chopped
1 medium red onion,
  thinly sliced, with slices
  cut in quarters
6¼-ounce can white tuna
  packed in water, drained
  and flaked
1 cup pitted black olives
1 cup coarsely chopped
  basil leaves

Dressing:
3 cloves minced garlic
2 tablespoons red wine
  vinegar
Salt to taste
⅓ cup olive oil

1. Place bread slices in a medium bowl and cover with water. Let soak for 5 minutes. Squeeze out the excess water well. Crumble the bread into salad bowl.

2. Add tomatoes, onion, tuna, olives and basil to the bread. Set aside.

3. In a food processor or small bowl, combine together garlic, vinegar and salt. Add olive oil in a stream and whisk until emulsified. Toss with the salad and serve at room temperature.

Note: You may substitute 8 ounces chopped cooked chicken breast or crabmeat for the tuna.

Potato Salad with Bleu Cheese and Walnuts

The Bleu cheese makes this distinctive and delicious.

Serves 6

2 pounds red potatoes, skinned and cut into 1-inch pieces
¼ pound Bleu cheese
⅓ cup mayonnaise
⅓ cup sour cream or plain yogurt
1½ tablespoons lemon juice
¼ teaspoon salt
¼ teaspoon pepper
1½ cups finely chopped celery
½ cup chopped green onions
½ cup coarsely chopped walnuts, lightly toasted and cooled
Paprika
Chopped walnuts for garnish

1. Boil potatoes in salted water, until tender, about 15 minutes. Drain well and cool.

2. In a blender, puree the Bleu cheese, mayonnaise, sour cream, lemon juice, salt and pepper.

3. Combine potatoes, celery, green onions and walnuts.

4. Toss potato mixture with dressing until well combined. Place into serving bowl and sprinkle with paprika and chopped walnuts.

Farmer's Market Potato Salad

Fresh, crisp and colorful.

Serves 6-8

2 pounds small red
  potatoes, scrubbed
½ teaspoon salt
1 15-ounce can corn,
  drained, or 3 ears fresh
  corn on cob, kernels
  removed
2 large carrots, peeled and
  cut into thin round slices
2 cups broccoli flowerets
Crisp lettuce leaves
4 ounces Fontina cheese,
  cut into strips

Dressing:
1 bunch green onions,
  sliced
2 tablespoons fresh
  chopped parsley
1 cup bottled vinaigrette
  dressing with Parmesan
  cheese

1. Boil potatoes in salted water until tender, about 15 minutes. Drain well. Quarter potatoes and place in large bowl.

2. Cook corn in salted water for 4 minutes. Add carrots during the last minute of cooking time, then rinse vegetables with cold water to stop cooking. Drain well and place in bowl with potatoes.

3. Blanch broccoli by cooking in boiling water for 30 seconds. Rinse with cold water to stop cooking. Drain well and place in bowl with potatoes.

4. In small bowl, whisk green onions, parsley and bottled dressing until blended. Add to vegetables in bowl. Toss to combine. Cover with plastic wrap and refrigerate 2 hours to blend flavors, stirring occasionally.

5. To serve, line platter with lettuce leaves and spoon potato salad on top. Scatter cheese strips on top as a garnish.

Cold Corned Beef, Potato and Green Bean Salad

A hearty winter salad that uses leftover beef for an easy salad entree.

Serves 6-8

¾ pound red potatoes, cut
   into ½ inch wedges
½ pound green beans,
   halved
1 pound corned beef,
   cooked (may use leftover
   brisket or pot roast)

Dressing:
⅓ cup mayonnaise
⅓ cup buttermilk
2 tablespoons prepared
   horseradish
2 tablespoons snipped
   fresh dill
2 tablespoons chopped
   fresh chives
½ teaspoon minced garlic
1 teaspoon Worcestershire
   sauce

1. Steam potatoes 15-20 minutes or until tender. Remove from pan and place in a large bowl.

2. Steam green beans for 10-15 minutes or until tender, yet crisp. Rinse under cold water to stop cooking and pat dry.

3. Mix dressing in a small bowl. Shred the corned beef and toss with potatoes and two-thirds of the dressing and chill one hour or overnight. Toss beans with remaining dressing in a separate bowl.

4. Serve on a platter with corned beef and potato mixture in center, surrounded by green beans.

Cranberry, Orange and Avocado Salad

This salad couldn't be prettier.

Serves 4

1 orange, peeled and
    divided into sections
1 avocado, peeled and
    sliced
Green leaf lettuce leaves

Dressing:
¾ cup cranberry sauce
1 heaping tablespoon
    mayonnaise
2 teaspoons lemon juice

1. Use individual salad plates and arrange orange sections and avocado slices alternately in a fan shape on lettuce leaves.

2. Combine dressing ingredients in a small bowl. Drizzle dressing on fruit.

Rose Queen Dressing

This dressing is fit for a queen!

1 cup vegetable oil
½ teaspoon sesame oil
¼ cup sugar
¼ teaspoon salt
1 teaspoon dry mustard
2 teaspoons finely ground
    pepper
½ cup seasoned rice wine
    vinegar

1. Put all ingredients in a covered jar and shake. Refrigerate until ready to use.

Vermouth Dressing for Spinach Salad

Vermouth and curry flavor this distinctive dressing.

⅓ cup olive oil
2 tablespoons white wine
  vinegar
1 tablespoon vermouth
2 teaspoons Dijon mustard
1 teaspoon soy sauce
½ teaspoon curry powder
½ teaspoon sugar
½ teaspoon salt
¼ teaspoon pepper

1. Whisk all ingredients in a small bowl. Cover and refrigerate until ready to use.

Creamy Bleu Cheese Dressing

Some of the calories are reduced in this classic dressing by substituting yogurt for sour cream.

Makes 2½ cups

¾ cup plain yogurt
½ teaspoon dry mustard
½ teaspoon pepper
½ teaspoon salt
⅓ teaspoon garlic powder
1 teaspoon Worcestershire
  sauce
1⅓ cups mayonnaise
4 ounces Bleu cheese,
  crumbled

1. Combine yogurt, mustard, pepper, salt, garlic powder and Worcestershire sauce. Blend in a food processor. Add mayonnaise and blend again. Slowly add Bleu cheese until emulsified. Refrigerate 24 hours before serving.

Sweet and Sour Sauce for Avocado Salad

An elegant salad featuring California's much-prized avocado.

Serves 4

2 tablespoons catsup
2 tablespoons vinegar
2 tablespoons butter or
  margarine
2 tablespoons sugar
2 tablespoons
  Worcestershire sauce
2-3 dashes hot pepper
  sauce
4 avocados, peeled and
  sliced
Red lettuce leaves
4 tablespoons sour cream
Julienned red bell pepper
  strips (optional)

1. Simmer catsup, vinegar, butter, sugar, Worcestershire sauce and hot pepper sauce for 5 minutes in a small saucepan.

2. Place avocados in a fan shape on red lettuce leaves. Drizzle with warm sauce and add a dollop of sour cream. If desired, garnish with red pepper strips.

Tarragon Dressing

A fabulous light dressing that will remind you of ranch dressing but without the sour cream and mayonnaise.

Makes 1 quart

1 tablespoon whipping
  cream
2 teaspoons tarragon
¼ cup fresh chopped
  parsley
½ tablespoon dry mustard
1½ teaspoons salt
½ teaspoon pepper
½ lemon, juiced
4 cloves garlic, minced
2 teaspoons minced green
  onions
⅔ cup tarragon vinegar
3 cups salad oil

1. Combine all ingredients except the salad oil in a small bowl or food processor.

2. Slowly add salad oil and continue blending until emulsified.

3. Store in covered jar. Refrigerate until ready to use.

Chapter 5

PASTAS ON
PARADE

Pasta

Here is a parade of

pasta dishes sure to

be memorable additions

to your next dinner

party or family gathering.

Penne and Chicken with Tomato and Leek Sauce

Special enough for company.

Serves 4-6

1 pound chicken breasts, skinned and boned
1 teaspoon salt
¼ pound pancetta or bacon, thinly sliced
2 small leeks, finely chopped
4 cups spaghetti sauce
½ cup whipping cream
2 teaspoons fresh thyme, finely chopped, or 1 teaspoon dried thyme
Pinch cayenne pepper
½ teaspoon salt
1 pound penne or other tubular pasta, cooked to package directions
½ cup grated Parmesan cheese for garnish

1. In a medium saucepan, bring to a boil enough water to cover chicken. Add chicken breasts and ½ teaspoon salt and simmer for 10 to 12 minutes, or until tender.

2. Remove pan from heat and cool chicken in liquid. Drain chicken and cut into ½-inch slices. Set aside.

3. Cook pancetta or bacon in a large skillet over medium-low heat until crisp and slightly brown. Drain on paper towels. Crumble and set aside. Discard all but 2 tablespoons drippings.

4. Add leeks to drippings and sauté over medium heat, stirring occasionally, until soft but not brown, about 5 to 7 minutes.

5. Add spaghetti sauce, cream, thyme, red pepper and ½ teaspoon salt. Bring to a boil, then reduce heat and simmer 3 to 5 minutes.

6. Just before serving, add pancetta and sliced chicken to sauce and heat briefly.

7. Pour sauce over drained pasta and toss. Serve immediately. Use Parmesan cheese for garnish.

California Pasta

This is a quick and easy pasta entree, sure to be a favorite of garlic lovers.

Serves 4-6

5-6 garlic cloves, minced
2 tablespoons olive oil
8-10 sun-dried tomatoes
    packed in oil, drained
    and chopped
8-10 Kalamata olives,
    chopped
½ cup fresh chopped basil
4 chicken breast halves,
    skinned, boned, cooked
    and julienned
Pinch red pepper flakes
6 medium tomatoes,
    chopped
1 pound angel hair pasta,
    cooked to package
    directions
Grated Parmesan cheese

1. Sauté garlic in oil.

2. Add sun-dried tomatoes, olives and basil. Simmer for 3 minutes.

3. Add prepared chicken and heat for 2 more minutes.

4. Add pepper flakes and tomatoes and continue heating for a few more minutes. Do not overcook. Combine sauce with drained pasta in a large bowl and toss well. Top with grated Parmesan cheese.

Creamy Chicken and Mushroom Fettucine

Serves 4

1 red bell pepper, cut into
    strips
3 tablespoons butter
1½ cups sliced mushrooms
1 teaspoon minced garlic
4 chicken breast halves,
    skinned, boned and cut
    into strips
½ cup chicken broth
⅛ cup sherry
2 cups heavy cream
1 teaspoon dried sweet
    basil
2 pinches cayenne pepper
1 pound fettucine noodles,
    cooked to package
    directions
Grated Parmesan cheese
    for garnish

1. Sauté red pepper in butter for 2 minutes, leaving peppers softened, but still firm. Remove peppers from pan. Add mushrooms and garlic; sauté until soft and remove from pan.

2. Cook chicken strips in the same pan at high heat, about 3-5 minutes, stirring often. Remove when done.

3. Add broth and sherry to pan, stirring to remove brown bits. Bring to a boil and reduce liquid by half. Let cool slightly and then add cream. Heat slowly and again reduce by half. Add basil, cayenne, vegetables and chicken. Serve over drained fettucine with grated Parmesan cheese for garnish.

Chicken Pasta Primavera

1 cup broccoli flowerets
⅓ cup chopped onion
2 cloves garlic, finely
    chopped
1 carrot, peeled and cut
    into julienne strips
4 tablespoons olive oil
2 cups cooked chicken, cut
    into bite size pieces
Salt to taste
3 tomatoes, diced
1 pound pasta, cooked to
    package directions
½ cup grated Parmesan
    cheese
2 tablespoons chopped
    fresh parsley

1. Cook the broccoli, onion, garlic and carrot in oil in a 10-inch skillet over medium heat, stirring frequently, until broccoli is crisp, yet tender, about 10 minutes.

2. Stir in chicken, salt and tomatoes. Heat for 3 minutes or until chicken is hot.

3. Spoon chicken mixture over drained pasta. Sprinkle with Parmesan cheese and parsley.

Chicken Pasta Al Pesto

Bountiful colors and flavor set apart this fresh-tasting pasta dish.

Serves 6

½ cup chopped fresh basil
  or spinach
1 tablespoon pine nuts or
  walnuts
4 cloves garlic, minced
4 tablespoons warm water
1 tablespoon butter
2 tablespoons grated
  Parmesan cheese
1 tablespoon olive oil
4 small zucchini, cut into
  julienne strips
4 small carrots, peeled and
  cut into julienne strips
½ cup Chinese pea pods
½ cup green peas, fresh, or
  frozen, thawed
½ sweet red bell pepper,
  cut into julienne strips
2 quarts chicken stock
8 ounces dry pasta
2 cups cooked chicken or
  turkey, cut into bite size
  pieces
Pepper to taste

1. Puree basil, pine nuts, garlic, water, butter and Parmesan cheese in a food processor or blender. Set aside.

2. Combine olive oil, zucchini, carrots, peapods, peas and red pepper in a skillet or wok. Stir-fry over medium-high heat until tender.

3. Bring chicken stock to boil. Add pasta and cook until tender, but firm to bite. Drain.

4. Toss together vegetables, pasta, chicken and basil mixture in a large bowl. Season with pepper.

Pasta with Sausage and Peppers

A sweet and savory combination.

Serves 4

1 pound mild Italian
   sausage
4 tablespoons olive oil
2 onions, sliced
1 green bell pepper, cut
   into julienne strips
1 red bell pepper, cut into
   julienne strips
¾ teaspoon salt
2 cloves garlic, minced
8 ounces linguine, cooked
   to package directions
Salt and Pepper to taste

1. Cut sausage into chunks and brown in a large frying pan over medium-high heat. Remove with a slotted spoon and drain on paper towels. Add oil to pan.

2. Reduce heat to medium, add onions and sauté until golden. Add pepper strips and salt and cook until softened. Stir in garlic and add sausage and cook for 2 minutes.

3. Add drained pasta to sausage mixture and toss to combine. Add salt and pepper.

Mediterranean Pasta

Serves 4

6 green onions, chopped
   fine
3 ounces sliced black olives
3 medium tomatoes,
   chopped
10 ounces marinated
   artichoke hearts,
   chopped, including
   marinade
10 ounces pasta shells or
   twists, cooked to package
   directions and drained
1 tablespoon mayonnaise
½ pound prosciutto, cut
   into julienne strips

1. Combine all ingredients and mix well. Chill and serve.

Shrimp and Scallop Linguine in Coriander Cream

Serves 4

3 tablespoons olive oil
½ cup onion, finely chopped
3-5 garlic cloves, minced
2 tablespoons flour
1 teaspoon ground coriander seeds
¼ cup vermouth
1 cup heavy whipping cream or half and half
½ pound shrimp, uncooked, peeled and deveined
½ pound bay scallops
1 pound fresh linguine, cooked to package directions
¼ cup parsley, chopped
Olive oil

1. Heat oil in a heavy skillet over medium heat. Add onion and garlic. Sauté until lightly browned, 4-6 minutes. Stir in flour and coriander seeds and cook 1 minute more. Add vermouth and cream. Bring to a gentle boil, stirring constantly. Add seafood and cook for about 5 minutes, until seafood turns opaque. Do not over cook. Set aside.

2. Toss drained pasta with a little olive oil and 2 tablespoons of the chopped parsley.

3. Divide pasta among four plates and top with seafood sauce. Garnish with remaining parsley. Serve immediately.

Pasta with Shrimp and Jalapeño-Orange Sauce

The imaginative pairing of jalapeños and orange juice makes this pasta unforgettable.

Serves 4

6 tablespoons butter
24 large shrimp, peeled
   and deveined
2 tablespoons minced
   green onions
1 small jalapeño pepper,
   seeded and thinly sliced
   or 1 7-ounce can whole
   green chiles, julienned
½ cup dry white wine
1½ cups orange juice
¾ cup whipping cream or
   half and half
Salt and Pepper to taste
12 ounces angel hair pasta,
   cooked to package
   directions
Parsley for garnish

1. Melt butter in a large skillet over medium heat. Add shrimp and cook until pink, about 1 minute per side. Remove from skillet and set aside.

2. Add green onions and jalapeño to skillet and sauté 1 minute. Add wine and bring to a boil. Mix in orange juice and cream. Boil until reduced to thin sauce, stirring occasionally, about 10 minutes. Add salt and pepper.

3. Add shrimp to sauce and cook until heated through. Add pasta and toss well. Sprinkle with minced fresh parsley and serve.

Pasta with Calamari

3 pounds squid, cleaned and rinsed

Coarse salt

6 tablespoons unsalted butter

3 medium garlic cloves, minced

4 medium green onions, finely chopped

¼ cup dry white wine

½ teaspoon salt

¼ teaspoon finely ground white pepper

1 pound fresh pasta, cooked to package directions (tomato pasta is especially good with this)

1. To clean squid, cut off tentacles. Pull out large white bones from body. Rinse squid in cold water. Remove head and pull, which should remove most of the innards. Discard head and innards. Scrape out any remaining material. Carefully remove and discard ink sac.

2. Rub coarse salt on squid to help remove skin, then pull off skin. Rinse squid once more.

3. Cut squid bodies crosswise in ½-inch slices. Cut tentacles into 2-inch pieces.

4. Melt butter in a 10-inch skillet. Add squid pieces and sauté over medium heat until slightly firm and pink, about 7-10 minutes. Add garlic, green onions and wine and bring to a boil. Add salt and pepper and taste for seasoning. Do not overcook; the squid pieces will get rubbery.

5. Pour squid sauce over drained pasta. Serve immediately.

Laguna Linguine with Clam Sauce

Serves 2-4

2 cloves garlic, cut in half

4 tablespoons olive oil

½ cup bottled clam juice

½ cup chopped fresh parsley

Pinch oregano

2 6-ounce cans chopped clams, juice reserved

8 ounces linguine, cooked to package directions

1. Sauté garlic in oil until light brown. Remove and discard garlic halves.

2. Add the bottled clam juice and the reserved clam juice from the canned clams. Heat thoroughly. Add parsley, oregano and clams. Heat until hot but do not boil. Serve over linguine.

Fettucine with Smoked Salmon and Black Pepper Sauce

Serves 6

1 bunch watercress,
    stemmed
1 medium red onion,
    peeled and quartered
1 tablespoon unsalted
    butter
2 cups heavy cream
2 teaspoons coarsely
    ground pepper
12 ounces fettucine
Salt to taste
4 ounces smoked salmon,
    cut into ⅜-inch pieces
Grated zest of 1 medium
    lemon

1. Chop the watercress finely with the metal blade of a food processor, about 5 seconds. Reserve. Chop the onion coarsely, about 5 pulses.

2. Cook the onion in butter in a skillet over low heat until softened, about 5 minutes. Set aside.

3. Simmer the cream and pepper in a skillet over medium heat until reduced to 1½ cups, about 7 minutes. Keep warm.

4. Cook the fettucine in boiling salted water until al dente, about 7 minutes. Drain, reserving ¼ cup of the water.

5. Toss the fettucine, reserved water, reduced cream mixture and salt in a serving bowl and top with the watercress, onion, salmon and lemon zest.

Linguine with Camembert, Tomato and Basil

Serves 4

5 Roma tomatoes, cut into
    small cubes
½ pound ripened
    Camembert cheese,
    remove rind and cut into
    small pieces
1 cup fresh basil leaves, cut
    into strips
3 cloves garlic
½ cup extra virgin olive oil
½ teaspoon salt
½ teaspoon pepper
1 pound linguine, cooked
    to package directions

1. Combine all ingredients except linguine. Let sit at room temperature in a covered bowl for 3 hours.

2. Drain pasta and, while still hot, pour sauce over and toss. Serve immediately.

Penne with Walnuts, Green Onions and Goat Cheese

Serves 4-6

¼ cup olive oil
1 cup chopped green onions
1 cup coarsely chopped walnuts
1 pound penne pasta, cooked to package directions
3-4 ounces mild goat cheese, crumbled
1 cup whipping cream
½ cup grated Romano cheese
Fresh ground pepper to taste

1. Heat olive oil in a large skillet. Add green onions and walnuts and sauté over medium heat until onions are tender, about 5 minutes.

2. Add cooked and drained pasta to skillet along with goat cheese. Reduce heat to low and stir gently until cheese melts.

3. Add whipping cream and Romano cheese. Season with pepper and stir well. Serve immediately.

Linguine Cheese Almandine

Serves 4-6

½ cup slivered almonds,
    blanched
1 cup low-fat cottage
    cheese
½ teaspoon Italian herb
    seasoning
¼ cup sliced green onions
2 tablespoons milk
1 cup chicken broth
2 tablespoons grated
    Parmesan cheese
1 cup frozen peas, thawed
2 tablespoons butter
8 ounces linguine, cooked
    to package directions
Freshly ground pepper to
    taste
Grated Parmesan cheese
    for garnish

1. Preheat oven to 350°.

2. Toast almonds on a cookie sheet in the oven for 5-7 minutes. Remove from oven and set aside.

3. In a bowl combine cottage cheese, Italian herbs, onion, milk, chicken broth, Parmesan cheese and peas. Stir well. Set aside.

4. Heat butter in a skillet over medium heat. Add cooked and drained linguine. Stir to mix well. While linguine is warm, add cheese mixture and stir gently until heated. Stir in pepper; top with toasted almonds and serve immediately. Serve with Parmesan cheese.

Spinach and Feta Cheese-Stuffed Pasta Shells

Serves 6

2 10-ounce packages
 frozen chopped spinach,
 thawed
10 ounces ricotta cheese
1 cup grated Parmesan
 cheese
3½ ounces Feta cheese
2 tablespoons chopped
 fresh basil
3 garlic cloves, minced
Salt and Pepper to taste
3½ cups bottled marinara
 or spaghetti sauce
32 jumbo pasta shells,
 cooked to package
 directions
Grated Parmesan cheese
 for garnish

1. Preheat oven to 350°.

2. Squeeze spinach dry. Transfer spinach to a large bowl. Add ricotta, ½ cup Parmesan, Feta, basil and garlic to bowl. Season mixture with salt and pepper. Blend.

3. Spoon ½ cup marinara sauce evenly over bottom of a 9x13x2-inch baking dish. Fill each pasta shell with spinach mixture. Place shells, filling side up, in dish. Spoon remaining sauce over shells. Sprinkle with remaining ½ cup Parmesan cheese. Cover loosely with foil and bake until heated through, about 30 minutes. Use additional Parmesan cheese for garnish.

Spinach, Gorgonzola and Walnuts over Fettucine

Serves 2

2 tablespoons olive oil
2 large garlic cloves,
 minced
4 ounces fresh or frozen
 spinach leaves, torn into
 small pieces
½ cup crumbled
 Gorgonzola cheese
¼ cup coarsely chopped
 walnuts
8 ounces fettucine, cooked
 to package directions
Salt and Pepper to taste

1. Heat olive oil in a large skillet and add garlic. Cook 5 minutes over low heat.

2. Add spinach and cook 5 minutes, stirring frequently.

3. Add cheese, walnuts and fettucine and toss well. Remove from heat and season with salt and pepper.

Spinach Fettucine with Goat Cheese, Broccoli and Cauliflower

2 cups broccoli flowerets
2 cups cauliflower
  flowerets
1½ cups chicken broth
8 ounces goat cheese
2 teaspoons chopped fresh
  thyme
½ teaspoon salt
¼ teaspoon finely ground
  white pepper
1 tablespoon all purpose
  flour
¾ pound spinach pasta,
  cooked to package
  directions
1 tablespoon finely
  chopped parsley

1. Immerse broccoli and cauliflower in large pan of boiling water and boil for 5 minutes or until cooked, but still crunchy. Drain and pour cold water over vegetables to stop cooking process. Drain thoroughly.

2. Boil chicken broth until reduced to 1 cup.

3. Remove rind from goat cheese, removing as thin a layer as possible. Cut cheese into small pieces. Whisk goat cheese into broth. Add thyme, salt and pepper and simmer about 5 minutes or until slightly thickened. Add flour and mix well. Add broccoli and cauliflower, reserving 8 flowerets of each.

4. Add drained pasta to sauce and toss until well combined.

5. Put pasta in serving bowl or on plates and garnish with reserved vegetables. Sprinkle with parsley and serve immediately.

Rancher's Pasta

Serves 4-6

¾ cup sun-dried tomato
  halves
2 tablespoons olive oil
4 cloves garlic, minced
1 cup black olive halves
1 teaspoon dried oregano
1 cup Feta cheese or
  Mozzarella cheese, grated
12 ounces fettucine,
  cooked to package
  directions

1. Soften tomato halves in very hot water. Drain. Cut tomato halves in strips.

2. Heat oil in a large skillet, add garlic and sauté for 2 minutes. Add olives, tomatoes and oregano; cook for 2 more minutes.

3. Add grated cheese and pasta. Mix until thoroughly blended and then serve.

Fettucine with Spinach Ricotta Sauce

Serves 4

2 tablespoons olive oil
1 medium onion, chopped
3 large garlic cloves,
   minced
1 tablespoon all purpose
   flour
2 cups whole milk (do not
   use nonfat or lowfat)
1 10-ounce package frozen
   chopped spinach,
   thawed and well drained
¾ cup ricotta cheese
⅓ cup freshly grated
   Parmesan cheese
10 oil packed sun-dried
   tomatoes, drained, cut
   into strips
3 tablespoons chopped
   fresh basil
¼ teaspoon ground
   nutmeg
Salt and Pepper to taste
1 pound fettucine, cooked
   to package directions
½ cup minced green
   onions
½ cup toasted pine nuts
Grated Parmesan cheese
   for garnish

1. Heat oil in a heavy medium saucepan over medium heat. Add onion and cook until translucent, stirring occasionally, about 4 minutes. Add garlic and cook 1 minute. Stir in flour and cook 1 minute.

2. Gradually whisk in milk and cook until sauce is smooth and bubbling, stirring constantly, about 4 minutes.

3. Mix in spinach, ricotta, Parmesan cheese, sun-dried tomatoes, basil and nutmeg. Season with salt and pepper.

4. Simmer over medium-low heat until heated through, stirring occasionally, about 5 minutes.

5. Toss drained fettucine with sauce. Garnish with green onions and pine nuts. Pass the Parmesan cheese at the table.

Baked Pasta with Spinach, Goat Cheese and Tomatoes

Serves 4-6

8 ounces fusilli pasta,
   cooked to package
   directions
5 tablespoons olive oil
1 28-ounce can diced
   peeled tomatoes,
   drained, reserving 3
   tablespoons liquid
¼ teaspoon red pepper
   flakes
2 cloves garlic
1 medium green onion
2 10-ounce packages
   frozen chopped spinach,
   drained, thawed and
   squeezed dry
1 egg
1 cup ricotta cheese
½ teaspoon salt
¼ teaspoon nutmeg
¼ teaspoon black pepper
¼ teaspoon dried rosemary
¼ teaspoon dried basil
¼ teaspoon dried oregano
7 ounces mild goat cheese,
   softened
Salt to taste

1. Preheat oven to 375°. Toss drained pasta in a bowl with 1 table-spoon olive oil. Set aside.

2. Toss tomatoes with 2 tablespoons olive oil and red pepper flakes in a small bowl. Set aside.

3. Mince garlic and green onion in a food processor. Add spinach, egg, ricotta, salt, nutmeg and pepper, then process until just combined. Spread mixture evenly in lightly oiled 2-quart shallow baking dish.

4. Spread pasta evenly over spinach and press gently in place. Drizzle reserved tomato liquid over pasta. Scatter tomatoes and any juices in bowl over pasta, pressing lightly in place.

5. Combine 1 tablespoon olive oil, rosemary, basil and oregano in small bowl. Cut goat cheese into small chunks and toss lightly in herb-oil mixture. Arrange cheese pieces on top of casserole so that pasta is completely covered with tomatoes and cheese. Drizzle with remaining olive oil and sprinkle lightly with salt.

6. Loosely cover dish with tented foil and place on baking sheet. Bake for 1 hour and 10 minutes. Remove foil. Bake uncovered for 10 minutes longer. Serve hot.

Fusilli with Tomato Mozzarella Sauce

Serves 4

1 pound ripe plum
    tomatoes, halved
8 ounces Mozzarella cheese
½ cup fresh sliced basil
6 tablespoons olive oil
2 tablespoons balsamic
    vinegar
2 large garlic cloves,
    minced
¼ teaspoon dried red
    pepper flakes
Pepper to taste
12 ounces fusilli pasta,
    cooked to package
    directions
¼ cup pine nuts, toasted
Fresh basil leaves for
    garnish

1. Cut tomatoes and cheese into ½-inch pieces and place in bowl. Mix in basil, olive oil, vinegar, garlic and red pepper flakes. Season with pepper. Let stand at room temperature 30 minutes.

2. Place drained pasta in a pot and add tomato mixture. Toss over low heat until cheese begins to melt.

3. Transfer pasta to platter or plates; sprinkle with pine nuts and garnish with basil leaves.

Southwestern Pasta Sauce

Serves 4

2 tablespoons olive oil
2 medium onions, sliced
2 cloves garlic, minced
28 ounce can tomatoes,
    crushed or coarsely
    chopped
¾ teaspoon hot pepper
    sauce
¼ teaspoon salt
¼ cup minced fresh
    cilantro
¼ teaspoon sugar
12 ounces angel hair pasta,
    cooked to package
    directions
Grated Parmesan cheese
    (optional)

1. Heat oil in a heavy skillet and sauté onions and garlic until limp.

2. Add tomatoes, hot pepper sauce, salt, cilantro and sugar. Boil, then reduce heat and simmer until thickened. Mix drained pasta with sauce. Pass grated Parmesan cheese separately.

Pasta Puttanesca

A dish to show off your red, ripe summer tomatoes.

Serves 6

2 large garlic cloves, minced
2 tablespoons olive oil
2½ pounds fresh tomatoes, seeded and chopped
1 tablespoon fresh minced basil
¼ cup white wine
1 teaspoon dried oregano, crumbled
¼ teaspoon dried red pepper flakes
½ cup sliced green stuffed olives
½ cup sliced black olives
1 tablespoon capers
1 pound linguine or spaghetti, cooked to package directions and drained

1. In a large skillet, sauté the garlic in oil until soft. Add tomatoes, basil, wine, oregano and red pepper flakes and simmer 10 minutes. Add olives and capers. Cover and simmer 10-15 minutes.

2. Toss the hot pasta with the sauce and serve.

Pesto Sauce

3 cups fresh basil leaves
4 cloves garlic
½ teaspoon salt
¾ cup grated Parmesan cheese
½ cup walnuts or pine nuts
½ cup olive oil

1. Puree all ingredients in a blender or food processor.

2. Toss pesto with your favorite cooked pasta (¼ cup per serving).

Easy Summer Pasta

Delicious served cold with a grilled entree on a summer night.

¼ cup red wine vinegar

1 tablespoon Dijon mustard

1 teaspoon sugar

2 teaspoons salt

⅓ cup plus 3 tablespoons olive oil

1 small onion, sliced

½ pound Chinese pea pods, cut in half

4 medium carrots, sliced

1 bunch broccoli, cut into bite size pieces

¼ cup water

1 pound rigatoni, cooked to package directions

3 small tomatoes, cut in wedges

½ cup chopped fresh basil

¾ cup grated Parmesan cheese

1. In a small bowl, mix vinegar, mustard, sugar, salt and ⅓ cup olive oil. Set aside.

2. In a large skillet, sauté onion in 1 tablespoon olive oil for 2 minutes. Add pea pods and cook 2-3 minutes until tender, yet crisp. Transfer to a large bowl.

3. In same skillet, add 2 tablespoons olive oil, carrots and broccoli. Add water. Reduce heat to medium, cover and cook 3 minutes. Uncover and cook 5 minutes until vegetables are tender, yet crisp.

4. Combine drained rigatoni, onion mixture, broccoli mixture, dressing, tomatoes, basil and Parmesan cheese. Toss and serve warm or cold.

Simple Pasta Sauce

Homemade "fast food" with style.

1 16-ounce jar marinated artichoke hearts, cut into small pieces

4-5 medium sized tomatoes, cut into small pieces

¼ cup chopped fresh basil

¼ cup grated Parmesan cheese

4 ounces sliced olives

8 ounces of your favorite pasta, cooked to package directions

1. Mix all ingredients together, except pasta.

2. Add pasta to sauce mixture and serve warm or cold.

Easy Pasta Sauce

A classic with all kinds of pasta. Make extra to keep on hand in the freezer.

Serves 4

2 tablespoons olive oil
2 onions, chopped
3 cloves garlic, minced
1 pound well flavored
   Italian sausage, cut in
   halves
8 ounces tomato sauce
14½ ounces whole
   tomatoes, peeled and
   chopped, reserving juice
Salt and Pepper to taste
1 teaspoon minced fresh
   rosemary
Pasta, cooked to package
   directions
Grated Parmesan cheese
   for garnish

1. Heat olive oil in a large skillet over medium heat. Add onion and sauté until translucent. Add garlic.

2. Squeeze sausage meat out of its casing into the skillet. Crumble and sauté briefly until meat loses red color. Add tomato sauce, tomatoes and reserved juice. Simmer, uncovered, for 15 minutes, stirring occasionally. Add salt, pepper and rosemary. Serve over hot pasta and sprinkle with Parmesan cheese.

Traditional Lasagna

Classic Italian fare for a crowd. This makes 2 pans.

Serves 16

1 1-pound box lasagna
noodles

1 tablespoon oil

1 pound ground beef

1 pound sweet Italian
sausage, without casing

1 onion, chopped

3 cloves garlic, chopped

12 ounces mushrooms,
chopped

1 teaspoon ground pepper

1 teaspoon salt

1 tablespoon dried
oregano

1 tablespoon dried basil

1 teaspoon dried thyme

2 14½-ounce cans peeled
and diced tomatoes

29 ounces tomato sauce

Filling:

16 ounces ricotta cheese

¼ cup sour cream

3 eggs

½ bunch parsley, chopped

½ cup grated Parmesan
cheese

16 ounces Mozzarella
cheese, shredded

1½ cups grated Parmesan
cheese

1. Cook lasagna noodles in boiling water, with oil, for 10 minutes.
   Drain noodles and cover in cold water until ready to use.

2. Sauté ground beef, sausage, onion and garlic in a large pan or
   Dutch oven until meat has browned. Drain excess fat. Return
   meat mixture to pan and add mushrooms, pepper, salt, oregano,
   basil, thyme, tomatoes and tomato sauce. Bring to a boil. Cover
   and reduce heat to simmer for 20 minutes.

3. Preheat oven to 350°.

4. To prepare Filling: Combine all ingredients in a bowl and mix
   well.

5. Using 2 9x13x2-inch baking pans, spoon ⅙ sauce on bottom of
   each pan (using a total of ⅓ of sauce). Next, put 4 noodles on top
   of sauce in each pan. Add ⅙ sauce over noodles in both pans. Pour
   ½ filling mixture oven noodles in each pan, using all filling.
   Sprinkle ¼ of the Mozzarella over filling in both pans (total cheese
   is ½). Place 4 more noodles in each pan. Pour remaining sauce
   evenly over noodles in both pans, then sprinkle remaining Mozzarella, evenly dividing between both pans. Sprinkle all Parmesan
   cheese over tops of lasagnas, dividing evenly.

6. Bake uncovered for 20 minutes.

Note: This recipe can be cut in half, if desired, or 1 pan of lasagna
can be cut into pieces and individually frozen.

Chicken Mushroom Lasagna

A creamy, subtly-flavored variation of a classic dish.

Serves 8

9 lasagna noodles, cooked to package directions

¼ cup butter or margarine

1 pound fresh mushrooms, sliced

½ teaspoon salt

¼ teaspoon white pepper

¼ cup flour

3 cups milk

½ cup chopped fresh parsley

2 chicken breast halves, skinned, boned, cooked and cut into small pieces

15 ounces ricotta cheese

12 ounces Mozzarella, shredded

½ cup grated Parmesan cheese

1. Drain and rinse cooked noodles and spread out over waxed paper to cool.

2. In a large saucepan, melt butter. Add mushrooms, salt and pepper and sauté until tender, about 5 minutes.

3. Stir in flour; then slowly add milk while stirring. Cook over medium-high heat until mixture thickens and boils, stirring constantly. Stir in ⅓ of parsley.

4. Preheat oven to 325°. Spread ⅓ cup of the mushroom sauce in the bottom of an ungreased 13x9x2-inch baking dish. Layer ⅓ of noodles, ⅓ of chicken, ⅓ of ricotta, ⅓ of Mozzarella, and then ⅓ of Parmesan. Repeat layers 2 more times, ending with Parmesan cheese on top. Sprinkle top with remaining parsley.

5. Bake for 45 minutes or until bubbly. Let stand 10 minutes to set before serving.

Lighter Lasagna

A healthier alternative without sacrificing flavor.

Serves 12

1 pound ground turkey
½ pound ground turkey
  sausage
1 clove garlic, minced
1 tablespoon dried basil
1½ teaspoons salt
1 16-ounce can tomatoes,
  cut up
1 12-ounce can tomato
  paste
3⅓ cups lowfat cottage
  cheese
2 eggs, beaten
1 teaspoon salt
½ teaspoon pepper
2 tablespoons dried parsley
  flakes
½ cup grated Parmesan
  cheese
8 wide lasagna noodles,
  cooked to package
  directions
1 pound lowfat
  Mozzarella, shredded

1. Preheat oven to 350°.

2. Brown turkey and sausage in a heavy pan. Drain off any fat. When meat is browned, add the garlic, basil, salt, tomatoes and tomato paste. Simmer uncovered until sauce is thick, about 30 minutes.

3. While sauce is thickening, combine the cottage cheese, eggs, salt, pepper, parsley and Parmesan cheese.

4. Place 4 noodles in a 13x9-inch baking dish. Spread ½ the cheese mixture over the noodles and sprinkle ½ the Mozzarella over the top. Cover with half the meat sauce. Repeat again, ending with the meat. Bake for 40 minutes. Let stand for 10 minutes.

Smoked Salmon and Caviar Pizza

A clever and classy pairing.

Pizza dough for 2 pizzas or
  2 large Boboli
¼ cup extra virgin olive oil
½ red onion, julienned
¼ bunch fresh dill, minced
⅓ cup sour cream or plain
  yogurt
Fresh ground pepper to
  taste
3-4 ounces smoked salmon
2 tablespoons caviar
4 small sprigs dill for
  garnish

1. Preheat oven to 500° for pizza dough or to 350° for Boboli. Sprinkle rolled pizza dough or Boboli with olive oil and red onion. Bake 8-12 minutes.

2. Combine dill, sour cream and pepper. Spread sour cream mixture on pizzas or Bobolis. Bake for 2 minutes.

3. Divide salmon and arrange over tops of pizzas.

4. Place 1 tablespoon caviar in center of each pizza. Place dill sprigs on each pizza for garnish.

Mushroom Pizza

Serves 6-8

2 tablespoons olive oil
1 medium onion, chopped
2 cloves garlic, minced
1 pound mushrooms,
  sliced
½ sweet red bell pepper,
  sliced
½ teaspoon dried basil
½ teaspoon dried oregano
¼ teaspoon crushed red
  pepper
¼ teaspoon garlic salt
1 large Boboli bread
⅓ cup chopped sun-dried
  tomatoes packed in oil
3 Roma tomatoes, sliced

1. Preheat oven to 450°.

2. Heat olive oil in a large skillet. Add onion and garlic and sauté until onion is tender. Add mushrooms and sauté about 15 minutes. Add bell pepper, basil, oregano, red pepper and garlic salt.

3. Place Boboli bread on baking sheet. Spread with mushroom mixture. Top with sun-dried and Roma tomatoes. Bake for 15 minutes.

Chapter 6

Birds of Paradise

Poultry

These carefully

selected poultry dishes are

distinctive enough for a

dinner in paradise.

Zorba Chicken

Light eating at its best!

Serves 8-10

3 pounds chicken breasts
and thighs, skinned (10-
12 pieces)
10½ ounces chicken broth
½ cup olive oil
¼ cup dry white wine
¼ cup lemon juice
4 garlic cloves, minced
1½ tablespoons fresh
thyme
1½ tablespoons fresh
rosemary
Salt and Pepper to taste
Rosemary sprigs for
garnish

1. Preheat oven to 350°. Wash chicken thoroughly. Place in a
10x14-inch baking dish.

2. Mix remaining ingredients in a bowl.

3. Pour mixture over chicken.

4. Cover baking dish tightly with foil and bake 1 hour or until done.
Garnish with fresh rosemary sprigs, if desired.

Gruyère Cheese and Pesto Filled Chicken Breasts

Ready made pesto sauce is a terrific time saver in the preparation of this sophisticated company dish.

Serves 4

4 chicken breast halves,
skinned and boned
½ cup grated Gruyère
cheese
⅓ cup ready made pesto
sauce
3 tablespoons pine nuts,
toasted
1 teaspoon minced green
onions
Flour
2 tablespoons olive oil

1. Preheat oven to 350°.

2. Pound chicken breasts between sheets of waxed paper. Mix
Gruyère cheese, pesto, pine nuts and green onions in a small bowl.

3. Spread 2 tablespoons of the cheese mixture on top of each chicken
breast and roll tightly.

4. Dredge chicken breasts in flour. Sauté rolled breasts in heated oil
at medium-high heat until golden brown, turning occasionally,
for approximately 6 minutes.

5. Place chicken in pan and bake until chicken is tender and cooked
through, about 20 minutes.

Baked Chicken Breasts with Mustard and Tarragon

Great served with Parmesan Rice with Walnuts from the "California Heritage Continues" cookbook.

Serves 2

1 cup fresh bread crumbs
1 tablespoon fresh minced
  parsley
2 teaspoons fresh tarragon
Salt and Pepper to taste
4 teaspoons coarse-grained
  Dijon mustard
2 tablespoons butter,
  melted and cooled
2 chicken breast halves,
  skinned and boned

1. Preheat oven to 475°.

2. Combine the bread crumbs, parsley, tarragon, salt and pepper together in a shallow dish.

3. Mix mustard and butter in a small bowl and coat chicken pieces with mustard mixture, then dip in crumb mixture, patting to help crumbs adhere to meat.

4. Put chicken on a broiling pan and bake for about 10 minutes on each side or until no longer pink. Allow 13 minutes on each side for thicker pieces of chicken.

Parmesan Chicken Florentine

A spinach stuffed chicken surprise.

Serves 6

10-ounce package frozen
  chopped spinach
3 tablespoons grated
  Parmesan cheese
3 ounces cream cheese
1 teaspoon garlic powder
⅛ teaspoon salt
⅛ teaspoon pepper
6 chicken breast halves or
  thighs, boned
2 tablespoons olive oil

1. Preheat oven to 350°.

2. Cook spinach per directions and drain excess water. While still hot, add 1 tablespoon Parmesan cheese, cream cheese, garlic powder, salt and pepper. Stir until melted.

3. Carefully lift one side of the skins to create a small pocket. Stuff pocket with 2 to 3 tablespoons of mixture. Drizzle olive oil over skin and sprinkle top of chicken breasts with remaining Parmesan cheese.

4. Put chicken in a casserole pan, cover and bake for 30 minutes.

5. Remove cover, drain grease and continue baking for 15 minutes or until done.

Note: Skinless chicken may be substituted if you coat one side of each piece with the filling and then roll it up.

California "No Fry" Chicken

A healthy "fried" chicken destined to be a family favorite, served hot or cold.

Serves 6

2 tablespoons olive oil
1 pint plain lowfat yogurt
¼ cup chopped fresh
  parsley
3 tablespoons chopped
  fresh chives
2 cups Italian bread
  crumbs
¼ teaspoon paprika
⅛ teaspoon cayenne
  pepper
Salt and Pepper to taste
6-8 large chicken breast
  halves, skinned

1. Line cookie sheet with foil. Brush foil lightly with 1 tablespoon olive oil.

2. Place yogurt in a medium bowl. Stir in parsley and chives. Set aside.

3. Combine bread crumbs, paprika and cayenne in shallow bowl.

4. Season chicken pieces with salt and pepper.

5. Thickly coat top of chicken breasts with yogurt mixture, then sprinkle chicken breasts with bread crumb mixture and pat crumbs to adhere. Place breaded chicken on prepared sheet.

6. Refrigerate chicken, uncovered, for at least 30 minutes. Preheat oven to 400° and position rack in top third of oven.

7. Drizzle chicken pieces lightly with remaining olive oil and bake until golden brown, about 35 minutes. Serve hot or at room temperature.

Grilled Chicken in Herbed Balsamic Marinade

The fresh and zesty marinade is the key to this delicious grilled chicken.

Serves 6-8

¼ cup Dijon mustard
¼ cup balsamic vinegar
¼ cup fresh lemon juice
4 large cloves garlic,
  minced
1 tablespoon minced fresh
  rosemary
½ teaspoon pepper
½ cup olive oil
4 chicken breast halves,
  skinned and boned

1. Combine mustard, vinegar, lemon juice, garlic, rosemary, pepper and oil in a medium bowl. Whisk together.

2. Wash chicken and pat dry. Place chicken in a glass or ceramic container and marinate at room temperature for 2 hours or in refrigerator for 4-6 hours or overnight.

3. Return chicken to room temperature before grilling. Grill chicken 5 to 6 minutes per side or until it springs to the touch.

Chicken Breasts with Lemon Caper Sauce

Serve with basmati rice.

Serves 4

4 chicken breast halves,
  skinned and boned
3 tablespoons unsalted
  butter
Seasoned salt and Pepper
  to taste
2 tablespoons chopped
  green onions
¼ cup dry white wine
½ cup chicken broth
½ cup whipping cream
1 lemon, peel grated and
  juice reserved
1 tablespoon drained
  capers
Lemon slices for garnish
Capers for garnish

1. Flatten chicken breasts between waxed paper. Brown chicken in melted butter in large skillet over medium-high heat, 3-4 minutes per side. Sprinkle with seasoned salt and pepper. Remove from pan and keep warm.

2. Add green onions to butter in skillet, sauté until soft. Stir in wine, scraping brown bits from pan. Add broth. Bring to boil and cook until reduced by one half. Stir in cream and heat thoroughly.

3. Remove from heat and stir in lemon peel, juice and capers. Pour over chicken breasts and garnish with lemon slices and extra capers.

Pine Needle Chicken

You're guaranteed a standing ovation when you serve this dish.

Serves 4

2½ pounds assorted
  chicken pieces
1 cup sherry
½ cup olive oil
1 large onion, minced
1 tablespoon
  Worcestershire sauce
2 tablespoons fresh
  rosemary leaves
½ tablespoon coarse black
  pepper
1 tablespoon garlic salt
1 tablespoon soy sauce

1. Put all ingredients in a large zip-lock bag, including chicken, and shake well.

2. Leave chicken in bag and marinate overnight in the refrigerator.

3. Drain off marinade and reserve for basting. Broil chicken on lower rack, 20-30 minutes, basting often.

Catalina Grilled Chicken Club

Delicious for a picnic or casual poolside lunch.

Serves 4

¼ cup light mayonnaise

1½ teaspoons Dijon or honey mustard

4 large chicken breast halves, skinned and boned

Salt and Pepper to taste

2 teaspoons oil

4 pita bread rounds, extra large

⅓ cup softened goat cheese

5 strips bacon, cooked and crumbled

4 leaves Boston lettuce

1 medium tomato, thinly sliced

1 red onion, sliced

1. Combine 2 tablespoons mayonnaise and mustard. Flatten chicken breasts between waxed paper. Coat both sides of chicken breasts with mayonnaise mixture, dividing evenly. Season with salt and pepper.

2. Grill 1 side about 2 minutes. Turn and grill until cooked through, about 3 more minutes or until moist but done. Quarter each chicken breast.

3. Heat 1 teaspoon oil in non-stick skillet. When hot, lightly brown both sides of pita bread over medium-high heat, about 3 minutes. Repeat with remaining oil and pita bread. Cut rounds in half. (If not using immediately, wrap in foil and keep warm in 200° oven.)

4. Combine remaining 2 tablespoons mayonnaise and cheese in small dish until smooth. Stir in bacon.

5. Spread mixture inside each pita half, dividing evenly. Fill halves with lettuce, chicken, tomato and onions, dividing evenly.

Raspberry Chicken

Delightfully different. Serve with wild rice.

Serves 4

4 chicken breast halves
½ cup raspberry preserves
½ cup pineapple juice
½ teaspoon soy sauce
2 tablespoons rice vinegar
½ teaspoon curry powder
½ teaspoon garlic powder
¼ cup fresh raspberries,
  mashed
½ cup fresh basil
Cornstarch
¼ cup whole raspberries

1. Combine all ingredients, except whole raspberries and cornstarch. Marinate overnight.

2. Remove chicken from marinade, reserving liquid. Broil 15 minutes or until done.

3. While chicken is cooking whisk cornstarch into reserved liquid and heat in a saucepan, stirring, until thickened. Pour sauce over broiled chicken and serve. Garnish with whole raspberries.

Chicken in Port Wine

So delicious, and no fat!

Serves 8

3 pounds chicken breasts,
  boned
1 cup white port wine
½ cup white vinegar
1 medium onion, minced
1 clove garlic, minced
3 tablespoons soy sauce
1 tablespoon
  Worcestershire sauce
1 teaspoon salt
1 bay leaf
½ teaspoon ground cloves
1 4-ounce can sliced
  mushrooms, drained

1. Mix all ingredients and marinate chicken breasts for 24 hours, in refrigerator.

2. Preheat oven to 325°.

3. Bake chicken and marinade in 9x13-inch pan for 1 hour, uncovered.

Rosemary Chicken in Herb Vinaigrette

The whole neighborhood will be over when they smell this cooking on the grill.

Serves 6

Herb Vinaigrette:
1½ tablespoons whole
    grain Dijon mustard
½ cup dry white wine
2 cloves garlic, minced
½ cup rice vinegar
1 tablespoon
    Worcestershire sauce
½ cup olive oil
½ cup corn oil
Salt and Pepper to taste

6 chicken breast halves,
    skinned and boned
⅓ cup fresh finely chopped
    rosemary leaves
⅓ cup fresh finely chopped
    marjoram leaves
Salt and Pepper to taste

1. Prepare Herb Vinaigrette: Blend mustard, wine, garlic, vinegar and Worcestershire in blender or deep bowl of electric mixer. Slowly add olive oil and corn oil to mixture until thickened. Season with salt and pepper.

2. Cover chicken breasts with enough Herb Vinaigrette to marinate well in a flat 8x10-inch glass dish. Cover dish and refrigerate, turning chicken occasionally, 6-8 hours or overnight.

3. When ready to cook, remove chicken from marinade and roll in mixture of rosemary and marjoram. Season with salt and pepper.

4. Grill quickly, until done, turning once, on well-oiled rack over hot coals, about 15-20 minutes.

Braised Lemon Chicken with Green Olives

Serves 8

8 chicken pieces
⅓ cup flour
1½ teaspoons salt
1 teaspoon pepper
2 tablespoons olive oil
2 tablespoons butter
2 garlic cloves, minced
1 small onion, chopped
2 ounces coarsely chopped
    stuffed green olives
1 cup diced celery
1 teaspoon chili powder
1 teaspoon Worcestershire
    sauce
½ teaspoon dry mustard
1 tablespoon sugar
Zest of 1 lemon
Juice of 1 lemon
¼ cup red wine vinegar
1½ cups chicken broth,
    unsalted

1. Preheat oven to 350°.

2. Wash and pat chicken dry. Combine flour with ½ teaspoon salt and ½ teaspoon pepper. Flour the chicken pieces, shaking off the excess.

3. Heat oil and butter in a 10-12 inch skillet and sauté the chicken until golden brown on both sides. Transfer chicken to a heavy 12-inch casserole with a cover.

4. Pour off the browning fat. In the same skillet, simmer the garlic, onion, olives, celery, chili powder, Worcestershire, dry mustard, sugar, lemon zest, lemon juice, vinegar, broth and remaining salt and pepper for 5 minutes.

5. Pour sauce over browned chicken and bake, covered, for 30 minutes.

6. Remove cover, baste, and continue baking for approximately 15 minutes. The chicken is done when the thickest part is pierced with a fork and the juices run clear.

Baked Herbed Chicken with Mushrooms

Chicken and vegetables simmering in a delicious herb-garlic sauce...something wonderful to come home to.

Serves 6

¼ cup butter
½ **pound mushrooms,**
  sliced
1 onion, sliced
2 garlic cloves, minced
¼ cup flour
1½ cups milk
½ cup dry white wine
1 teaspoon dried sage
1 teaspoon dried marjoram
2 tablespoons beef broth
  concentrate
2 tablespoons tomato paste
Salt to taste
½ teaspoon white pepper
6 chicken breast halves,
  boned
8-10 small carrots, peeled
  and cut in ¼-inch sticks
1 green bell pepper, sliced
6 small red potatoes,
  washed and halved
¼ cup chopped fresh
  parsley

1. Preheat oven to 350°.

2. In a medium saucepan, melt butter and sauté mushrooms, onion and garlic for 1-2 minutes. Sprinkle with flour and sauté until golden.

3. With a wire whisk, stir in the milk, wine, herbs, beef concentrate and tomato paste. Cook over low heat, stirring until thickened. Season with salt and pepper. Set aside. The sauce can be made ahead and refrigerated up to 24 hours.

4. Arrange chicken breasts in a large flat baking dish and surround with the vegetables. Pour sauce over the chicken and vegetables.

5. Bake, covered, for 30 minutes.

6. Remove cover and continue baking until chicken is well browned, the juices run clear, and the carrots are tender, approximately 25 minutes. Sprinkle with parsley and serve.

Mexican Chicken Kiev

Serves 6-8

8 chicken breast halves,
  skinned and boned
7 ounces green chiles,
  diced
4 ounces Monterey Jack
  cheese, cut into 8 strips
⅔ cup finely ground dry
  bread crumbs
½ cup grated Parmesan
  cheese
1½ tablespoons chili
  powder
½ teaspoon salt
½ teaspoon ground cumin
¼ teaspoon pepper
6 tablespoons butter,
  melted

Tomato Sauce:
32 ounces tomato sauce
½ teaspoon ground cumin
⅓ cup sliced green onions
Salt and Pepper to taste
Hot pepper sauce to taste

1. Flatten chicken breasts between waxed paper. Put about 2 table-spoons chiles and 1 cheese strip in center of each chicken piece. Roll up and tuck ends under.

2. Combine remaining ingredients, except butter, to make crumb mixture. Dip each stuffed chicken in shallow bowl containing melted butter and roll in crumb mixture.

3. Place chicken rolls seam side down in oblong baking dish. Cover and chill 4 hours or overnight.

4. Preheat oven to 400°. Bake uncovered for 20 minutes or until done.

5. Prepare Tomato Sauce: Combine all ingredients in a pan and heat well. Pour heated Tomato Sauce over chicken.

Chicken LaBamba

The best of Mexican flavors finished with California flair.

Serves 6-8

1 cup sour cream
⅓ cup milk
¼ cup chopped onion
½ teaspoon garlic salt
¼ teaspoon cumin
½ cup cilantro
Dash hot pepper sauce
1 can cream of chicken
   soup
10 ounces frozen chopped
   spinach, thawed and
   drained
4 ounces diced green
   chiles, drained
½ cup chopped red bell
   pepper
2-3 cups cooked chicken,
   cubed
4 ounces shredded
   Monterey Jack cheese
2 ounces shredded Sharp
   Cheddar cheese

Special Topping:
2 eggs, separated
1 cup all-purpose flour
1½ teaspoons baking
   powder
¾ cup milk
¼ cup margarine, softened
1 cup prepared salsa

1. Preheat oven to 350°.

2. Lightly grease 8x8-inch casserole dish. In large bowl, combine sour cream, ⅓ cup milk, onion, garlic salt, cumin, cilantro, hot pepper sauce, soup, spinach, chiles and red pepper and mix well.

3. Combine chicken with cheeses and toss lightly. Spoon half of spinach mixture into prepared casserole, sprinkle with ½ chicken mixture. Repeat layers.

4. Prepare Special Topping: Beat egg whites in a small bowl until stiff. Remove whites from bowl and set aside.

5. Lightly spoon flour into measuring cup and level off. In same small bowl, with same beaters, combine flour, baking powder, ¾ cup milk, margarine and egg yolks. Beat at low speed until moistened. Beat 4 minutes at highest speed, scraping sides of bowl occasionally. Fold in egg whites.

6. Pour Special Topping over filling, followed by salsa on top. Bake 40-45 minutes.

Asian Diced Chicken with Lettuce Cups

Beautiful!

Serves 6

½ cup plus 1 teaspoon
  light soy sauce
2 teaspoons cornstarch
6 tablespoons plus 2
  teaspoons sesame oil
Pepper to taste
1 pound chicken breasts,
  boned and finely diced
½ cup olive oil
4 cloves minced garlic
½ cup diced water
  chestnuts
½ cup diced onion
½ cup diced green onion
¼ cup chopped cilantro
½ teaspoon oyster sauce
1 teaspoon sugar
6 tablespoons pine nuts,
  toasted
Hoisin sauce
6 lettuce cups or radicchio
  cups

1. Combine ½ cup soy sauce, cornstarch, 6 tablespoons sesame oil and pepper in a medium bowl. Add diced chicken. Let stand for 30 minutes at room temperature. Remove from marinade.

2. Heat skillet or small wok over high heat. Add olive oil. Add ½ of the garlic to chicken mixture. Stir-fry 3 minutes. Remove chicken with slotted spoon onto plate.

3. Remove all but 2 tablespoons oil from skillet. Add remaining garlic and stir-fry until golden. Add water chestnuts, onion, green onions and cilantro. Stir-fry 1 minute.

4. Add remaining soy sauce, oyster sauce, sugar and remaining 2 teaspoons sesame oil. Stir-fry 2 minutes. Add pine nuts and chicken mixture. Heat 1 minute.

5. To serve, spread Hoisin sauce in each lettuce or radicchio cup. Top with a serving of chicken mixture. Roll up to eat.

Hot Peanut Chicken

Serves 4

4 chicken breast halves,
   skinned and boned
⅓ cup creamy peanut
   butter
1 tablespoon honey
3 tablespoons lime juice
2 tablespoons soy sauce
½ teaspoon ground cumin
½ teaspoon ground
   coriander
¼ teaspoon hot pepper
   sauce
3 cups rice, cooked
2 tablespoons sliced green
   onions (tops only)

1. Place chicken in 13x9x2-inch baking dish. Mix peanut butter and honey in a small bowl. Gradually stir in lime juice and soy sauce. Stir in cumin, coriander and pepper sauce.

2. Brush chicken with about half of the peanut butter mixture. Turn chicken, brush with remaining mixture. Cover and refrigerate for at least 2 hours. Remove chicken from refrigerator ½ hour before cooking.

3. Preheat oven to 375°.

4. Cover with foil and bake chicken for 30 minutes. Remove from oven and spoon sauce over chicken. Cover and return to oven and bake about 20 minutes longer.

5. Skim fat from drippings and discard. Spoon remaining drippings over chicken and serve over rice. Sprinkle with onion tops.

Thai Town Chicken and Broccoli with Peanut Sauce

An Asian delicacy from sunny California.

Serves 4-6

½ cup dry white wine
4 chicken breast halves,
   skinned and boned
4 cups broccoli flowerets,
   fresh or frozen
2 tablespoons oil
3 cups coconut milk
4 tablespoons sugar
1 teaspoon salt
6 tablespoons peanut
   butter, smooth
2-3 teaspoons curry
   powder
Cayenne pepper to taste
4-6 cups rice, cooked

1. Heat wine in large non-stick skillet. Place chicken in wine and cook, uncovered, over medium heat, stirring occasionally, for 15 minutes.

2. Add broccoli to skillet, cover, and simmer for 10 minutes, or until desired tenderness.

3. While chicken is cooking, prepare the sauce. Place oil in a medium saucepan and heat slightly, over a low flame. Whisk in the coconut milk. Add the sugar, salt and peanut butter. Bring to a boil, stirring constantly.

4. Add the curry powder and cayenne pepper. Lower the heat and cook for an additional 5 minutes to blend flavors.

5. To serve, place rice on a platter. Cover with the chicken-broccoli mixture and then top with the peanut sauce.

Toasted Almond Orange Chicken

A sure winner.

Serves 2

2 teaspoons cornstarch
3 tablespoons soy sauce
½ cup chicken broth
¼ cup water
¼ cup dry white wine
⅓ cup fresh orange juice
1 teaspoon sugar
2 teaspoons rice vinegar
1 teaspoon sesame oil
2 tablespoons olive oil
2 chicken breast halves, skinned and boned and cut into ¼-inch thick slices
6 2-inch strips of orange zest, cut into fine julienne strips (use a vegetable peeler)
1 clove garlic, minced
¼ teaspoon red pepper flakes
1 red bell pepper, cut into thin strips
1 cup trimmed snow peas
¼ cup slivered almonds, toasted
Rice, steamed

1. In a small bowl, stir together the cornstarch, soy sauce, broth, water, wine, orange juice, sugar, vinegar and sesame oil until the mixture is combined well.

2. In a large skillet, heat the olive oil over medium-high heat until it is hot, but not smoking. Add the chicken and stir-fry for 3 minutes. Transfer the chicken to a bowl.

3. Reduce heat to medium. Add the orange zest to the remaining oil in the skillet, stirring for 1 minute.

4. Add garlic and red pepper flakes and cook mixture, stirring, until the garlic is golden. Add bell pepper and snow peas. Stir the soy sauce mixture and then add it to the vegetables. Simmer mixture, stirring, for 3 minutes.

5. Add the chicken and toasted almonds. Simmer the mixture, stirring, for 2 minutes.

6. Serve the chicken mixture over rice.

Almond Chicken Curry

Coconut milk is the secret ingredient in this full-flavored dish.

Serves 4-6

4 chicken breast halves,
  skinned and boned
Pepper to taste
½ cup soy sauce
3 cloves garlic, crushed
6 small red onions or 6
  small white onions,
  chopped
2 teaspoons crushed ginger
1 tablespoon olive oil
2 cups water
1 cup coconut milk
3 teaspoons curry powder
½ teaspoon chili powder
1 tablespoon cornstarch
¼ cup diced green onions
¼ cup sliced almonds,
  toasted
½ cup golden raisins

1. Cut chicken in cubes. Marinate 1 hour with pepper and soy sauce.

2. Sauté garlic, onions and ginger in olive oil until slightly browned.

3. Add chicken to mixture and continue cooking until browned. Add 2 cups of water and boil for 15 minutes.

4. Add coconut milk, curry powder, chili powder and cornstarch. Simmer for 20 minutes, stirring as necessary.

5. Place green onions, almonds and raisins on top and serve.

Bombay Chicken

A spirited entree that would be set off nicely by a cool fruit salad.

Serves 8

8 chicken breast halves,
  skinned and boned
3 tablespoons lemon juice
3-4 tablespoons curry
  powder
¼ cup olive oil
4 cloves garlic, crushed
4 green onions, chopped
Seasoned salt and Pepper
  to taste
1 teaspoon cumin
1 cup chicken broth
2 medium tomatoes,
  chopped coarsely
1 tablespoon butter
Rice, steamed
½ cup chopped peanuts
Chopped green onions to
  garnish
½ cup raisins
Chutney

1. Pound chicken breasts between waxed paper. Rub chicken with lemon juice. Sprinkle chicken pieces with curry powder.

2. Heat oil in skillet on medium heat. Add garlic and sauté until lightly browned. Add chicken, onions, salt, pepper and cumin. Stir lightly to coat chicken with ingredients. Add chicken broth, cover, and continue to cook for approximately 30 minutes.

3. When chicken is tender, add tomatoes and butter. Heat through and serve over rice in a casserole dish, pouring liquid on top.

4. Garnish with peanuts, green onions, raisins and chutney.

Tantalizing Turmeric Chicken

An exciting blend of unusual flavors.

Serves 4

4 chicken breast halves,
    skinned and boned
Salt and Pepper to taste
1 tablespoon soy sauce
1½ teaspoons honey
2 tablespoons fresh lemon
    juice
1 tablespoon ground
    cumin
¼ teaspoon cayenne
    pepper
½ teaspoon turmeric
1 tablespoon ground
    coriander
2 teaspoons finely chopped
    garlic
2 tablespoons olive oil

1. Place the chicken in a mixing bowl. Add salt, pepper, soy sauce, honey, lemon juice, cumin, cayenne, turmeric, coriander and garlic. Blend well so that the pieces are well coated.

2. Cover with plastic wrap and refrigerate for at least 30 minutes or overnight.

3. Heat the oil in a skillet large enough to hold the pieces without crowding. Over medium-high heat, add chicken and cook until browned on one side. Turn the pieces and reduce the heat to medium. Cook until done, about 10-15 minutes. Serve hot.

Chorizo Stuffed Chicken Breasts

Serves 6-8

1 pound chorizo sausage,
   coarsely ground
4 ounces pine nuts, toasted
1 bunch green onions,
   chopped
8 chicken breast halves,
   skinned and boned
Salt and Pepper to taste
1 tablespoon margarine
2 tablespoons flour
½ cup skim milk
½ cup chicken broth
12 ounces prepared salsa
Cilantro to taste
8 ounces Colby Cheddar
   cheese

1. Preheat oven to 350°.

2. Thoroughly cook and drain chorizo of all fat. Add pine nuts and green onions to sausage.

3. Flatten chicken breasts between waxed paper. Lightly salt and pepper chicken.

4. Place chorizo mixture on chicken and fold over.

5. Melt margarine and add flour, making a paste. Add milk and broth, stirring until thick and smooth. Remove from heat and add salsa to sauce.

6. Pour ½ cup sauce on bottom of 10x13-inch baking dish. Carefully place stuffed breasts on top of sauce, pouring remaining sauce over chicken. Sprinkle cilantro and Cheddar cheese on top.

7. Bake for 45 minutes to 1 hour until chicken is slightly firm.

Chicken in Chili Tomato Sauce

A memorable sauce and healthy to boot.

Serves 4

2 teaspoons olive oil
1 small onion, chopped
6 chopped celery ribs
1 chopped green bell
  pepper
¼ cup white wine
2 cups tomatoes, peeled
  and seeded
½ tablespoon soy sauce
2 teaspoons chili powder
2 tablespoons lemon juice
2 cloves garlic, chopped
¼ teaspoon red pepper
  flakes
¼ cup tomato juice
Dash hot pepper sauce
4 chicken breast halves,
  skinned and boned

1. Preheat oven to 375°.

2. Heat the oil in a pot and sauté the onion, celery and bell pepper. As more liquid is needed, add the wine.

3. Stir in the remaining ingredients, except chicken, cover, and simmer for 15 minutes.

4. Cool slightly and then puree. (Recipe makes about 5 cups of sauce, freeze remainder.)

5. Place chicken in a baking dish, cover with 1 to 1½ cups sauce and bake for 40-50 minutes.

Baja Norte Chicken with Peach and Chile Salsa

For chicken with a spicy south of the border flavor.

Serves 6-8

1 tablespoon ground
  cumin
1¼ cups fresh orange juice
¼ cup olive oil
3 teaspoons hot chili
  powder
8 chicken breast halves,
  boned
1 4-ounce can diced green
  chiles
1 cup honey
1 cup chicken broth
2 peaches, peeled, pitted
  and chopped (can use
  canned peaches in juice)
1 teaspoon minced garlic

1. In a small bowl, whisk together the cumin, orange juice, oil and 1 teaspoon chili powder.

2. Arrange chicken in a large shallow baking dish and pour marinade over it, turning chicken to coat well. Let the chicken marinate in the refrigerator, covered, for at least 1 hour or overnight.

3. In a saucepan, combine the remaining 2 teaspoons chili powder, chiles, honey, broth, peaches and garlic, bring the liquid to a boil and simmer the mixture, stirring occasionally, for 30 minutes, or until it is slightly thickened. (The salsa may be made ahead and reheated or served at room temperature.)

4. Grill the chicken on an oiled rack set about 4 inches above glowing coals, turning it occasionally and basting it with marinade, for 25-30 minutes, or until it is just cooked through.

5. Serve the chicken with the salsa.

Creamy Chicken Stroganoff

Serves 4

3 tablespoons margarine
¼ cup chopped onion
1 4-ounce can of
  mushroom pieces,
  drained with liquid
  reserved
⅓ cup milk
½ teaspoon garlic powder
¼ teaspoon pepper
¼ teaspoon cayenne
  pepper
1 teaspoon chopped thyme
  leaves
1 can cream of chicken
  soup
2 cups diced chicken,
  cooked
¼ cup stuffed green olives
10 ounces spinach noodles,
  cooked to package
  directions
1 cup plain lowfat yogurt
½ cup chopped green
  onions

1. In a skillet, melt one tablespoon margarine and cook onions and mushrooms for about 5 minutes, stirring frequently. Stir in milk, garlic powder, peppers, thyme, soup and reserved liquid from mushrooms. Add chicken and olives, heat until hot.

2. Drain noodles and toss with 2 tablespoons margarine.

3. Stir yogurt into chicken mixture, heat until hot. Serve over noodles. Garnish with green onions.

Palos Verdes Chicken Pie

Easier and more elegant than a chicken pot pie, this marvelous dish alternates layers of flaky crust with creamy chicken and vegetables.

Serves 2

4 teaspoons butter
4 teaspoons flour
½ cup chicken broth
½ cup diced carrots, peeled
½ cup green peas
2 chicken breast halves,
   skinned and diced
⅛ teaspoon dried thyme
Salt and Pepper to taste

Biscuit Batter:
¾ cup flour
1 teaspoon sugar
½ teaspoon salt
1 teaspoon baking powder
1 tablespoon grated
   Parmesan cheese
2 tablespoons butter, cut
   into pieces
¾ cup milk or half and
   half

1. Preheat oven to 375°.

2. Melt butter in a medium pan and stir in flour. Stir in broth and cook over low heat until mixture is smooth and thickened, about 5 minutes. Stir in carrots, peas and chicken. Add thyme and season with salt and pepper.

3. Simmer 5 minutes for flavors to blend and remove from heat. Set aside.

4. Prepare Biscuit Batter: Place flour, sugar, salt, baking powder and cheese in bowl and stir to mix well. Cut in butter until crumbly. Pour in milk and stir briefly until batter is sticky and holds together.

5. Spoon half of chicken mixture into buttered 1-quart casserole. With spoon, drop half of batter over chicken. Cover with remaining chicken mixture and top with remaining batter.

6. Bake until golden brown, about 30 minutes.

Hollywood Bowl Chicken in a Basket

Perfect for a picnic dinner before an evening concert. The picnickers near you will be envious.

Serves 4

4 teaspoons Italian herbs
1 teaspoon garlic powder
1 teaspoon celery seed
2 tablespoons chopped
  Italian parsley
4 tablespoons butter
8 inch round sourdough
  loaf bread
4 chicken breast halves,
  skinned and boned
Seasoned salt to taste
½ cup all purpose flour
¼ teaspoon pepper
1 tablespoon paprika

1. Preheat oven to 350°.

2. Mix Italian herbs, garlic powder, celery seed, parsley and butter together.

3. Cut lid off bread and remove most of the dough from the loaf, leaving a soft crust around sides. Butter inside with herb mixture.

4. Season chicken with seasoned salt and dip into flour seasoned with pepper and paprika. Sauté in skillet about 7 minutes on each side.

5. Place chicken in bread. Put lid on and wrap in foil. Bake for 30-40 minutes.

6. Overwrap foil with newspaper or other insulating material to transport to your picnic spot. Serve each person a piece of chicken and a piece of the "basket".

Spicy Marmalade Squab

Easy and stylish.

Serves 3-4

6 squabs
Seasoned salt and Pepper
  to taste
2 apples, quartered and
  sliced
1 small jar orange
  marmalade
2½ tablespoons Hoisin
  sauce

1. Clean squabs, seasoning with seasoned salt and pepper in the cavities and on top. Stuff with apples. Combine marmalade and Hoisin sauce. Marinate squabs in sauce for 24 hours, in refrigerator.

2. Grill squabs, lightly covered with foil, on medium coals for 15-20 minutes on each side. Baste frequently with marinade.

Note: Serve with wild rice.

Holiday Hens with Apricots and Cranberries

Serves 2

½ cup dried apricots
½ cup dried cranberries
½ cup dry white wine
2 tablespoons olive oil
1 small onion, finely
   chopped
2 cloves garlic, finely
   chopped
2 rounded teaspoons
   grated ginger root
½ teaspoon ground
   cinnamon
8 ounces tomato sauce
1 tablespoon packed
   brown sugar
Seasoned salt and Pepper
   to taste
2 Cornish hens

1. Combine apricots and cranberries in a small bowl. Add wine and let stand for 1 hour. Drain, reserving wine.

2. Preheat oven to 375°.

3. Heat 1 tablespoon olive oil in medium pan. Add onion, garlic and ginger root and sauté for 5 minutes over medium heat. Add reserved wine, fruit, cinnamon, tomato sauce and brown sugar. Season with salt and pepper. Simmer for 5 minutes. Pour mixture into a small roasting pan.

4. Rinse hens with cold water and pat dry with paper towels. Discard any obvious fat. Sprinkle hen cavities with seasoned salt and pepper. Rub skins lightly with olive oil.

5. Arrange hens over sauce in pan. Bake until golden, basting occasionally with pan juices, 1 hour to 1 hour and 15 minutes.

Savory Oven Roasted Cornish Hens

They'll think you worked all day on this. Don't tell!

Serves 2

2 plum tomatoes, seeded
   and diced
2 tablespoons grated
   Parmesan cheese
Hen giblets, chopped
1 teaspoon crushed
   rosemary
¼ teaspoon pepper
½ teaspoon garlic powder
½ cup seasoned and finely
   crushed croutons
1 Cornish game hen
Seasoned salt to taste
2 tablespoons olive oil

1. Preheat oven to 375°.

2. Mix first seven ingredients in a small bowl. Stuff mixture into the bird. Place hen, breast side up, on rack in a shallow roasting pan. Sprinkle breasts with seasoned salt.

3. Brush hen with olive oil.

4. Roast for 1 hour. Baste often with oil.

5. To serve, split hen in half and mound stuffing attractively around halves.

Duck in Wine Sauce

You'll please the hunter in your house with this dish.

Serves 2

3-4 pound duck, domestic
    or wild
Seasoned salt and Pepper
    to taste
1 apple, quartered
1 onion, quartered
3 celery stalks, diced
1½ cups dry red wine
½ cup butter, melted
½ pound mushrooms,
    sliced
Salt and Pepper to taste

1. Preheat oven to 550°.

2. Wash duck and sprinkle seasoned salt and pepper on outside and in cavity. Stuff with apple, onion and celery.

3. Put duck in pan, breast up, in oven for 10 minutes. Turn down oven to 325°. Remove pan and add one cup wine and cook for 40 minutes.

4. While duck is cooking, in skillet add ½ cup wine and melted butter. Bring to boil, stirring often. Reduce sauce by half. Add mushrooms, salt and pepper. Cook for 4-5 minutes.

5. Pour sauce over duck or serve as a condiment.

Torrey Pines Turkey Tostadas

Top with sour cream, sliced avocados, salsa and chopped olives. Delicious!

Serves 4

8 6-7 inch flour tortillas
1 10-ounce can refried
    beans
2 teaspoons chili powder
1 teaspoon ground cumin
3½ cups diced turkey,
    cooked (about 1 pound)
1 cup chopped green
    onions
1 cup chopped plum
    tomatoes
Salt and Pepper to taste
4 ounces shredded
    Cheddar cheese
4 ounces shredded
    Monterey Jack cheese
2 fresh jalapeño chiles,
    thinly sliced
1 cup fresh cilantro

1. Preheat oven to 425°.

2. Arrange tortillas on 2 large baking sheets and bake until crisp, about 5 minutes.

3. Heat refried beans, 1 teaspoon chili powder and ½ teaspoon cumin in small saucepan over medium heat, stirring constantly.

4. Combine turkey, green onions, tomatoes and remaining ½ teaspoon cumin in medium bowl. Season with salt and pepper.

5. Spread ¼ cup warm bean mixture over each tortilla, within 1 inch of edge. Spoon turkey mixture over beans and sprinkle with cheeses, jalapeño slices, cilantro and remaining chili powder. Bake tostadas until cheese melts and filling is heated through, about 7 minutes.

Tempting Turkey Meatloaf

Where's the beef? Leave it behind with this delicious and healthy alternative.

Serves 4

1 pound ground turkey
1½ cups chopped onion
1 cup fresh bread crumbs
2 egg whites, beaten
½ cup pine nuts, toasted
12 chopped sun-dried
    tomatoes, drained of oil
⅓ cup milk
2 teaspoons fresh chopped
    rosemary, or ½ teaspoon
    dried, crumbled
2 teaspoons fresh chopped
    oregano or ½ teaspoon
    dried, crumbled
Salt and Pepper to taste

1. Preheat oven to 375°.

2. Combine all ingredients in bowl, seasoning with salt and pepper. Mix well.

3. Transfer mixture to a loaf pan and bake until loaf pulls away from sides of pan and top is golden brown, about 50 minutes.

Breast of Duck with Cherries in Port Wine

Easy and colorful.

Serves 4

4 duck breast halves
Seasoned salt and Pepper
    to taste
6 ounces cherry jam, with
    whole cherries
½ cup Port wine

1. Preheat oven to 350°.

2. Rub the duck breasts with salt and pepper. Prick the skin of the duck breasts. Place in oven and cook for 50 minutes.

3. Place the jam and wine in a saucepan and bring to a boil. Reduce heat and simmer for about 10 minutes.

4. To serve, spoon a little sauce over each duck breast. Serve the remaining sauce separately.

Timesaver Turkey Breast

What once was an all day effort is now a snap, thanks to readily available small cuts of turkey and imaginative methods of preparation such as this one.

Serves 6

3 large cloves garlic, minced

4 large green onions, minced

2 teaspoons ground cinnamon

2 teaspoons ground allspice

2 teaspoons pepper

1¼ teaspoons salt

2 tablespoons canola oil

1 large turkey breast, skinned and boned (about 2¼ pounds)

1 large onion, thinly sliced

½ cup golden raisins

3 tablespoons white wine vinegar

1 tablespoon minced parsley

1. Preheat oven to 500°.

2. Grind together into a paste the garlic, green onions, cinnamon, allspice, pepper, salt and oil. Wash turkey breast and dry with paper towels. Rub spice paste evenly into entire surface of turkey.

3. Separate onion slices into rings and place in center of large piece of heavy duty aluminum foil. Add raisins and sprinkle with vinegar. Place turkey breast on top of onions and raisins. Wrap turkey, leaving small amount of airspace between foil and breast.

4. Place meat on a baking sheet in the center of oven and roast for 30-35 minutes or until meat thermometer reads 160°.

5. Carefully open foil. Let turkey rest 10 to 20 minutes and then cut into thin diagonal slices. Arrange slices on warm platter. Spoon juices and onions over the turkey and garnish with parsley.

CALIFORNIA

LIFESTYLES

It is a clear winter day, a sunny 75° at California's picture postcard time of year. While the rest of the nation lies buried under snow and sleet, Californians are out and about,

their car tops down and their spirits light. Morning might begin with coffee and croissants under the colorful umbrellas of L.A.'s open-air Farmers Market, where diners and strollers are surrounded by every kind of fruit and flower on which to feast the eye and appetite.

The freeways are quiet, inviting a cruise to Malibu or Melrose Avenue, to ski slopes or desert fairways. Which will it be? Come on. Hop in.

It's a day to catch that glorious California spirit.

❧

A world-famous attraction for alfresco dining,
shopping, and browsing, L.A.'s Farmers Market was started in the 1930's when
farmers gathered in a field to sell their produce directly to the people.

START YOUR ENGINES

Company Brunch

Perhaps more than anything else, Southern California

is the land of the automobile. Angelenos think nothing of hour-long freeway commutes

in traffic that would make a New Yorker blanch. The narrow, curvy Pasadena Freeway,

the nation's oldest, is an "E" ride at Disneyland to a region born to drive.

Negotiating complicated freeway mazes without a qualm, zipping down to the

beach for dinner or out to Palm Springs for the weekend,

Southern Californians love the freedom of their own set of wheels and bask in the

privilege of living within arm's reach of mountains, beaches, and deserts.

Sneak Previews

Award-Winning Appetizer Party

Living in SoutHern California brings the glitz and glamOur of Hollywood cIose to home. Whether it's running into Kevin Costner in the grocery store Iine or rounding Your own street corner to find a camera creW filming a TV movie, Hollywood casts its magical glOw all across Southern CalifOrnia. Everyone has a story to tell about sharing the sanDbox at the park with Robin Williams and his children or seeinG Cher at the car wash. For inbetween Iocation shooting in exotic plAces, appearing on talk shows, and working out at the gyM, these box office herOes live much as the rest of Us do, and they call this neighboRhood home.

BOWL ME OVER

Box Supper for the Bowl

Garden Gazpacho   page 71
Catalina Grilled Chicken Club   page 146
Potato Salad with Bleu Cheese and Walnuts   page 111
Iced Cinnamon Raisin Bars   page 295

It is said that each January first, legions of snowbound Easterners decide to pack up and move West after seeing the panorama of the Rose Bowl, the towering mountains, the blue sky, and the delicious 70 degree sunshine on their TV screens. We don't blame them. To Californians, the Rose Bowl is more than the collegiate athletic event of the year. Part spectacle, part celebration, it is a festival of food and friendship, and, in the best years, a chance to root for the home team in the balmy winter sunshine. On fragrant fall afternoons, the Rose Bowl hosts lavish tailgate picnics and spirited football rivalries that have become Southern California traditions.

Botanical Gardens

*N*estled in a quiet residential area close to Pasadena

is the jewel known as the Huntington Library, Art Collections, and Botanical Gardens.

Acclaimed by scholars and art historians for its distinguished art collection

and original literary works, it is beloved to Pasadenans for its acres of quiet gardens,

its tall cool halls lined with beautiful paintings, and for its observance of the most

civilized of British traditions: afternoon tea.

Salad Sampler

Summer Garden Salad   page 88   ❧   Baja Salad   page 93

Curried Rice and Shrimp Salad   page 98   ❧   Rosemary Buttermilk Biscuits   page 34

Double Delight Lemon Pie   page 280   ❧   Palisades Iced Tea   page 38

PASTAS ON

PARADE

Post-Parade Get-Together

Who doesn't love a parade? And when the parade features a three-story high, flower-bedecked

robot who blinks his eyes, spouts smoke, and then suddenly transforms himself into a race car, it must

be the nation's favorite display of engineering skill and floral artistry, the Tournament of Roses Parade.

Floats in this New Year's Day parade don't just float down Pasadena's Colorado Boulevard. They turn,

they whirl, they feature rock climbers scaling a sheer cliff of flowers or acrobatic skiers who ski down a

slope and turn flips in mid-air. Humorous, whimsical, or breathtakingly beautiful, each year they manage

to surpass the seemingly unbeatable entries of the year before.

Birds of Paradise

Dinner Under the Palms

For generations, the warm, dry air, rolling miles of green golf courses, and sparkling blue swimming pools of Palm Springs have drawn snowbirds from icy climes the world over. With boutiques to rival Rodeo Drive and world-class restaurants on every corner, Palm Springs offers pleasures to the most sophisticated tastes. Southern Californians have always cherished this desert paradise. Close enough for a weekend jaunt and sunny and warm even when L.A. skies are gloomy, Palm Springs is an escape to sunshine and relaxation.

Surf's Up

Seafood Soirée

Since the Beach Boys immortalized California girls, woodies, and surfin' safaris, California has meant white sand and blue water to much of the world. Though every local doesn't plaster zinc oxide on his nose, strap his surfboard on his car and head out to catch the waves, the beach's appeal is so widespread that it could be called the favorite destination of native and visitor alike. What do they find when they get there? Huge, crashing waves, fresh sea air, light shining on the water, and an open, free-wheeling sense of space. Most beaches offer sand volleyball courts with pick-up games at any time of day. Cyclists and roller bladers have a field day on miles of paved bike paths. Out in the water, surfers are joined by windsurfers and an occasional jet skier. Children dart in and out, gleefully racing the waves. Sunbathers, kite fliers, and solitary strollers dot the landscape. California beaches are more than a place to wriggle your toes in the sand: they are the ultimate refuge from fast-paced lives.

BEEF ING IT UP

Dinner on the Grill

Pass by the vast green lawns surrounding the Rose Bowl on a Saturday morning or weekday at twilight and you'll witness what Californians do best: exercise. Swarms of fleet cyclists in black and neon flash past in close herds. Joggers in raggedy cut-offs or matched jogging suits circle huge fields in one long continuous rotation. In the center of these lawns are pint-sized soccer players, middle-aged touch football devotees and golfers practicing their drives into nets hauled from home. Is it the year-round good weather? Is it the value placed on health and fitness? Or is it California's sense of fun, its energy and vitality, that draw those secretaries and CPA's, those grocery clerks and college students, out from behind their desks and onto the playing fields of Pasadena? Whatever their reasons, and in all seasons, Californians are beefing it up.

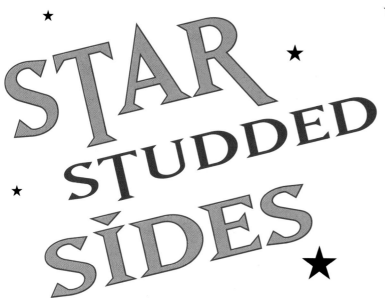

STAR STUDDED SIDES

Supper after Stargazing

Roasted Eggplant   page 242
Bulgur Pilaf with Mushrooms and Olives   page 253
Jicama Carrot Salad   page 90
Very Berry Spinach Salad   page 101
Refreshing Custard Pie   page 279

When you think of California's stars, you might think of
Jane Fonda, Jack Nicholson, or even Zsa Zsa. But Southern
California's clear skies and fair weather provide choice viewing
of stars of the celestial variety. Mt. Wilson Observatory, set high
on a peak in the San Gabriel Mountains, is the perfect spot for a
mountain picnic on a starry night. Griffith Park Observatory,
not far from downtown L.A. in the vast expanse of Griffith
Park, features hands-on exhibits, planetary shows, and
educational programs for the star-struck. A bustling hive of
top-notch scientists and engineers, Pasadena's Jet Propulsion
Laboratory is NASA's center for unmanned exploration of the
solar system. A fascinating facility to visit, JPL truly brings the
wonders of the universe close to home.

Aftershocks

Faultless Finales
A Holiday Dessert Party

Thanks to its position straddling several fault lines, California has been known to rattle and roll from time to time. While our Midwestern cousins worry that someday California will break off into the ocean in one big chunk, Californians seem to enjoy living on the edge. School children learn to duck and cover as routinely as they learn their ABC's, and residents' only apparent concessions to the quake threat are to tie their china cabinet doors closed with rubber bands and store bottles of water in the garage. Californians, you see, are hard to rattle. Any region that has given birth to such wild and wacky variations in fashion, music, hair styles, and speech could not easily be shocked by anything. This openness to adventure, this spirit of originality and innovation, are hallmarks of the California character. Is it any wonder that no other state is so often in the national eye?

There are many Californias: glittering and sophisticated, outdoorsy and carefree, zany and unpredictable. In no other corner of the world is so much creative energy, so much sizzle, packed into one region. What, then, do these wildly differing elements, the television producer and the bungee jumper, the symphony conductor and the triathlete, have in common? They share a quality as Californian as that ever-present sunshine—a free-wheeling vitality, an openness to adventure and innovation, and the sheer delight of living in the bountiful garden that is Southern California.

Chapter 7

Surf's up

Seafood

Californians are as

passionate about their

seafood as they are

about their miles of

picture-perfect coastline.

Wherever you live, these

delectable dishes will make the

most of the day's catch.

Scallop Sauté with Prosciutto and Dill

For the perfect accompaniment, serve with saffron rice.

Serves 4

4 tablespoons butter
2 green onions, minced
1 clove garlic, minced
3 slices prosciutto, diced
1 cup thinly sliced
　mushrooms
1 pound bay scallops,
　rinsed and dried
½ cup whipping cream
Salt and Pepper to taste
2 tablespoons minced fresh
　dill

1. Melt 1 tablespoon of the butter in a large skillet. Add onions and garlic; sauté 1 minute. Add prosciutto and mushrooms. Sauté until mushrooms are soft but not brown, about 3 minutes. Remove with a slotted spoon to bowl.

2. Add ½ of the remaining butter to skillet.

3. Add ½ of the scallops and sauté over high heat for 1 minute. Remove with slotted spoon to bowl. Add remaining butter to skillet. Add remaining scallops and sauté for 1 minute. Remove with slotted spoon to bowl.

4. Drain all juices from mushrooms and scallops and pour liquid into skillet. Add cream and boil gently until sauce is slightly reduced and lightly coats the back of a spoon. Taste and adjust seasonings, adding salt and pepper.

5. Stir dill, scallops and mushrooms into sauce.

6. Remove from heat. Serve immediately.

Baked Scallops with Swiss Cheese and Fennel

Serves 4

2 pounds bay scallops
2 tablespoons minced
　shallots
¼ cup minced fennel bulb
½ cup butter
1 tablespoon lemon juice
4 ounces grated Swiss
　cheese
2 tablespoons grated
　Parmesan cheese
¼ cup seasoned fine bread
　crumbs
2 tablespoons chopped
　fennel greens

1. Preheat oven to 400°.

2. Rinse scallops in cold water. Pat dry with paper towels. Place in buttered casserole.

3. Sauté shallots and fennel in butter until soft but not brown. Add lemon juice. Pour over scallops.

4. Sprinkle ½ of both cheeses, ½ of the bread crumbs and all the fennel greens over the scallops. Toss gently to coat evenly.

5. Sprinkle top with remaining cheeses and bread crumbs.

6. Bake for 15-20 minutes until scallops are tender when pierced with a knife and cheeses are golden and bubbly.

Note: May also be baked and served in 4 individual ramekins.

Seafood Curry with Coconut Milk

Serves 6

1½ pounds medium
   uncooked shrimp,
   shelled and deveined
   with tails left on
¾ pound scallops
¾ pound red snapper or
   orange roughy fillets
Juice of 1 lemon
28 ounces canned coconut
   milk
1 small onion, thinly sliced
1 teaspoon curry powder
¼ cup dark raisins
¼ teaspoon cinnamon
3 cloves, whole
Dash of hot pepper sauce
Salt and Pepper to taste
¼ cup toasted slivered
   almonds
6 cups cooked basmati or
   long grain white rice
2-3 diced green onions
   (optional)

1. Clean shrimp thoroughly. Rinse scallops. Rinse fish and cut into 2x1-inch strips.

2. Place seafood in a bowl, squeeze lemon juice over it and toss gently to mix. Set aside.

3. Place coconut milk in a large skillet or wok. Add onion, curry powder, raisins, cinnamon, cloves, hot pepper sauce, salt and pepper. Bring this to a boil and cook 5 minutes longer.

4. Reduce heat to medium. Add seafood and lemon juice from bowl. Cook until shrimp are pink and scallops and fish are firm, about 8-10 minutes. Do not overcook.

5. If desired, remove seafood with slotted spoon and reduce sauce slightly, then return seafood to pan.

6. Sprinkle toasted almonds on top. Serve over hot basmati or white rice. Garnish with more raisins, almonds and green onions, if desired.

Chilled Mussels Vinaigrette

Serves 4

½ cup finely minced onion
3 cloves garlic, minced
1 bay leaf
¼ teaspoon thyme
2 sprigs parsley
1 cup dry white wine
Salt and Pepper to taste
2½ pounds mussels
1 tablespoon Dijon
  mustard
2 teaspoons fresh chopped
  basil
2 hard boiled eggs
2 tablespoons red wine
  vinegar
1 cup light olive oil

1. Scrub and debeard the mussels.

2. Put ¼ cup onion, 2 cloves of garlic, bay leaf, thyme, parsley, wine, salt and pepper in a large pot. Add the mussels, cover and bring to a boil. Let steam 4-5 minutes or just until mussels open. Drain and discard any that remain unopened. Remove top shell of each mussel and discard. Leave the mussels on the half shell. Arrange them on a serving platter and let cool slightly.

3. Mix mustard, ¼ cup onion, 1 clove garlic and 1 teaspoon basil in a mixing bowl. Place eggs in a sieve and push through with fingers or very finely chop them. Add half the eggs to the mustard mixture. Reserve the other half for garnish.

4. Add the vinegar, salt and pepper to the mustard mixture. Whisk rapidly, slowly drizzling the oil so that it will blend thoroughly.

5. Pour the sauce over the mussels. Sprinkle with the remaining eggs and chopped basil.

Ginger Scallops with Cilantro

Fresh and flavorful.

Serves 4

1 pound bay scallops
2 tablespoons butter
2 tablespoons peanut oil
1 tablespoon fresh minced
   ginger, peeled
2 tablespoons chopped
   fresh cilantro
1 tablespoon lemon juice
   or rice wine vinegar
Salt and Pepper to taste

1. Rinse, then pat scallops dry on paper towels.

2. Heat butter with oil in a large skillet over medium to high heat. When sizzling stops, add ginger. Stir for 30 seconds.

3. Add scallops and stir until scallops turn white and begin to become firm, about 1½ minutes.

4. Add cilantro, lemon juice or vinegar, salt and pepper and stir to mix. Remove from heat at once.

Note: Serve alone as a first course or with rice and a green vegetable as a main course.

Black and Red Peppered Shrimp

Serves 4

¼ cup butter
3 cloves garlic, peeled and
   minced
1 teaspoon dried red
   pepper flakes
1 teaspoon fresh ground
   pepper
½ teaspoon salt
1 pound medium
   uncooked shrimp, in
   shells
1 lemon, thinly sliced

1. Preheat oven to 400°.

2. In a large cast iron skillet, melt butter over medium heat. Add garlic and sauté until tender, but not browned. Stir in red pepper flakes, pepper and salt. Add the shrimp and lemon slices. Toss to coat thoroughly.

3. Place shrimp mixture in a casserole dish and bake for 15 minutes, stirring occasionally.

Note: Serve with a crusty French or sourdough bread to soak up the drippings.

Baked Greek Shrimp with Feta Cheese

Serves 4

¼ cup olive oil
1 medium onion, chopped
1 pound plum tomatoes,
   chopped
4 cloves garlic, minced
½ teaspoon dried thyme
½ teaspoon dried oregano
Salt and Pepper to taste
1 cup fresh spinach leaves,
   cut julienne style
2 ounces anchovies in olive
   oil
1 pound medium
   uncooked shrimp,
   shelled and deveined
   with tails left on
4 ounces Feta cheese
Grated Parmesan cheese

1. Preheat oven to 450°.

2. Heat oil in large skillet over medium heat. Add onion, tomatoes, garlic, thyme, oregano, salt, pepper, spinach leaves and anchovies with oil. Sauté 8-10 minutes until saucy and all vegetables are wilted.

3. Add shrimp and simmer until shrimp turn opaque, about 2-4 minutes. Divide all of the skillet ingredients equally among 4 individual ramekins. Sprinkle with the Feta and Parmesan cheeses.

4. Bake on top rack of oven for 15 minutes.

Thai Shrimp Satay

Perfect for entertaining.

Serves 6

4 cloves garlic
2 tablespoons peanut oil
3 tablespoons peanut
   butter
¼ cup lemon juice
1 teaspoon chili powder
1 teaspoon turmeric
Salt to taste
3 dozen large, uncooked
   shrimp, shelled and
   deveined

1. In a bowl, mix all ingredients, except shrimp, into a paste. Add the shrimp and mix well. Let stand 1 hour at room temperature.

2. Thread shrimp on skewers and grill 3-4 minutes on each side or until the shrimp are brown and crisp, but not overcooked. Serve hot.

Southwestern Shark Seviche

A wonderful entree for a summer evening.

Serves 4

1 pound shark fillets
1-1½ cups fresh lime or
   lemon juice
1 medium onion, thinly
   sliced and separated into
   rings
3 jalapeño or serrano
   chiles, chopped
1 large avocado, diced
¼ cup chopped cilantro
¼ cup olive oil
2 tablespoons white wine
   vinegar
Salt and Pepper to taste
Cilantro leaves

1. Cut shark into ½-inch cubes and place in a medium glass bowl and cover with lemon or lime juice. Refrigerate 12 hours, turning a few times so that all surfaces of fish are "cooked" by the juice.

2. Gently mix onion, chiles, avocado, cilantro, oil, vinegar, salt and pepper and add to the shark after it has "cooked" for 12 hours. Return to refrigerator.

3. Serve chilled, garnished with cilantro leaves.

Note: Serve with your favorite black bean recipe and warm flour tortillas.

Grilled Prawns in Marinade

For an elegant dinner off the grill.

Serves 4

½ cup olive oil
¼ cup sherry
1 teaspoon dry mustard
¼ teaspoon pepper
½ teaspoon salt
1 tablespoon fresh chopped
   parsley
1 large clove garlic, minced
16 jumbo shrimp or
   prawns, uncooked

1. Combine oil, sherry, mustard, pepper, salt, parsley and garlic, for marinade in a glass dish. Shell and devein shrimp or prawns. Split down the backs leaving the tails on. Place shrimp or prawns in marinade for at least 4 hours, or overnight.

2. Grill shrimp or prawns over hot coals turning every 2 minutes, just until they turn opaque, about 5 minutes. Do not overcook.

Note: These are great by themselves or may be served over garlic buttered linguine as a light entree.

Poached Striped Sea Bass with Savory Herbs and Wine

Serves 4

2 cups white wine
2 cups coarsely chopped
   onions
2 cups coarsely chopped
   carrots
2 cups coarsely chopped
   celery
2 tablespoons lemon juice
2-3 cloves garlic, minced
3-4 allspice, whole
½ teaspoon each: dried
   dillweed, thyme, basil,
   parsley, marjoram and
   tarragon
1 pound skinless striped
   bass fillets
1 tablespoon cornstarch
   (optional)
2 tablespoons wine or
   water (optional)
2 tablespoons cold butter
   (optional)

1. Combine wine, onions, carrots, celery, lemon juice, garlic and seasonings in a large skillet. Bring to a boil, cover and simmer for 15 minutes. Place fish fillets in simmering liquid and cook covered for 8-10 minutes, just until fish flakes easily. Do not overcook. Remove fish. Arrange on a serving platter.

2. Leftover pan liquid may be thickened by whisking in cornstarch mixed with wine or water, while cooking over medium heat. The butter may also be whisked in if a richer sauce is desired. Spoon sauce over fish and serve. Fish and sauce (without butter) may be served cold.

Sherried Shrimp En Casserole with Artichoke Hearts

Serves 4

2 14-ounce cans artichoke hearts, drained and quartered
½ cup grated Parmesan cheese
1 pound small shrimp, cooked
½ pound fresh mushrooms, sliced
4 tablespoons butter
2 tablespoons flour
1½ cups milk
¼ cup dry sherry
½ teaspoon thyme
1 teaspoon Worcestershire sauce
¼ teaspoon paprika
Salt and Pepper to taste
Fresh thyme sprigs for garnish

1. Preheat oven to 375°.

2. Arrange artichoke hearts to cover bottom of buttered baking dish. Sprinkle lightly with ¼ cup Parmesan cheese.

3. Arrange cooked shrimp on top of artichokes. (Reserve 2-3 shrimp for garnish.)

4. In a large skillet, sauté mushrooms in the butter over medium-high heat until soft, about 5-10 minutes. Sprinkle mushrooms with flour, tossing gently to coat.

5. Gradually add the milk to skillet, stirring constantly. Add sherry, thyme, Worcestershire, paprika, salt and pepper. Continue stirring until mixture comes to a very low boil. Cook 1 minute longer.

6. Spoon sauce over shrimp in baking dish. Sprinkle top lightly with remaining Parmesan and paprika.

7. Bake for 20-30 minutes until golden and bubbly.

8. Garnish with shrimp and fresh thyme sprigs.

Note: May also be prepared in 4 individual ramekins.

Blackened Cajun Catfish with Tequila Lime Sauce

A very unique "South of the Border" flavor.

Serves 4

1 cup unsalted butter
1 teaspoon lemon pepper
1 teaspoon thyme
1 teaspoon basil
1 teaspoon garlic powder
1 teaspoon onion powder
½ teaspoon seasoned salt
⅛ teaspoon cayenne
  pepper
2 pounds catfish fillets, ½-
  inch thick
2 limes, cut into 8 wedges

Tequila Lime Sauce:
¼ cup tequila
½ cup sweet and sour bar
  mix
¼ cup triple sec
2 teaspoons cornstarch
1 tablespoon chopped
  cilantro

1. In a saucepan, over low heat, melt the butter. Add lemon pepper, thyme, basil, garlic powder, onion powder, salt and cayenne. Dip each fillet in butter mixture, thoroughly coating both sides. Place fish fillets in a shallow dish and pour remaining seasoned butter over fish. Cover tightly with plastic wrap and refrigerate 1 hour.

2. Preheat a cast iron skillet over high heat 10 minutes. Place 2 fish fillets at a time in the very hot skillet (there will be smoke) and cook over high heat 2 minutes per side until blackened.

3. Place fish on a serving platter and repeat with remaining fillets.

4. Prepare Tequila Lime Sauce: Combine tequila, bar mix, triple sec and cornstarch in a saucepan, stirring until cornstarch is well blended. Cook over medium heat until slightly syrupy and translucent, stirring constantly. Just before serving, add cilantro. Makes 1 cup.

5. Serve fish topped with Tequila Lime Sauce and garnish with lime wedges.

Cold Spinach-Wrapped Salmon with Chive Mayonnaise

Serves 6

½ cup lemon juice
½ cup dry vermouth
½ cup water or bottled
   clam juice
6 salmon steaks
24 or more large spinach
   leaves, washed and
   stemmed
1½ cups mayonnaise
¼ cup lemon juice
1 tablespoon Dijon
   mustard
¼ cup fresh minced chives
½ teaspoon salt
¼ teaspoon white pepper
Chives for garnish
12 niçoise (black) olives for
   garnish

1. In a large skillet combine the lemon juice, vermouth and water or clam juice. Bring to a simmer and place salmon steaks in the simmering liquid and cover. Poach 10 minutes for each inch of thickness. Carefully turn the fish once while simmering. Remove fish with a slotted spatula and chill in refrigerator.

2. Bring a large pot of water to a boil. Add the spinach leaves and blanch for 2-3 seconds until just beginning to wilt. Drain immediately and rinse with very cold water to retain color and prevent further cooking. Spread the leaves flat on paper towels.

3. Mix the mayonnaise, lemon juice, mustard, chives, salt and pepper. When the salmon is completely chilled, wrap completely in the spinach leaves. Place salmon steaks on a platter and spoon sauce over the top of each one. When ready to serve, garnish with more chives and niçoise olives.

Sesame Smelts

Crunchy and delicious.

Serves 4-6

1 cup pancake mix
¼ cup cornmeal
½ teaspoon salt
½ teaspoon pepper
1 teaspoon cinnamon
⅛ teaspoon cayenne
   pepper
1¼ cups milk
2¼ ounces sesame seeds
2 pounds fresh smelts,
   cleaned
1½ cups flour
Peanut oil
Sesame oil

1. In a shallow bowl, combine pancake mix, cornmeal, salt, pepper, cinnamon and cayenne.

2. Add milk, stir until blended. Add sesame seeds.

3. Roll smelts in flour, then in batter.

4. Place fish in single layer in large skillet in ½-inch hot peanut oil to which 1 teaspoon of sesame oil has been added. Fry 3-4 minutes until golden brown and fish flakes easily with a fork.

5. Drain on paper towels. Repeat process until all fish are fried, adding more peanut and sesame oils, as necessary.

Grilled Salmon Steaks with Creamy Bouquet Garni

Serves 6

1 tablespoon olive oil
Juice of ½ lemon
6 salmon steaks

Bouquet Garni Sauce:
1 cup plain lowfat yogurt
1 tablespoon chopped
  fresh parsley
1 tablespoon chopped
  fresh chives
1 teaspoon each: dried
  oregano, basil and thyme
¼ teaspoon pepper
Salt to taste
Juice of ½ lemon
1 tablespoon capers
  (optional)
Milk (optional)
Fresh herb sprigs for
  garnish

1. Combine olive oil and lemon juice in a small bowl. Brush salmon steaks on both sides with oil mixture. Place on grill over hot coals. Grill 5 minutes on each side or until fish flakes easily when tested with a fork.

2. For Bouquet Garni Sauce: Combine all ingredients in a small bowl. Mix well. Chill at least 30 minutes or more to allow flavors to blend. Makes 1 cup.

3. Arrange fish steaks on a serving platter; spoon sauce over tops. If sauce seems too thick; thin it with a little milk. Garnish with sprigs of fresh herbs.

Seafood Paella

Spectacular for a dinner party.

Serves 4-6

2 tablespoons olive oil
2 cloves garlic, minced
1 medium onion, coarsely
    chopped
½ teaspoon turmeric
½ teaspoon oregano
½ teaspoon fresh pepper
1 bay leaf
1 hot red pepper, dried
1¼ cups long grain white
    rice, uncooked
3 cups chicken stock
½ pound bay scallops
12 medium size shrimp,
    uncooked, in shells
12 small clams, in shells
12 mussels, in shells
12 crab claws
2 medium tomatoes,
    seeded and diced
10 ounces frozen peas
2 ounces sliced pimentos
1 tablespoon capers
½ cup vermouth

1. Preheat oven to 325°. Heat oil in 10-12-inch skillet over medium heat. Add garlic, onion, turmeric, oregano, pepper, bay leaf, red pepper and rice. Cook, stirring often, until rice begins to look opaque, about 3-5 minutes.

2. Pour in stock and simmer over low heat for 10 minutes, so the rice absorbs some stock.

3. Coat inside of 3 to 4-quart casserole with olive oil. Place ½ of the seafood, tomatoes, peas, pimentos and capers in the casserole. Top with ¾ of the rice mixture. Arrange rest of seafood, tomatoes, peas, pimentos and capers on top.

4. Spoon remaining rice on top. Sprinkle with vermouth, cover and bake for 30 minutes.

5. Check once or twice and if it seems too dry, add some hot stock. Uncover and bake 10-15 minutes longer, until rice is fluffy.

Note: Serve from the casserole with hot garlic bread.

Sausage-Stuffed Squid in Wine

Serves 4

8 squid mantels, cleaned
(white triangular body
tubes)
½ pound Italian sausage
4 tablespoons olive oil
1 cup chopped onion
1 teaspoon minced garlic
¼ cup plus 2 tablespoons
fresh chopped parsley
1 cup seasoned bread
crumbs
1 egg
¼ teaspoon red pepper
flakes
Salt and Pepper to taste
1 cup diced tomatoes,
seeded
1 cup dry white wine
1 bay leaf
2 sprigs fresh thyme
1 sprig fresh parsley
2 tablespoons butter

1. Rinse squid mantels under cold water. Pat dry with paper towels. Set aside.

2. Remove sausage from casings. Put in mixing bowl.

3. Heat 2 tablespoons of the oil in a small skillet. Add ½ cup onion and the garlic. Cook until soft, but not brown. Add the onion mixture, ¼ cup parsley, bread crumbs, egg, pepper flakes, salt and pepper to the sausage in mixing bowl. Blend well.

4. Using a small spoon, stuff mixture into the squid bodies. Do not overstuff as the squid will shrink a little while cooking.

5. Either sew up the openings or secure with a toothpick. Heat the remaining 2 tablespoons oil in a large skillet and add the stuffed squid. Cook, turning the pieces often, about 5 minutes.

6. Add the remaining ½ cup onion, tomatoes, wine, bay leaf, herb sprigs, salt and pepper. Cover and bring to a boil. Simmer gently for 30 minutes.

7. Remove the squid with a slotted spatula to a large shallow serving bowl. Discard strings or toothpicks.

8. Over high heat, reduce the sauce in the skillet by ½. Swirl in the butter. Spoon sauce over and around squid. Serve sprinkled with the remaining 2 tablespoons chopped parsley.

Panfried Trout with Lemon and Capers

A hit with some fishermen we know who cook this over an open fire under the stars.

Serves 4

4 whole trout, cleaned
  with head and tail left on
½ cup milk
½ cup flour
Salt and Pepper to taste
½ cup vegetable or corn oil
1 lemon, with peel, diced
6 tablespoons butter
2 tablespoons lemon juice
¼ cup capers, drained
2 tablespoons fresh
  chopped parsley
Lemon slices for garnish
Parsley sprigs for garnish

1. Rinse the trout inside and out with cold water and pat dry. Using a pair of kitchen shears, cut off the fins. In 2 shallow dishes, place the milk and flour which has been seasoned with salt and pepper. Take each fish and dip it first in the milk and then dredge completely in the seasoned flour. Shake to remove excess flour.

2. Heat the oil in a large skillet and add the trout. Cook over medium-high heat until golden brown, about 4-5 minutes on each side or 10-15 minutes total cooking time. Allow fish to fully cook. Baste them with oil in the skillet as they cook so they do not dry out. Transfer the fish to a warm serving dish. Sprinkle with the diced lemon.

3. Remove the cooking oil from the skillet and wipe it out. Heat the butter in the skillet until it just starts to brown. Then add the lemon juice and the capers. Cook about 15 seconds, then pour the butter over the trout. Sprinkle all over with the chopped parsley. Garnish with lemon slices and parsley sprigs.

NOTE: To dice lemon, quarter it lengthwise, then cut each quarter crosswise into little triangles. This should make a very attractive presentation.

Toasted Macadamia Mahi-Mahi

So Easy!

Serves 4-6

8 ounces pineapple yogurt
2 tablespoons rum
2 pounds mahi-mahi fillets
½ teaspoon salt
1 tablespoon butter
¼ cup coconut, toasted
1 cup macadamia nuts,
  toasted

1. In a shallow baking dish, mix together yogurt and rum.

2. Add fish and coat thoroughly on all sides. Cover and refrigerate several hours or overnight.

3. Preheat oven to 350°. Sprinkle fish lightly with salt. Bake for 25 minutes or until fish flakes easily when tested with a fork.

4. Toast coconut and nuts by melting butter in a skillet over medium heat, adding coconut and nuts, and stirring until lightly browned.

5. Remove fish to a serving platter. Sprinkle with coconut and nuts and serve.

Herbed Stuffed Trout with Orange and Onion

Worthy of the best of the day's catch.

Serves 4

4 trout, cleaned
Salt and Pepper to taste
2 teaspoons each: minced
fresh parsley, tarragon,
chives and thyme or ½
teaspoon each, dried
4 thin onion slices, cut in
half
4 thin orange slices, cut in
half
½ cup butter, melted
1 teaspoon paprika
2 tablespoons cognac
Juice of 1 orange
Fresh herb sprigs for
garnish

1. Preheat oven to 350°.

2. Score each trout (slash diagonally) 3 times. Sprinkle trout lightly with salt and pepper.

3. In a small bowl, combine herbs and use the mixture to stuff the slashes in the trout.

4. Place the trout side by side in a buttered shallow baking pan. Top each fish with 4 alternating half slices of onion and orange.

5. Mix butter, paprika, cognac and orange juice. Spoon over trout. Bake for 20-25 minutes until trout are lightly browned. Garnish with sprigs of the same herbs used to stuff trout.

Swordfish Baked in Spicy Peanut Mole

You will be delighted with this easy but gourmet fish entree.

Serves 6

3 tablespoons peanut oil
6 swordfish steaks, about 3
pounds
3 cups chicken broth
15 ounces Dona Maria
mole paste (found in
Mexican food section of
grocery store)
Toasted peanuts for
garnish
Cilantro leaves for garnish

1. Preheat oven to 350°.

2. In a large skillet, heat peanut oil until very hot. Sear swordfish steaks for 1 minute on each side. Remove to platter and set aside.

3. Place chicken broth and mole paste in saucepan over medium heat, stirring until paste is completely dissolved and sauce is heated through.

4. Pour ½ the warm sauce into a large glass baking dish. Place the swordfish in a single layer on top. Cover with the remaining sauce, then bake until fish just flakes when firmly pressed with the back of a fork, about 10 minutes for 1-inch thick steaks. Do not overcook.

5. Garnish with peanuts and cilantro leaves.

Fillet of Sole in Grape Sauce

A wonderful combination of flavors!

Serves 6

2 pounds sole fillets
1½ cups water
1 cup dry white wine
1 medium onion,
    quartered
1 bay leaf
4 whole peppercorns
½ teaspoon salt
4 tablespoons butter
4 tablespoons flour
1 cup cream
2 tablespoons cognac or
    dry sherry
1 teaspoon lemon juice
1 teaspoon Worcestershire
    sauce
Salt and Pepper to taste
1 cup canned seedless
    green grapes, drained
    and juice reserved
Lemon slices, bay leaves,
    peppercorns and grapes
    for garnish

1. Rinse fish with cold water, pat dry with paper towels. In a large skillet, combine water, wine, onion, bay leaf, peppercorns and salt. Bring to a boil. Add fish to liquid, reduce heat, cover and simmer 4-5 minutes or until fish flakes easily when tested with a fork. Remove fish with slotted spatula to a serving platter, keep warm.

2. Strain reserved liquid, return to skillet and boil rapidly until reduced to about 1 cup. Remove from heat and set aside.

3. In a small saucepan, melt butter and blend flour to make a roux. Gradually stir in reduced liquid and cream. Continue cooking, stirring constantly, until mixture thickens. Do not boil. Add cognac or sherry, lemon juice, Worcestershire sauce, salt and pepper. Gently stir in grapes just until heated through. Adjust sauce to desired consistency with reserved juice from grapes.

4. Spoon sauce over fillets on serving platter. Garnish with lemon slices, bay leaves, peppercorns and grapes. Serve extra sauce on the side.

Mousseline of Crab with Tarragon

For your most discriminating guests.

Serves 6

1 pound cooked crab meat
   or imitation crab meat
½ cup whipping cream
¼ teaspoon salt
¼ teaspoon pepper
¼ teaspoon paprika
½ teaspoon tarragon
Dash of nutmeg
1 egg

Mustard Sauce:
1 tablespoon butter
1 tablespoon flour
1 cup milk or cream
1 tablespoon Dijon
   mustard
Salt and Pepper to taste

1. Preheat oven to 350°.

2. Pat crab meat dry with paper towels. Set aside. Whip cream until stiff and set aside. Place crab in bowl of food processor. Add all spices. Turn processor on and off until crab approaches puree state. Add egg and process until pureed.

3. Transfer to medium bowl and gently fold in whipped cream. Spoon mousseline mixture into 6 well buttered individual 1 cup ramekins.

4. Fill large oblong pan with 1-inch boiling water. Place mousselines in pan. Bake for 25-35 minutes or until toothpick inserted in center comes out clean. Allow to cool 3-5 minutes.

5. Prepare Mustard Sauce: In a small saucepan over medium heat, melt butter. Blend in flour. Gradually stir in milk. Continue cooking, stirring constantly, until sauce thickens. Remove from heat and blend in mustard, salt and pepper. Makes 1 cup.

6. Run sharp knife around edges of mousselines and invert onto serving plates. If mousselines will not come out of ramekins easily, then serve directly from casseroles. Serve with Mustard Sauce.

Grilled Halibut with Ginger Butter

Serves 4

2 tablespoons sesame oil
2 tablespoons soy sauce
2 tablespoons lemon juice
   or rice wine vinegar
2 tablespoons chopped
   parsley
½ teaspoon dried thyme
2 green onions, chopped
Dash of cayenne pepper
4 halibut steaks, 1½-inches
   thick

Ginger Butter:
2 green onions, finely
   chopped
1 tablespoon peeled and
   minced ginger
½ cup butter
Salt and Pepper to taste
Juice of 1 lemon

1. Combine the first 7 ingredients for marinade in a shallow glass dish and add the halibut steaks turning once to coat thoroughly. Cover and refrigerate 1-4 hours.

2. Grill the fish over hot coals for 10 minutes for each inch of thickness, turning midway through the cooking time. The fish should be firm to the touch. Or, if you wish, broil the fish 6 inches from the source of heat for the same length of time.

3. Remove the fish to a warm platter.

4. Prepare Ginger Butter: Process all ingredients in food processor and let stand at room temperature until ready to use.

5. To serve, top each warm steak with a generous dollop of Ginger Butter.

Red Snapper with Champagne and Truffles

Serves 6

1 6-8 pound red snapper,
   dressed, boned, head and
   tail left intact.
Salt and Pepper to taste
2 cod fillets (about 6
   ounces)
1 egg
2 tablespoons minced
   truffles (any dark woody
   mushroom will do)
1 large green onion,
   minced
1 cup champagne or dry
   sparkling wine
¼ cup butter, melted
Juice of 1 lemon

1. Preheat oven to 350°.

2. Sprinkle snapper inside and out with salt and pepper.

3. In a food processor, blend cod until they have a pastelike consistency. Add egg, truffles, and green onion to cod, and fold in gently with spatula.

4. Stuff snapper with the mixture. Secure openings with skewers.

5. Place snapper on a greased foil-lined shallow baking pan.

6. In a bowl, combine champagne, butter and lemon juice. Pour over snapper. Bake for 40-50 minutes, basting with pan juices. Transfer to a large serving platter.

Note: Serve with Hollandaise sauce, if desired. Asparagus tips make a lovely accompaniment, especially when used to garnish the platter.

Chapter 8

BEEF
ING
IT UP

Beef, Lamb and Pork

What do Californians

eat after they hang up their

cleats, their tennis rackets, or

their aerobic shoes for the

day? These tempting meat

entrees are sure winners in a

world where everyone is

beefing it up.

Green Peppercorn Steak

Easy and delicious.

Serves 4

¼ cup green peppercorns
2 tablespoons Dijon
   mustard
4 steak fillets
3 tablespoons butter
¼ cup red wine
1 cup heavy cream
½ teaspoon salt
2 tablespoons chopped
   parsley

1. Drain the peppercorns and rinse them. Pat dry on paper towel and crush them with a mortar and pestle.

2. Mix the crushed peppercorns with the mustard and spread this on both sides of the steaks.

3. Melt the butter in a large frying pan over high heat. When the foam subsides, add the steaks and fry for 2 minutes on each side. (This will produce rare steaks. Double the time for medium-rare and allow about 12 minutes for well-done steaks.)

4. Remove the steaks from the pan and place on a serving dish. Keep them warm while you make the sauce.

5. Add the wine to the pan and cook briskly, scraping meat pieces. Reduce heat and add the cream and salt to the pan and cook gently for a few minutes.

6. Remove the pan from the heat and pour the sauce over the steaks. Sprinkle with parsley and serve at once.

Sautéed Steak

Serves 4

1½ tablespoons butter
4 pieces white bread,
   rectangles
½ tablespoon oil
4 steak fillets
Salt and Pepper to taste
2 tablespoons minced
   green onions
½ pound mushrooms,
   sliced
⅓ cup Madeira wine

1. Heat butter in frying pan and sauté bread in clear melted butter. Remove from pan.

2. Add oil to butter and heat until butter foam has almost subsided. Dry steaks on paper towels, then sauté for 3 to 4 minutes on each side. Meat is medium rare as soon as a little pearling of juice appears on top, and meat feels slightly springy when pressed.

3. Place steaks on toasted rectangles and arrange on a hot platter. Season with salt and pepper.

4. Pour fat out of pan, add green onions, mushrooms and wine. Boil down rapidly, scraping meat juices, then pour over steaks and serve.

Steak in Pastry with Mushroom Sauce

Just right for an intimate dinner party.

Serves 4

4 steak fillets, ¾-inch thick
Salt and Pepper to taste
6 tablespoons butter
2 cups finely chopped
 mushrooms
Pinch of dried thyme
1 tablespoon fresh
 chopped parsley
1 pound flaky pastry
 (Pepperidge Farm)
1 egg, lightly beaten
1 clove garlic, crushed
1 cup red wine
2 tablespoons whipping
 cream
Cornstarch

1. Rub salt and pepper into the steaks.

2. Melt 4 tablespoons of the butter in a large frying pan over medium heat and, when sizzling, cook the steaks for 1 minute on each side. Remove from the pan and allow them to get cold. Place cold steaks in the refrigerator.

3. Lightly sauté 1 cup of the mushrooms in the pan juices. Add the thyme and parsley, and allow to cool.

4. Roll out the flaky pastry until fairly thin and cut into 4 equal-sized rectangles that are large enough to cover the top and sides and to tuck under the steaks.

5. Preheat oven to 325°. Remove the steaks from the refrigerator and place on an oiled baking sheet with space between each one. Put a spoonful of mushroom mixture on the top of each steak and entirely wrap each steak with a rectangle of pastry. Cut a few slits in the tops to allow the steam to escape.

6. Brush the pastry with a little beaten egg and place the baking sheet in the center of the oven for 15-30 minutes, according to how well done you like your meat.

7. Melt the remaining butter in the frying pan and add the remaining mushrooms, garlic, wine, salt and pepper. Cook the sauce until it reduces by roughly one quarter and then, just before serving, stir in the whipping cream. Thicken with cornstarch.

8. Pour mushroom sauce over the pastry and serve.

Broiled Roquefort Steaks

A fabulous open-faced sandwich for a casual meal with friends.

Serves 4

4 ounces Roquefort cheese,
  crumbled
6 tablespoons butter,
  softened
Dash or two of
  Worcestershire sauce
4 8-ounce strip steaks or
  fillets, ½ to ¾-inch thick
  and at room temperature
Pepper to taste
4 slices rye bread, toasted
  and lightly buttered
  (butter optional)

1. Place cheese in a small bowl. Add 4 tablespoons of butter and Worcestershire sauce and mix with wooden spoon until smooth.

2. Wipe steaks dry and sprinkle with pepper. (The Roquefort topping will provide enough salt.) Sauté steaks over high heat 2-3 minutes on each side in remaining butter. Remove pan from heat.

3. Spoon Roquefort mixture over steaks, and put under broiler for a few seconds, until mixture melts.

4. Toast rye bread and butter lightly. Arrange steaks on top of toast and serve at once.

Steak Provençal

Serves 4

2 red bell peppers, sliced
3 yellow bell peppers,
  sliced (2 seeded, 1 with
  seeds)
2 green bell peppers, sliced
2 jalapeño peppers, diced
8 mushrooms, sliced
1 tablespoon diced garlic
3 medium onions, chopped
¼ cup butter
¼ cup olive oil
4 tomatoes, peeled, seeded
  and chopped
½ cup white wine
8 ounces tomato puree
½ teaspoon bouquet garni
4 steaks, individual fillets
  or strip steaks

1. Combine peppers, jalapeños, mushrooms, garlic and onions in a large skillet and sauté in butter and oil until almost tender.

2. Add tomatoes, wine, tomato puree and bouquet garni to vegetables and simmer 10 minutes.

3. Broil or barbecue steaks.

4. Pour sauce over steaks and serve.

Pinwheel Steaks

Delectable! And sure to get compliments.

Serves 3-4

1 beef flank steak, 1½
    pounds

Marinade:
2 cups dry red wine
½ cup finely chopped
    green onions
2 bay leaves, crumbled
1 tablespoon
    Worcestershire sauce
1 clove garlic, crushed
1 teaspoon salt
½ teaspoon freshly ground
    pepper

½ pound bacon
2 cloves garlic, minced
1 teaspoon salt
½ teaspoon coarsely
    ground pepper
¼ cup minced parsley
¼ cup finely chopped
    onion

1. Pound flank steak to ½-inch thickness.

2. Combine all Marinade ingredients and mix well. Place flank steak in 9x13-inch pan and pour Marinade over meat. Marinate in refrigerator overnight or up to 72 hours.

3. Remove steak from Marinade.

4. Fry bacon until almost done but not crisp.

5. Score steak on both sides.

6. Sprinkle steak with garlic, salt, pepper, parsley and onion. Place bacon lengthwise on steak.

7. Roll-up steak, starting with narrow end. Skewer with wooden toothpicks at 1-inch intervals.

8. Cut into 1-inch slices and grill over medium-hot coals for 5-7 minutes, turning once.

Grilled Stuffed Flank Steak with Marinara Sauce

This looks and tastes like you spent all day on it.

Serves 4

Marinara Sauce:
1 tablespoon olive oil
½ medium onion, chopped
2 medium garlic cloves, minced
1 pound plum tomatoes, chopped, or 1 28-ounce can plum tomatoes, drained
2 red bell peppers, cored, seeded and chopped
¾ cup fresh chopped basil
Salt and Pepper to taste

1 flank steak, 1½ - 2 pounds
2 teaspoons dried marjoram
¼ pound hard salami, sliced
⅔ cup thinly sliced red onions
2 cups grated Mozzarella cheese
Freshly ground pepper
1 cup dry red wine

1. Prepare Marinara Sauce: In a medium saucepan, heat the oil over medium heat, and sauté the onion and garlic until translucent. This will take about 5 minutes.

2. Stir in the tomatoes, peppers and basil. Cover pan, reduce heat, and simmer 25 minutes.

3. Puree mixture in a blender or food processor. Return to the saucepan and simmer, uncovered, until thick, about 20 minutes.

4. Season sauce with salt and pepper. May be made a day ahead.

5. Place the flank steak on a flat surface.

6. With a sharp knife, slice lengthwise along the grain to make a pocket. This may be done by the butcher. Rub the inside of the pocket with the marjoram.

7. Open the pocket and in it layer the salami, onions and cheese. Secure tightly with wooden toothpicks to close the opening.

8. Put the meat in a shallow dish and season with the pepper.

9. Pour the wine over the meat and marinate at room temperature for several hours, turning once.

10. Grill over medium coals for about 8-10 minutes on each side for rare.

11. Remove to a carving board and cut across the grain of the meat in ½-inch slanting slices. Serve with warm Marinara Sauce.

Citrus Marinated Flank Steak

Zesty and fresh-tasting.

Serves 4

1 flank steak, 1¼-1½
   pounds

Marinade:
½ cup oil
¼ cup lemon juice
¼-½ cup parsley
1 teaspoon salt
Pepper to taste
2 cloves garlic, minced

1. Trim fat off steak.

2. Combine all Marinade ingredients and marinate flank steak for 4
   hours or overnight.

3. Grill steak on barbecue, about 6 minutes per side.

4. Cut meat at a 45° angle, to grain and serve.

Marinated Flank Steak

A classic on the grill.

Serves 4

1 flank steak, 1½ pounds

Marinade:
1 cup soy sauce
1 tablespoon olive oil
1 tablespoon red wine
   vinegar
1 teaspoon ginger
1 clove garlic, minced or 1
   teaspoon dry minced
   garlic

1. Pierce flank steak several times on each side so Marinade can
   penetrate.

2. Mix together all ingredients for Marinade and pour over flank
   steak.

3. Let meat marinate for several hours.

4. Barbecue for 5 minutes on each side.

Chuck Wagon Steak with Beer

Serves 15-20

1 cup oil
2 cups beer
¼ cup lemon juice
2 cloves garlic, crushed
1½ teaspoons salt
2 bay leaves
1 teaspoon pepper
1 teaspoon dry mustard
1 teaspoon basil
1 teaspoon oregano
1 teaspoon thyme
1 10-pound chuck steak or
   tri tip steak

1. Combine oil, beer, lemon juice and seasonings. Pour over meat.

2. Refrigerate several hours or overnight.

3. Preheat oven to 425°. Place steak in roasting pan and brush with marinade.

4. Roast in oven for 2½ hours for rare steak.

Roast Beef with Fresh Garlic

Serves 6

3 large garlic cloves,
   minced
1½ tablespoons salt
½ teaspoon Hungarian
   sweet paprika
½ teaspoon turmeric
½ teaspoon ground thyme
½ teaspoon pepper
1 7-pound beef rib roast,
   cut from small end
   (about 3 ribs), trimmed
2 tablespoons vegetable oil

1. In a small bowl, mix garlic, salt, paprika, turmeric, thyme and pepper.

2. Wipe beef dry and rub all sides with oil. Rub garlic mixture over sides and top of beef.

3. Transfer to shallow pan. Cover loosely with foil. Refrigerate overnight.

4. Let roast stand at room temperature 1 hour.

5. Preheat oven to 450° and position rack in lowest third of oven.

6. Roast beef 30 minutes to sear. Reduce oven temperature to 325° and continue cooking for 1 hour and 15 minutes, the roast will be medium rare.

7. Remove from oven and let meat stand at least 15 minutes. Carve meat into ½-inch slices and serve.

Rainy Day Pot Roast

Serves 4-6

3 pounds beef chuck
2 tablespoons vegetable oil
1 medium onion, sliced
2 tablespoons granulated
    beef bouillon, or more to
    taste
Salt and Pepper to taste
Dried basil (optional)
Water

1. Preheat oven to 350°.

2. Brown roast in Dutch oven over medium heat, in oil. Add onion and brown.

3. Pour bouillon over browned roast, allowing some to drop into bottom of pan. Sprinkle meat with salt, pepper and basil. Add enough water to cover bottom of pan, ½-inch in depth.

4. Cover and bake until roast is very tender, 2-3 hours. Do not allow liquid to boil away. If necessary, add more water to pan.

Note: Drippings make a delicious base for gravy.

Mexican Beef Stir Fry

Serves 4-6

1 pound beef flank steak
1 teaspoon ground cumin
1 teaspoon garlic salt
1 teaspoon crushed
    oregano
2 tablespoons oil
1 sweet red bell pepper,
    cut into thin strips
1 medium onion, chopped
1-2 jalapeño chiles, seeded
    and cut into slivers
1 tomato, seeded and cut
    into chunks
8-12 flour tortillas
Sour cream, guacamole
    and Monterey Jack
    cheese for garnish

1. Cut steak across the grain, into thin slices.

2. Combine cumin, garlic salt and oregano. Heat 1 tablespoon of the oil and spice mixture in a large frying pan or wok. Add red pepper, onion and chiles. Fry over medium-high heat, stirring constantly, for about 2-3 minutes, or until the vegetables are tender, yet crisp. Remove vegetables from pan and set aside.

3. Add remaining oil and spice mixture to pan and fry beef strips, in two batches, for about 2 minutes.

4. Return vegetables to pan and heat mixture through, stirring constantly. Add tomato chunks at end.

5. Serve with heated tortillas and garnish with sour cream, guacamole and cheese.

Santa Barbara Shish Kabobs

There is such an abundant variety of good things on these skewers that this recipe calls for a party. The marinade is sensational.

Serves 8

Marinade:
½ cup vegetable oil
¼ cup soy sauce
½ cup red wine
1 teaspoon ground ginger
3 small garlic cloves, crushed
1½ teaspoons curry powder
2 tablespoons catsup
¼ teaspoon pepper
¼ teaspoon hot pepper sauce

Kabobs:
1 pound sirloin steak, cut into 1-inch thick squares
1 pound boneless leg of lamb, cut into 1-inch thick squares
1 pound pork tenderloin, cut into ½-inch thick squares
1 eggplant, sliced in ½-inch squares
2 apples, peeled and cut into 6 wedges
1 green bell pepper, seeded and cut
1 cup cut pineapple
10 mushrooms
½ pound bacon, sliced

1. Prepare Marinade: Blend all ingredients in a blender or food processor. Set aside.

2. Place meat in a shallow dish, keeping each type of meat separate.

3. Pour ¾ of the Marinade over the meat. Cover and refrigerate 24 hours, stirring once or twice.

4. A few hours before serving, place eggplant, apples, green pepper, pineapple and mushrooms in a medium bowl. Add remaining Marinade. Marinate 2-3 hours at room temperature, stirring occasionally.

5. To cook Kabobs, wrap a half slice of bacon around each piece of lamb. On large skewers, alternate beef, mushrooms, lamb, eggplant, pineapple, pork, green pepper and apple.

6. Barbecue or broil for 5-10 minutes on each side.

Spicy Latin American Kabobs

Serves 6-16

3-8 pounds sirloin, cut in ½-inch cubes

Marinade:
1 bottle Pico Pica Hot Sauce
2 large red chile peppers, seeded and finely chopped
1 onion, chopped
2 large garlic cloves, crushed
1 teaspoon ground cumin
1 teaspoon oregano
1 teaspoon paprika
1 teaspoon cinnamon
4 cloves
1 tablespoon sesame seeds
Juice of several limes
¼ cup chopped cilantro, loosely packed

1. Prepare Marinade: Mix all ingredients together.

2. Place sirloin in a plastic or glass container and add Marinade. Marinate in the refrigerator overnight. To dilute Marinade, add water and more lime juice to taste.

3. Skewer meat as individual kabobs and broil or barbecue to desired doneness.

4. Count on ½ pound or less total meat portions for each person.

Tijuana Torte

A great mid-week supper. Your kids will love it.

Serves 6-8

1 pound ground beef
1 small onion, chopped
1 8-ounce can tomato
   sauce
1 pound can stewed
   tomatoes
1 small can mild salsa
1 7-ounce can diced green
   chiles
1 package Lawry's Taco
   Seasoning
12 corn tortillas
1 pound Cheddar cheese,
   grated

1. Preheat oven to 350°.

2. Brown ground beef with onion. Drain grease.

3. Add tomato sauce, stewed tomatoes, salsa, green chiles and taco
    seasoning to the meat and mix well.

4. Tear tortillas into pieces and lay in bottom of 9x9-inch dish.
    Spoon ⅓ of meat sauce on top of tortillas and sprinkle with ⅓ of
    the cheese. Layer two more times with tortillas, meat sauce and
    cheese.

5. Top with remaining Cheddar cheese covering entire top.

6. Bake for 30-45 minutes. Cool 15 minutes before serving.

Belgian Meatballs

Another hit with the kids!

Serves 8

Meatballs:
1 medium white onion, finely diced
1 tablespoon butter
1 pound ground beef
1 pound ground veal
1 egg
1 clove garlic, crushed
¾ teaspoon nutmeg
3 ounces tomato sauce
½ cup bread crumbs
Salt and Pepper to taste
Flour, as needed

Sauce:
4 onions, sliced
2 cloves garlic, crushed
5 tomatoes, peeled, seeded and chopped
½ cup white wine
Worchestershire sauce to taste
1 8-ounce can tomato sauce
1 teaspoon beef bouillon powder
1 bay leaf
1 teaspoon tarragon
1 teaspoon parsley

1. In a frying pan sauté onion in butter.

2. Place sautéed onions in a medium bowl. Add remaining Meatball ingredients, except flour, to bowl. Roll mixture into balls and sprinkle with flour until coated.

3. Add Meatballs to frying pan, brown on all sides. Remove from pan.

4. Prepare Sauce: Sauté onions and garlic in skillet with remaining butter from the Meatballs. When soft, add tomatoes and remaining ingredients.

5. Cover and simmer the sauce for ½ hour.

6. Add the Meatballs and continue to simmer for ½ hour.

Note: Meatballs may be served over rice.

Veal Escalopes with Artichoke Hearts

Turkey slices can be substituted for the veal in this rich, subtly flavored dish.

Serves 4

5 tablespoons butter
½ pound veal escalopes
Flour for dusting
1 pint half and half, or
   whipping cream
2 tablespoons tarragon
½ teaspoon salt
Pepper to taste
1 package frozen artichoke
   hearts
Arrowroot or cornstarch
   for thickening

1. Melt 2 tablespoons butter in large skillet. Dust veal with flour, and place in hot skillet. Brown veal on both sides.

2. Remove cooked veal and place on hot plate, keeping warm.

3. Add half and half, remaining butter, tarragon, salt and pepper to medium-hot skillet.

4. Cook frozen artichokes according to package directions, and drain. Add to skillet.

5. Bring sauce to a boil and simmer. Add arrowroot or cornstarch, as needed, to thicken sauce.

6. Pour thickened sauce over cooked veal and serve at once.

Broiled Ginger Lamb Chops

The whole family will love the sweet and sour flavor.

Serves 4

1 teaspoon minced ginger
   root
1 teaspoon minced garlic
4 teaspoons oil, preferably
   canola oil
1 teaspoon soy sauce
1 teaspoon red wine
   vinegar
½ teaspoon brown sugar
Pepper to taste
4 small loin lamb chops,
   1-inch thick

1. Preheat broiler.

2. Combine ginger, garlic, oil, soy sauce, vinegar, sugar and pepper in a bowl.

3. Place lamb chops in a dish and coat with ginger mixture, reserving a portion of ginger mixture for basting.

4. Broil chops for 7 minutes on one side, then turn and brush with remaining ginger mixture. Broil an additional 5-7 minutes or until done, as desired.

Lamb Chops in Caper Sauce

Serves 4

2 tablespoons butter
4 large loin lamb chops
2 tablespoons flour
½ cup chicken stock
3 tablespoons medium
  sherry
4 tablespoons capers,
  drained
Salt and Pepper to taste
1 teaspoon brown sugar

1. Heat butter in skillet. Fry the chops on both sides in the butter for 5 minutes. Remove from the pan.

2. Stir the flour into the pan juices and cook for 2-3 minutes. Stir in the stock and sherry and then add the capers, salt, pepper and sugar. Bring slowly to a boil, stirring continuously. Reduce heat until the sauce is at simmering point.

3. Place the chops back into the pan, cover with a lid and simmer for 15 minutes.

Lamb with Eggplant

Serves 6-8

3 1-pound eggplants
4-6 tablespoons olive oil
2½ pounds leg of lamb,
  cut into 1½-inch cubes
1 medium onion, chopped
2 cloves garlic, minced
¼ cup chopped parsley
1 bay leaf
Salt and Pepper to taste
1 tablespoon dried
  oregano
4 large tomatoes, cut into
  wedges
Juice of 1 lemon

1. Preheat oven to 325°.

2. Peel the eggplants and cut off the stems. Cut eggplants into 1½-inch cubes.

3. Heat 2-3 tablespoons oil in a skillet. Add the eggplant cubes and brown on all sides, turning as needed. Set aside on paper towel.

4. Add and heat remaining 2-3 tablespoons oil in the skillet. Add the lamb in batches and completely brown each piece. Put the lamb pieces, as they are done, in a large quart casserole. Add the onion and garlic to the skillet. If the pan is dry, add another tablespoon oil. Cook for 30 seconds.

5. Scrape the contents of the skillet over the lamb. Add the parsley, bay leaf, salt, pepper and oregano and stir to mix.

6. Arrange the eggplants in a single layer over the lamb and top with the tomatoes. Season with salt and pepper. Add the lemon juice.

7. Cover the casserole and bake for 1½ hours.

Butterflied Lamb with Peppercorns

The crisp crust makes this lamb special.

Serves 6

3 tablespoons crushed
　green peppercorns,
　preserved in salt water
1 tablespoon fresh
　rosemary
¼ cup fresh mint leaves
5 cloves garlic, crushed
½ cup red wine vinegar or
　lemon juice
½ cup light soy sauce
4-5 pound leg of lamb,
　boned and butterflied
2 tablespoons Dijon
　mustard
½ teaspoon sea salt

1. Preheat oven to 350°.

2. Combine 1 tablespoon of the crushed peppercorns with the rosemary, mint, garlic, vinegar and soy sauce in a shallow bowl. Marinate the lamb in the mixture for 8 hours, turning occasionally.

3. Remove lamb from marinade and drain. Reserve the marinade.

4. Spread mustard over skin side of meat, sprinkle with sea salt and pat remaining peppercorns into the mustard. Set the lamb in a shallow roasting pan large enough to hold the meat comfortably and carefully pour the reserved marinade around the meat.

5. Bake until medium rare, approximately 1½ hours, or until meat thermometer registers 140°. Let stand for 20 minutes before carving.

6. Serve the pan juices in a gravy boat with the lamb.

Marinated Butterflied Lamb

An elegant entree for spring's first warm weekend.

Serves 8-10

1 5½-pound leg of lamb,
　boned and butterflied
½ cup Dijon mustard
2 tablespoons soy sauce
3 large garlic cloves,
　minced
1 tablespoon fresh
　rosemary
½ teaspoon powdered
　ginger
2 tablespoons olive oil

1. Flatten out meat and put into a 9x13-inch glass dish. If the meat is too large, cut in half and put into 2 dishes.

2. Whisk together the mustard, soy sauce, garlic, rosemary, ginger and oil to make a paste. Spread the paste on both sides of the meat and cover with plastic wrap. Refrigerate for 24 hours.

3. Cook for 15-20 minutes per side on barbecue grill over medium coals.

Lamb Shanks

Lamb is available all year long, but somehow spring lamb is better for this traditional meal. A lovely Sunday dinner that smells good all afternoon.

Serves 6

4 lamb shanks (3 pounds)
3-4 tablespoons flour
2 tablespoons oil
1 clove garlic, crushed
2 teaspoons salt
1 teaspoon oregano
¼ teaspoon pepper
1 cup chicken bouillon
1 tablespoon lemon juice
4 carrots, pared and halved
4 small onions
2 stalks celery, quartered
2 potatoes, quartered
1 tablespoon flour
¼ teaspoon Kitchen Bouqet

1. Preheat oven to 350°.

2. Remove fat from shanks, wipe with a damp towel, and coat with flour.

3. Slowly heat oil in Dutch oven. Brown shanks well, turning several times.

4. Add garlic, salt, oregano, pepper, bouillon and lemon juice. Cover and bake for 1½ hours.

5. Turn shanks and add carrots, onions, celery and potatoes.

6. Cover and bake for 35-45 minutes.

7. Remove meat and vegetables to warm platter and cover.

8. Reserve 1½ cups of liquid from Dutch oven. Skim off fat from liquid and put 1 tablespoon in a saucepan.

9. Blend in flour and gradually stir in remaining skimmed liquid. Add Kitchen Bouqet, bring to boil, stirring, for 1 minute. Pour over meat and vegetables.

French Lamb Chops

Simple to make, yet sophisticated in taste.

Serves 4-6

6 small loin lamb chops, boned
1 small bottle Dijon mustard
1 egg, beaten
2 cups bread crumbs
2 tablespoons oregano
2 tablespoons rosemary
2 tablespoons powdered garlic
Salt and Pepper to taste

1. Preheat oven to 450°.

2. Brush chops on all sides with mustard, then dip in egg.

3. Combine bread crumbs, oregano, rosemary and garlic. Mix well.

4. Roll chops in bread crumb mixture.

5. Put chops in buttered baking dish and sprinkle with salt and pepper. Bake for 20 minutes.

Easy Mushroom Pork Chops

Serves 4

2 tablespoons butter
4 1-inch large pork chops,
  boned
2 cups sliced button
  mushrooms
Juice of ½ lemon
1 tablespoon flour
Salt and Pepper to taste
½ teaspoon dried thyme
4 tablespoons heavy cream
Parsley, chopped to
  garnish

1. Preheat oven to 350°.

2. In a frying pan, melt butter and brown the chops on both sides.

3. Transfer each one to a piece of aluminum foil large enough to enclose the chops loosely.

4. Add mushrooms to the pan and sauté quickly. Pour in lemon juice. After 1 minute, stir in flour and cook for 1-2 minutes.

5. Season the chops with salt, pepper and thyme. Spoon the mushroom mixture and then the cream onto the chops.

6. Wrap chops securely in foil. Place the chops on a baking sheet or in a roasting pan and bake for 1 hour.

Cranberry Pork Chops

Tangy and terrific.

Serves 6

1 tablespoon butter
1 onion, chopped
3 pounds pork chops,
  1-inch thick
⅔ cup bottled chili sauce
3 tablespoons brown
  sugar, firmly packed
1 tablespoon red wine
  vinegar
1 teaspoon dry mustard
1½ cups cranberries, fresh
  or frozen
1 orange, thinly sliced for
  garnish

1. Preheat oven to 400°.

2. Melt butter in 9x13-inch baking dish and add onions. Bake uncovered for 10-15 minutes or until onion is limp. Stir occasionally.

3. Place pork chops in dish and place onions around meat, not under. Reduce oven temperature to 350° and bake for 25 minutes, uncovered.

4. Stir together remaining ingredients, except orange slices, in a bowl. Add onions from baking dish, then spoon sauce over the chops. Continue baking until meat is fully cooked and cranberry sauce has slightly caramelized, about 25-30 minutes longer.

5. Garnish meat with orange slices.

Southwestern Pork with Red Chiles

Serves 4

5 dried red chiles, seeded
   and stems removed
1 cup water
2 tablespoons vegetable oil
2 pounds pork, cut into 1-
   inch cubes
½ teaspoon fresh minced
   oregano
¼ teaspoon garlic powder
Salt to taste

1. Place chiles in a blender with water and blend into a paste. Set aside. If chile paste is too thick, add a little water.

2. Add oil to skillet and lightly brown pork. Add chile paste, oregano, garlic and salt to meat. Mix well.

3. Cover skillet and simmer slowly until done, approximately 30-40 minutes.

4. Sauce may be thickened with cornstarch, if necessary.

Note: Serve with rice, tortillas or noodles.

Orange and Maple Glazed Ribs

Who doesn't love ribs? This citrus and maple glaze is exceptionally good.

Serves 4

⅔ cup pure maple syrup
½ cup orange juice
¼ cup minced onion
2 teaspoons grated orange
   peel
2 teaspoons fresh lemon
   juice
1 teaspoon dry mustard
2 racks baby back pork ribs
   (about 3 pounds)
Salt and Pepper to taste

1. Combine first 6 ingredients in a heavy saucepan. Cook slowly over medium-low heat for 5 minutes, stirring occasionally. Pour sauce into a large bowl and let cool. Sauce can be prepared 24 hours ahead, covered and refrigerated.

2. Preheat oven to 350°. Season rib racks with salt and pepper. Arrange on a large baking sheet. Bake for 35 minutes. Cool for 15 minutes. Cut racks into individual ribs.

3. Add ribs to the sauce in the bowl and turn them to coat. Return ribs to baking sheet. Bake 15 minutes longer, basting three times with remaining sauce.

Empanadas

Fun to make and they disappear so fast.

Serves 6

4 cups flour
1 cup butter, softened
¾ cup water
1 teaspoon salt

Meat Filling:
2 medium onions, minced
1 pound ground pork
¼ cup oil
1 cup water
¼ cup currants
1 teaspoon dried chiles,
  crushed
¼ teaspoon cumin seeds
¼ teaspoon cayenne
  pepper
Garlic to taste
Salt and Pepper to taste
Vinegar
2 egg yolks, slightly beaten

1. Place flour on wooden board and make a well in center. Place butter, water and salt in well and mix with fingertips, working in enough flour as needed to form smooth dough. Let dough rest 1 hour in refrigerator.

2. Divide dough into 6 portions and roll out until each one is very thin. Cut circles of dough, 8-10 inches in diameter, cutting around a plate as a guide.

3. Preheat oven to 400°. Prepare Meat Filling: Over medium heat, brown pork and onions in oil, crumbling meat finely until meat is cooked through and onions are translucent. Drain fat from mixture, then return to pan and add water, currants and spices. Blend well and simmer, stirring occasionally, for 30 minutes or until moisture has evaporated. Let mixture cool.

4. Place ⅙ of meat mixture onto ½ of each dough circle, leaving a ½-inch border. Moisten border of circle with vinegar, then fold 1 side over and seal with a fork. Place empanadas on baking sheet and brush with egg yolk. Bake for 20-25 minutes or until golden.

Note: Prepared empanadas may be tightly covered in plastic wrap on baking sheet and refrigerated for up to 4 hours before baking. (Do not brush with egg until just before baking.) To freeze: Unbaked, prepared empanadas may be wrapped in plastic and frozen up to 2 months. Defrost in refrigerator overnight, then brush with egg and bake.

Crêpes Ensenada

A versatile recipe delightful for brunch, lunch or dinner. Tortillas are a welcome alternative to homemade crêpes for busy cooks.

Serves 12

12 thin slices ham
1 pound Monterey Jack cheese, cut into ½-inch strips
1 can whole green chiles, cut into ¼-inch strips
12 flour tortillas

Cheese Sauce:
¼ pound butter
½ cup flour
1 quart milk
¾ pound Cheddar cheese, grated
1 teaspoon prepared mustard
½ teaspoon salt
Dash of pepper
Paprika

1. Divide ham, cheese and chile strips among tortillas. Place on top of tortillas; roll and secure, if necessary, with a toothpick.

2. Place tortilla rolls into a lightly greased 9x13-inch baking dish, separating them slightly.

3. Preheat oven to 350°.

4. Prepare Cheese Sauce: Melt butter in saucepan. Blend in flour and cook, stirring, for a few minutes.

5. Add milk slowly, stirring constantly to avoid lumps, then add cheese, mustard, salt and pepper. Stir until smooth.

6. Pour Cheese Sauce over tortillas and sprinkle with paprika. Bake for 45 minutes.

Sausage Pie Provençal

Great after a day of skiing. A snap to make.

Serves 6

1 pound sausage
3 eggs, beaten
1 cup shredded cheese
   (your choice)
Salt and Pepper to taste
¼ cup onion, chopped
½ cup milk
1 frozen pie shell

1. Preheat oven to 350°.

2. Cook sausage in skillet until completely cooked. Drain grease and let cool.

3. Mix all ingredients in a large bowl, including cooked sausage.

4. Place sausage mixture in the unbaked pie shell.

5. Bake for 40-45 minutes until golden and bubbly.

Burke's Bar-B-Q Sauce for Ribs

A great sauce for summer barbecues.

1½ cups catsup
¾ cup wine vinegar
8 tablespoons brown sugar
6 tablespoons
   Worchestershire sauce
1 teaspoon dry mustard
Dash of hot pepper sauce
1 6-ounce can crushed
   pineapple in syrup
1 clove garlic, crushed

1. In a medium pan, mix all ingredients and cook over medium heat for 5 minutes. Brush sauce on ribs before and during barbecuing.

Dijon Mustard Marinade

This recipe will make enough marinade for a 4 pound lamb.

2 cloves garlic, crushed
½ teaspoon salt
2 tablespoons Dijon mustard
1 tablespoon soy sauce
2 tablespoons fresh lemon juice
1½ tablespoons rosemary, thyme or oregano
¼ cup olive oil

1. Put garlic and salt into a small bowl.
2. Whisk in the remaining ingredients.
3. Paint both sides of your meat. Cover and marinate overnight, in the refrigerator.

Kathy's Spicy Sauce

This is delicious with smoked chicken, pork or beef.

2 cups mayonnaise
2-3 teaspoons Chipotle peppers, to taste (canned and packed in adobo sauce)

1. Combine ingredients in food processor until well blended.
2. Serve cold in a sauce boat.

Tri Tip Marinade

2 tablespoons vegetable oil
⅓ cup soy sauce
2 tablespoons brown sugar
1 tablespoon red wine vinegar
½ teaspoon powdered ginger
1 clove garlic, crushed

1. Combine marinade ingredients and pour over your beef.
2. Marinate in the refrigerator for 8 hours, or overnight for a more pronounced flavor.

Note: Can also use on chicken, ribs or fish.

Chandler Horseradish Sauce

Makes 1⅓ cups

3 ounces fresh horseradish
¼ cup white wine vinegar
½ teaspoon Dijon mustard
2 teaspoons powdered
    sugar
½ cup bread crumbs
¼ cup milk
Salt and Pepper to taste
½ cup heavy cream,
    whipped

1. In a bowl, combine the horseradish, vinegar, mustard and sugar.

2. Put the bread crumbs in the milk and then squeeze the bread dry.

3. Add bread to the horseradish mixture. Add salt and pepper.

4. Fold in the whipped cream and serve.

Lolly's Delight

This sauce is delicious on ham, or makes a great sausage appetizer. Fry 2 pounds sausage links, then add to sauce.

2 cups currant jelly
1 cup prepared mustard
    (add less if you would
    like it sweeter)

1. In a double boiler add both ingredients and cook over medium heat until sauce thickens. Place sauce in a sauce bowl and serve.

Chapter 9

STAR
STUDDED
SIDES

Vegetables and Rice

You needn't be a stargazer

or budding astronaut to

appreciate the star-studded

side dishes that follow,

and we guarantee that

they will add a certain

sparkle to your table.

Flavorful Cranberries

Excellent with pork.

Serves 4

2 cups cranberries
½ cup sugar
¼ cup water
1 cinnamon stick
2 cloves, whole
¼ teaspoon ground mace
½ teaspoon grated orange
   rind

1. Wash and drain cranberries.

2. In a saucepan, combine sugar, water, cinnamon stick, cloves and mace.

3. Bring water and spices to a boil and simmer 3 minutes.

4. Add cranberries and orange rind. Simmer until cranberries begin to split open, stirring constantly.

5. Remove cloves and cinnamon stick from cranberry mixture.

6. Chill before serving.

Hot Curried Fruit

Serves 12

16 ounces cling peaches
20 ounces pineapple slices
16 ounces pear halves
5 maraschino cherries with
   stems
⅓ cup butter
¾ cup light brown sugar,
   packed
4 teaspoons curry powder

1. Preheat oven to 325°.

2. Drain fruits until dry on paper towels. Arrange fruit in a 1½ quart casserole. Melt butter in a saucepan. Add brown sugar and curry, mixing well. Spoon curry mixture over fruit.

3. Bake 1 hour uncovered, then refrigerate.

4. 30 minutes prior to serving, reheat casserole in a 350° oven, until warm.

Cinnamon Pears

A colorful garnish for holiday plates.

Serves 6

2 cups water
1 cup crushed cinnamon
  candies
½ teaspoon cloves
½ teaspoon nutmeg
6 pears, peeled, cored and
  halved

1. Heat water in saucepan. Gradually add cinnamon candies, stirring constantly until dissolved.

2. Add cloves and nutmeg, mixing well.

3. Add pears and cook until just tender, turning often.

4. Let pears cool in syrup.

5. Serve or store in refrigerator, up to 2 weeks.

Broccoli with Lemon Dill Sauce

Serves 6

1 head of broccoli, cut in
  flowerets
2 tablespoons butter
2 tablespoons flour
1 teaspoon grated lemon
  peel
½ teaspoon dried dill
¼ teaspoon salt
Dash of paprika
1 cup milk

1. Steam broccoli in a medium saucepan until tender. Set aside.

2. Melt butter in a medium saucepan. Remove from heat and stir in flour, lemon peel, dill, salt and paprika.

3. Return to medium heat and gradually whisk in milk.

4. Cook and whisk until mixture is thickened.

5. Arrange cooked broccoli on a platter. Pour sauce over broccoli and serve.

Glazed Carrots and Grapes

Choose small green grapes for this interesting combination of flavors.

Serves 8

2 pounds fresh carrots,
    julienned or sliced or 2
    16-ounce packages
    frozen sliced carrots
2 tablespoons butter
3 tablespoons brown sugar
3 tablespoons vodka
1½ teaspoons cornstarch
2 teaspoons water
1½ cups green grapes,
    seedless

1. Steam or cook carrots until tender and drain.

2. In a medium saucepan, melt butter and stir in brown sugar and vodka. Add carrots.

3. In a small bowl, mix cornstarch and water until smooth. Stir into carrots.

4. Bring carrots to a boil, stirring constantly.

5. Add grapes just before serving and cook vegetables until heated through.

Zippy Carrots

Here's the secret for getting your kids to eat their carrots!

Serves 6-8

1 pound baby carrots,
    peeled (fresh or frozen)
2 tablespoons butter or
    margarine, melted
¼ cup brown sugar
2 tablespoons dry mustard
¼ teaspoon salt

1. Steam carrots until crisp, yet tender, and place in a medium saucepan.

2. Combine the remaining ingredients in a small bowl and add to carrots.

3. Cook over medium heat for 5-7 minutes.

4. Serve warm.

Carrots with Cognac

A sophisticated taste, but oh so easy!

Serves 6-8

1 pound baby carrots, fresh
 or frozen, peeled
4 tablespoons butter
2 tablespoons cognac or
 brandy
¼ cup minced parsley
Salt and Pepper to taste

1. In a wide frying pan lay carrots flat and add water to cover.

2. Bring to a boil and simmer until tender, drain.

3. Add butter and cognac or brandy, and cook over medium heat, shaking pan until carrots are coated and barely browned.

4. Mix in parsley and season with salt and pepper.

Brown Buttered Corn with Herbs

Excellent with poultry or grilled meats.

Serves 4

2 tablespoons butter
1½-2 cups fresh corn, cut
 from about 3 ears
2 tablespoons fresh finely
 shredded basil
½ cup chopped green
 onions
Salt and Pepper to taste

1. In a medium skillet, heat the butter over medium high heat until the foam subsides.

2. Sauté the corn for approximately 4 minutes. The corn will be partially browned.

3. Place corn in a serving bowl and add basil, green onions, salt and pepper. This can be served warm or cold.

Creamed Corn

Serves 4

1 tablespoon butter
1 tablespoon flour
1 pound corn, frozen
½ cup milk
½ cup whipping cream
3 tablespoons sugar

1. Melt butter in a medium saucepan and slowly add flour, making a roux. Set aside.

2. In a large skillet, on medium heat, mix corn, milk, cream and sugar, until warm.

3. While corn mixture is warm, add roux and heat to simmer. Serve warm.

Roasted Eggplant

Serves 4-6

1 large eggplant
4 small tomatoes
1 large onion
1 tablespoon minced garlic
1 tablespoon ground
  coriander
1 teaspoon dried thyme
1 teaspoon pepper
½ teaspoon salt
1 cup chicken broth
½ cup olive oil
½ cup red wine vinegar
Thyme and coriander
  sprigs for garnish

1. Preheat oven to 500°.

2. Cut the eggplant into 1-inch cubes, leaving skin on.

3. Cut tomatoes into eighths; seed and core. Cut onion into eighths; separate layers.

4. Place all the prepared vegetables in a large mixing bowl.

5. Sprinkle garlic, coriander, thyme, pepper and salt on top. Gently toss.

6. Pour chicken broth, olive oil and red wine vinegar over the vegetable mixture. Toss gently until completely coated and well mixed.

7. Spoon vegetables into shallow 9x13-inch pan coated with vegetable oil spray.

8. Roast for 1 hour, stirring gently every 20 minutes. Garnish with thyme and coriander.

Cucumbers with Sour Cream

A wonderful summer side dish.

Serves 4-6

1 cup sour cream
1 tablespoon sugar
¼ cup cider vinegar
¼ cup chopped fresh dill
¼ teaspoon white pepper
¼ teaspoon salt
½ teaspoon celery seed
2 large cucumbers, peeled
   and thinly sliced
½ small brown onion,
   thinly sliced
Dill for garnish

1. In a medium bowl, combine sour cream, sugar, vinegar, dill, pepper, salt and celery seed, blend well.

2. Add cucumbers and onions to sour cream mixture, toss lightly. Refrigerate at least 2 hours.

3. Sprinkle cucumbers with additional dill and serve chilled.

Red Pepper Halves Stuffed with Creamed Spinach

Beautiful for a holiday dinner.

Serves 6

3 large red bell peppers
2 10-ounce packages
   chopped frozen spinach
6 ounces white sauce
   (canned or homemade)
1 cup sour cream
2 tablespoons instant
   onion soup mix
1 teaspoon dry chicken
   stock base

1. Preheat oven to 350°.

2. Cut red peppers in half and remove seeds. Parboil in water for 3 minutes. Drain and cool.

3. Cook and drain spinach completely.

4. Blend sauce, sour cream, onion and chicken stock.

5. Stir sauce into spinach.

6. Stuff red peppers with spinach mixture.

7. Bake for 15-20 minutes or until heated through.

Cold Green Beans with Gruyère Cheese

Excellent for picnics and easily prepared a day ahead.

Serves 6-8

1½ pounds fresh green
   beans
⅓ cup olive oil
2 tablespoons white wine
   vinegar
1 tablespoon Dijon
   mustard
4 tablespoons chopped
   fresh parsley
Salt and Pepper to taste
1 cup sliced mushrooms
¼ pound Gruyère cheese,
   grated

1. Wash and blanch green beans for 1 minute or until very crunchy.

2. Place oil, vinegar, mustard, parsley, salt and pepper in a jar and shake well. Pour sauce over green beans, then refrigerate.

3. Prior to serving, add mushrooms and cheese. Toss well.

Green Beans à la Grecque

For an elegant picnic or cold buffet.

Serves 6

1 pound green beans,
   washed and trimmed,
   cut into 1-inch lengths
2 tablespoons olive oil
1 medium onion, thinly
   sliced and separated into
   rings
2 large garlic cloves,
   minced
¼ cup red wine vinegar
1 tablespoon dried
   oregano, crumbled
2 large tomatoes, peeled,
   seeded and coarsely
   chopped
6 tablespoons crumbled
   Feta cheese
Salt and Pepper to taste

1. Bring a large saucepan of water to a boil. Add the beans and simmer until tender, yet crisp, 3-5 minutes. Drain, refresh in ice water, and drain again. Set beans aside or if prepared early in the day, wrap in paper towels and store in a plastic bag in the refrigerator.

2. Heat the oil in a large skillet over medium heat. Add the onion and garlic. Sauté until soft, but not browned, about 5 minutes.

3. Add the vinegar, oregano and tomatoes. Simmer for 5 minutes, stirring frequently.

4. Add green beans and simmer, stirring frequently, until heated through. Remove from heat.

5. Sprinkle with Feta cheese and toss gently. Taste first (Feta can be salty) and then season with salt and pepper.

6. Serve immediately or cool and serve at room temperature.

Pink Onions

Excellent with grilled meats.

Serves 4-6

4 red onions, peeled and
  thinly sliced
1 cup white vinegar
1 cup sugar

1. Cover onions with boiling water. Let stand 5 minutes. Drain.

2. Cover again with boiling water for another 5 minutes. Drain.

3. Combine vinegar and sugar and pour over onions. Store in jars in refrigerator.

4. Serve cold.

Marinated Grilled Vegetables

A delicious accompaniment to any grilled entree.

Serves 6

3 Japanese eggplants, sliced
  in half lengthwise
3 red bell peppers, sliced in
  half lengthwise
1 large red onion, sliced
  ¼-inch thick
3 small to medium
  zucchini, sliced in half
  lengthwise
Olive oil
Salt and Pepper to taste
1 teaspoon oregano
2 tablespoons balsamic
  vinegar
8 tablespoons virgin olive
  oil
1 cup grated Mozzarella or
  crumbled goat cheese
  (optional)

1. Grill vegetables over medium coals on barbecue, basting with olive oil until cooked through, but still firm. Cut into strips and toss in large bowl with salt, pepper, oregano, vinegar and olive oil.

2. Serve vegetables and pass cheese separately, if desired, to sprinkle on top.

Coronado Potatoes

Serves 10

24 small red potatoes
4 tablespoons butter
1 green onion, minced
2 cloves garlic
¼ cup chopped parsley
½ teaspoon lemon juice
1 chive, minced
Parsley sprigs for garnish

1. Boil potatoes approximately 25 minutes.

2. Melt butter in an 8-inch skillet. Sauté green onion and garlic for 3 minutes. Stir in parsley and lemon juice.

3. Drain potatoes and place in serving dish. Pour butter mixture over potatoes, to thoroughly coat. Sprinkle chives on top of the potatoes. Garnish with parsley sprigs.

Parmesan Potatoes

A favorite of all ages.

Serves 8

4 large potatoes, peeled and cut into ¼-½ inch slices
7 tablespoons butter, melted or olive oil
1½ cups grated Parmesan cheese
⅓ cup flour
2 teaspoons chopped rosemary
Parsley
Green onions (optional)

1. Preheat oven to 350°.

2. Put potatoes in saucepan with water to cover. Bring to a boil and cook 15 minutes. Drain.

3. Pour melted butter or oil in a glass oblong baking dish. Mix Parmesan cheese, flour and rosemary together. Pat potatoes with cheese mixture on all sides.

4. Place potatoes over butter in dish in a single layer.

5. Bake for 30-45 minutes. Garnish with parsley and green onions, if desired.

Fat Rascal Potatoes

Serves 4

4 large Idaho potatoes
4 tablespoons butter
1 cup grated Cheddar
cheese
¾ cup sour cream
3 chives, chopped
4 bacon strips, chopped

1. Preheat oven to 350°.

2. Bake potatoes wrapped in aluminum foil for 30 minutes. Remove potatoes and let cool.

3. Open aluminum and make one cut lengthwise and one across the top of the potatoes. Gently squeeze the potato to loosen.

4. Spoon out the potato pulp, making sure not to tear the skin, and place pulp in a medium mixing bowl.

5. Add butter, cheese and sour cream, to the bowl. With a mixer, beat the potato mixture until fluffy.

6. Spoon mixture back into the potato skins. Reclose with aluminum foil and bake in the oven on a cookie sheet for 20-30 additional minutes, at 350°.

7. Prior to serving, remove potatoes from foil and serve whole potatoes with chives and bacon bits sprinkled on top.

Crispy Potatoes

You can never make enough of these.

Serves 3-4

½ cup oil
3 medium white potatoes
Spicy salt seasoning of
your choice

1. Heat oil in frying pan until very hot.

2. Slice potatoes into very thin rounds, then stack several rounds on top of each other, and slice into very thin slivers.

3. Place potatoes in hot oil, then sprinkle seasoning on top (be generous here, seasoning makes it!) Let potatoes get brown, then flip and brown other side.

4. Reduce heat and continue to cook until potatoes are tender.

Spicy Vegetable Medley

A tasty and colorful way to show off your garden's bounty.

Serves 6-8

¼ cup olive oil
2 garlic cloves, crushed
¾ pound zucchini, cut
   lengthwise in quarters
3 yellow squash, cut
   lengthwise in quarters
4 ears of corn, kernels cut
   from the cob
6 green onions, sliced
4 ounces green chile salsa
1 small green bell pepper,
   diced
1 red bell pepper, diced
¼ cup diced red onion
1 teaspoon salt
1 teaspoon pepper
2 tomatoes, diced

1. Heat oil in large skillet with garlic. Cook for 5 minutes over moderately low heat. Remove and discard garlic.

2. Add zucchini, squash, corn, green onions, salsa, peppers and red onions.

3. Sprinkle mixture with salt and pepper and simmer, covered, over low heat for 15 minutes or until vegetables are tender but still crisp.

4. Top the mixture with tomatoes and cook an additional 1 minute. Place in a large bowl and serve hot.

Shortcut Spinach

A classic that continues to please.

Serves 4

20 ounces chopped frozen
   spinach
1 2.8-ounce can french
   fried onion rings
1 can cream of mushroom
   soup
8 ounces grated Cheddar
   cheese
½ cup almonds, toasted

1. Preheat oven to 350°.

2. Cook and drain spinach.

3. Put spinach into a medium mixing bowl and add remaining ingredients, except almonds.

4. Turn all ingredients into a greased covered casserole. Bake for 30 minutes. Top with toasted almonds.

Spinach Mushroom Bake

Serves 10

20 ounces chopped frozen
    spinach, thawed and
    drained
1 can cream of mushroom
    soup
1 pint sour cream
1 tablespoon minced
    parsley
¼ cup chopped green
    onions
¼ teaspoon Worcestershire
    sauce
1 cup sliced mushrooms
1 tablespoon butter
1 tablespoon lemon juice
½ teaspoon pepper
½ teaspoon garlic powder

1. Preheat oven to 400°.

2. Mix spinach with undiluted soup, sour cream, parsley, green onions and Worcestershire sauce.

3. Sauté mushrooms in butter and season with lemon juice, pepper and garlic powder.

4. Stir mushrooms into spinach mixture.

5. Turn mixture into a greased 2½-quart shallow baking dish. Bake for 30 minutes.

Note: May be prepared a day in advance and then baked.

Yams with Pineapple Glaze

Delicious with ham.

Serves 8-10

4 large yams
4 tablespoons butter
½ cup brown sugar
1 teaspoon salt
¼ teaspoon lemon rind
1 teaspoon grated orange
    rind
1 cup canned crushed
    pineapple in syrup
2 teaspoons cornstarch

1. Peel and slice yams. Boil in salted water for 10 minutes, then drain.

2. Melt butter in a large heavy skillet and stir in brown sugar, salt, lemon rind, orange rind and pineapple.

3. Dissolve cornstarch in 2 tablespoons cold water. Stir into pineapple mixture.

4. When mixture is thickened, add yams, turning until completely covered with pineapple sauce. Cook over medium heat until tender.

Yellow Squash

Serves 6-8

1 pound yellow squash,
  sliced
1 onion, finely chopped
1 cup grated Cheddar
  cheese
¼ cup half and half
2 tablespoons butter
1 egg, beaten
Dash of nutmeg
Salt and Pepper to taste
½ cup cracker crumbs
Paprika to taste

1. Preheat oven to 350°.

2. Steam squash and onion until done. Drain.

3. Combine squash and onion in a large bowl, add cheese, half and half, butter, egg, nutmeg, salt and pepper. Mix well.

4. Place mixture in a greased casserole dish.

5. Top with cracker crumbs and paprika.

6. Bake approximately 25-30 minutes until slightly brown.

Zucchini Bake

A meal in itself.

Serves 6-8

1 medium onion, chopped
⅓ cup butter
5 cups sliced zucchini
½ cup chopped fresh
  parsley, or 2 tablespoons
  dried
½ teaspoon salt
½ teaspoon pepper
¼ teaspoon garlic powder
½ teaspoon oregano
8 ounces refrigerated
  crescent rolls
2 teaspoons Dijon mustard
1 cup grated Mozzarella
  cheese
1 cup grated Swiss cheese
2 eggs, beaten

1. Preheat oven to 350°.

2. Sauté onion in butter.

3. Add zucchini and cook until tender.

4. Add spices and stir.

5. Press crescent rolls into 8x8-inch square or 9-inch round pan to form crust. Spread mustard on top of the dough.

6. Pour zucchini mixture into pan.

7. Sprinkle with cheeses and pour the eggs on top.

8. Bake for 20-25 minutes.

Poppy Seed Noodles

A nice change of pace from potatoes or rice.

Serves 8-10

1 cup margarine or butter
1½ cups blanched slivered
    almonds
½ cup poppy seeds
½ teaspoon salt
12 ounces wide egg
    noodles, cooked to
    package directions

1. Melt margarine and sauté the almonds. Brown slowly so they do not burn.

2. Stir in poppy seeds and salt.

3. Add almond mixture to cooked noodles and toss well, coating thoroughly.

Parmesan Rice

Easy and elegant with any entree.

Serves 8

½ cup butter
2 cups long grain white
    rice
2 10½-ounce cans beef
    consommé, or beef broth
6 green onions, chopped
¾ cup grated Parmesan
    cheese

1. Melt butter in medium pan. Add rice and brown over medium heat for 5 minutes.

2. Add beef consommé and cook, covered, over low heat until liquid has been absorbed, about 20 minutes.

3. Add green onions and stir. Top with Parmesan cheese.

4. Heat until cheese is melted. Mix thoroughly. Can be made ahead of time.

Mediterranean Pilaf

Turmeric and curry powder add golden color and a delightful flavor.

Serves 8

3 cups chicken broth
1½ cups long grain white
    rice
2 tablespoons vegetable oil
¾ cup golden raisins,
    seedless
½ teaspoon turmeric
1 teaspoon curry powder
1½ tablespoons soy sauce

1. In a 1-quart saucepan, bring chicken broth to a boil.

2. In a medium saucepan, mix rice, oil, raisins, turmeric, curry powder and soy sauce. Pour in chicken broth.

3. Cover and cook over low heat for 20 minutes or until all liquid is absorbed and rice is tender. Mix well.

Rice with Red Peppers and Nuts

Serves 6

2 cups chicken stock
1 cup long grain white rice
¼ teaspoon salt
⅛ teaspoon finely ground
  pepper
3 tablespoons pine nuts or
  almonds
2 tablespoons butter
2 tablespoons oil
1 finely chopped medium
  onion
½ cup diced red bell
  pepper
½ cup diced celery
2 tablespoons finely
  chopped parsley
Salt and Pepper to taste

1. Preheat oven to 350°.

2. Bring chicken stock to boil in medium saucepan over high heat. Add rice, salt and pepper, and stir with fork. Lower heat, cover and simmer 20 minutes.

3. Toast nuts in oven for 5 minutes or until lightly browned.

4. In medium skillet, heat butter and oil over medium heat. Sauté onion, stirring occasionally, until soft. Add red pepper and celery and continue cooking for about 5 minutes until vegetables are cooked but still slightly crisp.

5. When rice is cooked, add vegetables, nuts, parsley, salt and pepper. Toss and serve immediately.

Almost Fried Rice

Reminds one of fried rice. It can be made ahead of time.

Serves 6

3 tablespoons salad oil
2 eggs
Salt and Pepper to taste
½ pound thinly sliced
  mushrooms
2 tablespoons minced
  onion
4 cups cooked white rice
2 tablespoons soy sauce
1 cup whole blanched
  almonds
1 cup chopped green
  onions

1. Preheat oven to 350°.

2. Heat 1 tablespoon oil in frying pan. Add eggs, salt and pepper and stir just enough to break yolks.

3. Cook slowly until the eggs are very firm and can be cut into strips. Remove strips and set aside.

4. Add remaining oil to pan and sauté mushrooms and onion, stirring constantly until cooked. Add rice, soy sauce and egg strips. Mix thoroughly.

5. Place in casserole, top with almonds, cover, and bake for ½ hour.

Bulgur Pilaf with Mushrooms and Olives

Serves 4

1 cup bulgur wheat
3 tablespoons olive oil
½ pound fresh
  mushrooms, sliced
1 cup chopped onion
½ teaspoon oregano
½ teaspoon minced garlic
1 cup chopped pitted black
  oil-cured olives
1½ cups chicken stock or
  water
1 tablespoon chopped fresh
  parsley
½ tablespoon minced basil

1. Rinse bulgur wheat in water and drain.

2. Pour oil into a heavy-bottomed saucepan and place over high heat. Add mushrooms and cook, stirring, until they begin to brown.

3. Add onion; lower heat, and continue to sauté until the onion is soft and begins to brown.

4. Stir in oregano, garlic, olives and bulgur. Pour in stock or water, cover, reduce heat, and cook for about 20 minutes until water is absorbed and the bulgur is tender.

5. Stir in parsley and basil and serve.

Cinco de Mayo Rice

An easy side dish that adds zip to a barbecued dinner.

Serves 6

3 cups cooked white rice
1 4-ounce can diced green
   chiles
½ pound sharp Cheddar
   cheese, grated
1½ cups sour cream

1. Preheat oven to 350°.

2. Combine all ingredients and put into a greased casserole dish.

3. Bake for 30 minutes.

Chile Cheese Rice Bake

Serves 8

1 cup long grain white rice
2 medium zucchini, sliced
1 7-ounce can diced green
   chiles
12 ounces Jack cheese,
   grated
1 large tomato, chopped
Salt to taste
2 cups sour cream
1 teaspoon oregano
1 garlic clove, chopped
¼ cup chopped green
   onions
Chopped parsley

1. Preheat oven to 350°.

2. Cook rice and set aside. Steam zucchini until tender, then drain.

3. Butter 3-quart casserole. Layer rice, chiles, ½ of cheese, zucchini and tomato. Sprinkle with salt. Combine sour cream, oregano, garlic and green onions and spoon over tomato layer. Scatter remaining cheese on top.

4. Cover and bake for 45-50 minutes.

5. Sprinkle with chopped parsley and serve.

Browned Rice

One of Mom's old favorites that has stood the test of time.

Serves 2-4

½ cup butter or margarine
1 cup long grain white rice
1 cup canned onion soup
1 beef bouillon cube, dissolved in 1 cup hot water
1 small can button mushrooms
½ cup almonds, slivered

1. Preheat oven to 350°.

2. Melt butter in a skillet, add rice to brown.

3. Add remaining ingredients and mix well. Put into a casserole dish. Bake covered for 1 hour.

Santa Fe Rice

Serves 6

2 cups long grain white rice
2 tablespoons oil
5 cups chicken broth
Salt to taste
2 tablespoons chopped onion
2 tablespoons chopped tomato
2 tablespoons chopped green bell pepper
2 tablespoons chopped sweet red bell pepper
2 tablespoons chopped black olives
1 clove garlic, minced
6 tablespoons frozen peas, cooked and drained
6 green bell pepper slices
6 sweet red bell pepper slices

1. Fry rice in oil until browned. Add chicken broth and season with salt. Bring to boil, reduce heat, cover and cook 20 to 30 minutes.

2. Remove from heat and let stand, covered, for 5 minutes. Stir in onion, tomato, chopped green and red peppers, olives and garlic and heat to serving temperature.

3. Garnish each serving with a tablespoon of peas. Place pepper slices attractively around rice.

Note: This can be made in advance adding vegetables up to 1 hour before serving. Peas may be mixed into rice.

Confetti Rice

Serves 8

½ cup butter or margarine
1½ cups long grain white
   rice, uncooked
3 cups chicken broth
¾ cup chopped parsley
1 cup diced carrots
½ cup sliced green onions
1 cup chopped celery
   (optional)

1. Preheat oven to 350°.

2. Melt butter in pan, add rice and lightly brown for 3-5 minutes.

3. Pour chicken broth in a casserole. Add browned rice, cover, and bake for 45 minutes. Mix in vegetables and bake for an additional 10 minutes.

California Curried Couscous

A fabulous alternative to rice. It will become a favorite!

Serves 6-8

1½ cups chicken broth
2 teaspoons curry powder
1 cup couscous
2 large cloves garlic,
   minced
½ cup chopped celery
½ cup chopped onion
1 tablespoon olive oil
¼ cup chopped chutney
3 tablespoons lemon juice
¼ cup pine nuts, toasted
¼ cup dried currants
½ cup thinly sliced green
   onions

1. Boil chicken broth and curry powder in a medium saucepan. Add couscous, stir, cover, and reduce heat to low. Cook for 5 minutes more.

2. Remove from heat and fluff with a fork. Cover until ready to use.

3. While couscous cooks, sauté garlic, celery and onion in oil over medium heat until soft, but not browned, about 5 minutes. Combine chutney and lemon juice together in a small bowl.

4. Toss couscous with vegetable mixture. Stir pine nuts, currants and green onions into chutney mixture. (This can be done in a frying pan over low heat). Serve immediately or place in a casserole and briefly reheat at serving time.

Chapter 10

Aftershocks

Desserts

Guaranteed to make

your chin drop, if not

to make the ground

tremble, the following

tempting California desserts

are aptly named.

Penguin Cake

No one will guess that a purchased angelfood cake is the base for this showy, special occasion cake.

Serves 8-10

1 14-ounce package
   angelfood cake
5-6 tablespoons light rum
12 ounces semi-sweet
   chocolate chips
3 eggs
1 tablespoon vanilla extract
Dash of salt
1½ pints whipping cream,
   divided
2 tablespoons sugar
3 tablespoons powdered
   sugar
¼ cup toasted slivered
   almonds or chocolate
   shavings for garnish

1. Break cake into 2-inch pieces onto a cookie sheet. Sprinkle with rum. Set aside.

2. Melt chocolate over simmering water in a double boiler, stirring constantly. Add eggs 1 at a time. Add vanilla and salt and cook, stirring for 1 minute. Remove from heat and cool slightly.

3. Whip ½ pint of the whipping cream, adding the sugar gradually until stiff peaks are formed. Fold into chocolate mixture.

4. In a buttered 9-inch springform pan, layer cake with chocolate mixture, beginning and ending with the cake. There should be 3 layers of cake and 2 of chocolate.

5. Refrigerate cake for at least 6 hours. After that time, run a sharp knife around the sides of the pan and then remove pan sides. Whip remaining pint of whipping cream with 3 tablespoons powdered sugar and generously frost top and sides of cake. Sprinkle with chopped nuts or shaved chocolate. Store in refrigerator or cover and freeze.

California Carrot Cake

Could it be? A carrot cake with no carrots to grate!

Serves 10-12

4 eggs
2 cups sugar
10 ounces strained baby
  food carrots
1 cup vegetable oil
1 cup crushed pineapple,
  juice drained and
  reserved
2 cups flour
2 teaspoons cinnamon
2 teaspoons baking soda
1 teaspoon salt
1 teaspoon vanilla extract
1 cup raisins
1 cup chopped walnuts

Cream Cheese Frosting:
8 ounces cream cheese
4 tablespoons softened
  butter
1 teaspoon vanilla extract
2 cups powdered sugar
1-2 tablespoons milk (if
  needed)
Chopped walnuts for
  garnish (optional)

1. Preheat oven to 350°.

2. Beat eggs and sugar until well combined. Add carrots, oil, pineapple and ⅓ cup reserved pineapple juice. Sift together flour, cinnamon, baking soda and salt. Add to carrot mixture, beating well. Stir in vanilla, raisins and walnuts.

3. Pour batter into a lightly greased 9x13-inch pan. Bake in oven for 50 minutes. Cool completely and frost with Cream Cheese Frosting.

4. Prepare Cream Cheese Frosting: Mix together all ingredients until blended. If mixture appears too thick, thin with 1-2 tablespoons of milk.

5. Spread frosting liberally on top of cooled cake. Garnish with chopped walnuts, if desired.

Hawaiian Cake

A deliciously moist cake for a crowd.

Serves 10

3 cups flour
1 teaspoon baking soda
1 teaspoon salt
2 teaspoons cinnamon
2 cups sugar
1½ cups vegetable oil
3 large eggs, lightly beaten
8 ounces crushed
    pineapple, including
    juice
2 cups mashed bananas
    (approximately 5
    bananas)
3½ ounces flaked coconut
1½ teaspoons vanilla
    extract

Cream Cheese Glaze:
1¼ cups powdered sugar
3 ounces cream cheese,
    softened
1 tablespoon light corn
    syrup
½ teaspoon vanilla extract

Walnut halves or chopped
    nuts for garnish

1. Preheat oven to 350°. Butter and flour a 10-inch tube pan with removable bottom.

2. In a large bowl, sift together flour, baking soda, salt and cinnamon. Add sugar and combine well.

3. In a mixing bowl, combine vegetable oil and eggs. Add to dry ingredients and stir until just combined. Add pineapple and bananas to mixture. Stir in coconut and vanilla. Pour into prepared pan.

4. Bake 1 hour and 10 minutes to 1 hour and 20 minutes or until cake tester comes out clean. Cool cake on a wire rack for 15 minutes. Remove sides of pan and cool cake completely on tube. Run knife around bottom of pan and tube; invert cake onto a plate. Top with Cream Cheese Glaze when cool.

5. Prepare Cream Cheese Glaze: At low speed, beat together all ingredients until smooth.

6. Spread glaze on top of cooled cake, letting excess drip down sides. Decorate top with walnut halves or chopped nuts.

Pear Cake

Serves 8

1½ cups plus 2
  tablespoons flour
1½ cups sugar
1½ teaspoons baking soda
½ teaspoon salt
¼ teaspoon ground cloves
½ teaspoon ground ginger
2 eggs
¾ cup pear nectar (or juice
  from canned pears)
½ teaspoon vanilla extract
1 pound 13 ounce can
  pears in heavy syrup,
  sliced

Topping:
¾ cup brown sugar,
  packed
3 tablespoons butter,
  softened
1 cup slivered blanched
  almonds

1. Preheat oven to 350°.

2. Sift together flour, sugar, baking soda, salt, cloves and ginger. Set aside.

3. Beat eggs slightly and add pear nectar and vanilla. Mix in sifted dry ingredients. Pour batter into buttered 9x13-inch pan. Press sliced pears evenly into batter, pushing down slightly.

4. Prepare Topping: Combine brown sugar, butter and almonds until mixture is crumbly. Sprinkle evenly over pears.

5. Bake for 40-45 minutes or until golden brown.

Applesauce Cake with Caramel Sauce

Wonderful! The caramel sauce makes this cake distinctive.

Serves 8

1 cup butter, softened
2 cups sugar
2 eggs
3 cups flour, sifted
1½ teaspoons nutmeg
1 tablespoon cinnamon
1 teaspoon ground cloves
1 tablespoon baking soda
2½ cups applesauce
2 tablespoons corn syrup
1 cup raisins
1 cup chopped walnuts

Caramel Sauce:
½ cup butter
1 cup brown sugar, packed
2 tablespoons light cream
2 teaspoons vanilla extract
¼-½ cup powdered sugar,
   sifted

Chopped nuts

1. Preheat oven to 350°. Butter and flour a 10-inch tube pan.

2. Cream together butter and sugar. Add eggs one at a time, beating for 30 seconds after each egg.

3. Sift together flour, nutmeg, cinnamon, cloves and baking soda. Set aside.

4. Combine applesauce and corn syrup in a small bowl. Add to creamed mixture alternately with sifted ingredients. Fold in raisins and nuts.

5. Pour into prepared pan. Bake 1½ to 2 hours until cake tests done when tester is inserted.

6. Cool cake in pan on wire rack for 10 minutes. Remove from pan and cool completely. Drizzle Caramel Sauce on top.

7. Prepare Caramel Sauce: In a medium saucepan, combine butter, brown sugar and light cream. Heat until melted. Add vanilla and remove from heat.

8. Using a hand mixer, beat in powdered sugar and mix thoroughly. Pour sauce over cooled cake and sprinkle with chopped nuts to decorate.

Apple Spice Cake with Brown Sugar Glaze

Perfect for a fall gathering.

Serves 8

2¼ cups flour, sifted
1 teaspoon baking soda
¼ teaspoon salt
2 teaspoons cinnamon
1 teaspoon allspice
1 teaspoon nutmeg
¾ cup chopped pecans,
  lightly toasted
⅓ cup butter
1 teaspoon grated lemon
  peel
⅓ cup vegetable
  shortening
¾ cup sugar
⅔ cup light brown sugar,
  lightly packed
2 large eggs
⅔ cup tart green apple,
  peeled and chopped
1¼ teaspoons vanilla
  extract
1 cup applesauce
Chopped pecans for
  garnish (optional)

Brown Sugar Glaze:
3 tablespoons butter
3 tablespoons brown sugar
3 tablespoons heavy cream
¾ cup sifted powdered
  sugar
½ teaspoon vanilla extract

1. Preheat oven to 350°. Position rack in lower ⅓ of the oven. Butter and flour a 9-inch fluted tube pan.

2. Sift together flour, baking soda, salt, cinnamon, allspice and nutmeg. Stir in chopped pecans and set aside.

3. Soften butter in mixer at low speed. Add grated lemon peel and cream until smooth, approximately 1 minute. Add shortening and beat an additional minute. Add sugar and light brown sugar, blending very well. Add eggs and beat until mixture is smooth and well combined. Beat in fresh apple and vanilla.

4. On low speed, add flour mixture to creamed mixture alternately with applesauce. Blend well. Spoon batter into prepared pan, smoothing the top.

5. Bake 55-60 minutes until cake leaves side of pan or until tester inserted in center comes out clean. Remove from oven and cool for 10-15 minutes. Invert cake onto rack and remove pan.

6. Prepare Brown Sugar Glaze: Melt butter and brown sugar in medium saucepan over low heat. Stir in heavy cream. Cook slowly until mixture boils. Simmer 1 to 2 minutes. Whisk in powdered sugar; add vanilla. Glaze cake with Brown Sugar Glaze and sprinkle with chopped pecans, if desired.

Blueberry Cake with Lemon Buttercream

This is a very pretty cake, luscious with blueberries.

Serves 8

1½ cups fresh blueberries
  or frozen, thawed and
  well-drained
2 tablespoons flour
1 egg
½ cup sugar
2 tablespoons butter or
  margarine, softened
1 teaspoon vanilla extract
1½ cups flour
2 teaspoons baking powder
¼ teaspoon salt
1 cup warm milk

Lemon Buttercream:
½ cup butter or margarine,
  softened
1 cup powdered sugar,
  sifted
2 tablespoons fresh lemon
  juice

1 cup blueberries for
  garnish

1. Preheat oven to 350°. Generously grease and flour a 6-cup ring mold. Set aside.

2. In a small bowl, toss blueberries with 2 tablespoons flour. Set aside.

3. In a medium bowl, beat egg, sugar, butter and vanilla with a mixer on high speed until fluffy. In a separate bowl, thoroughly stir together 1½ cups flour, baking powder and salt.

4. Alternately add flour mixture and milk to creamed mixture, beginning and ending with the flour mixture. Mix well after each addition. Fold in blueberries.

5. Pour batter into prepared mold. Bake 30-35 minutes or until wooden pick inserted near center comes out clean. Cool in mold for 10 minutes. Remove from mold and cool on rack for 10 minutes. Transfer to platter.

6. Prepare Lemon Buttercream: In a small bowl, beat butter and powdered sugar on high speed until fluffy. Beat in lemon juice.

7. Spread Lemon Buttercream on top of cooled cake, letting it drizzle over sides. Place blueberries in center of ring for garnish.

Beachcomber Banana Nut Cake

Easy, packable and portable for an outing to the beach.

Serves 8

1 cup mashed bananas
  (about 3 small bananas)
½ cup sour cream
2¼ cups cake flour, sifted
1 teaspoon baking soda
1 teaspoon salt
½ teaspoon nutmeg
1½ teaspoons cinnamon
1 cup pecans, chopped
½ cup unsalted butter
1 cup sugar
½ cup light brown sugar,
  lightly packed
2 large eggs
1¼ teaspoons vanilla
  extract
Powdered sugar (optional)

1. Preheat oven to 350°. Butter and flour a 9x13-inch pan.

2. Mash bananas well and stir in sour cream.

3. Sift together flour, baking soda, salt, nutmeg and cinnamon. Stir in the chopped nuts and set aside.

4. Cream butter for 1½ to 2 minutes. Add the sugars, blending well. Add the eggs one at a time. Stir in vanilla. Add the flour mixture alternately with the banana mixture. Mix well. Spoon batter into the prepared pan and smooth surface.

5. Bake for 40-45 minutes or until cake is golden brown on top and comes away from sides of pan.

6. Cool completely on cake rack. Just before serving, dust top with powdered sugar, if desired.

Pecan Pound Cake

Serves 8-10

1 cup pecan pieces
2¼ cups flour, sifted
1 teaspoon baking powder
¼ teaspoon salt
1 cup unsalted butter
1⅓ cups sugar
5 large eggs
1¾ teaspoons vanilla
  extract
¼ cup sour cream
2-3 tablespoons pecan
  pieces for garnish
2 teaspoons sugar

1. Preheat oven to 350°.

2. Break pecans into ¼ inch pieces, toast for 6-8 minutes in oven. Remove and cool.

3. Lower oven temperature to 325°. Butter and flour a 9-inch flat-bottomed tube pan.

4. Sift together flour, baking powder and salt. Set aside.

5. Cream butter; add the sugar and blend. Add eggs one at a time. Blend in vanilla. Add ½ of the flour mixture and sour cream, mixing for about 30 seconds. Add remaining flour mixture. Mix batter for 20-30 seconds. Fold in the toasted pecans and pour batter into prepared pan, smoothing top. Sprinkle remaining pecans and sugar on top of cake. Place pan in lower ⅓ of the oven.

6. Bake for 60 minutes or until cake is golden brown on top and is starting to pull away from sides or until tester in center comes out clean.

7. Cool in pan on cake rack for 10-15 minutes. Remove from pan and cool completely.

Zesty Orange Cake

Serves 12

1½ cups orange juice
1 cup rolled oats,
    uncooked
½ cup butter
1 cup sugar
½ cup molasses
2 eggs
1 teaspoon vanilla extract
1¾ cups flour
1 teaspoon baking powder
1 teaspoon baking soda
½ teaspoon salt
1 teaspoon ground
    cinnamon
1 teaspoon grated orange
    zest
1 cup chopped nuts
    (optional)

Topping:
½ cup brown sugar
¼ cup butter
1 tablespoon orange juice
½ teaspoon orange zest,
    grated
1 cup coconut
½ cup nuts, coarsely
    chopped

1. Preheat oven to 350°. Bring orange juice to a boil and pour over oats. Set aside. Cream butter with sugar. Beat in molasses, then eggs and vanilla.

2. Combine flour, baking powder, baking soda, salt and cinnamon. Add dry ingredients to butter mixture alternately with orange juice mixture. Add orange zest and nuts.

3. Spread batter in greased 9x13-inch pan. Bake for 40 minutes.

4. Prepare Topping: Place brown sugar, butter, orange juice and zest in saucepan and bring to boil. Cook 1 minute, stirring. Add coconut and nuts.

5. Spread topping over warm cake and place under broiler for 1 minute.

6. Serve cake warm or at room temperature.

Lemon Frosted Apple Cake

Serves 10

3 cups flour, sifted
1 teaspoon salt
½ teaspoon ground cloves
1 teaspoon cinnamon
3 cups grated Golden
  Delicious apples (about
  3 large apples)
2 teaspoons baking soda
½ cup vegetable shortening
2 cups sugar
2 eggs
1 cup chopped walnuts

Lemon Butter Frosting:
½ cup butter, softened
16 ounces powdered sugar,
  sifted
½ teaspoon grated lemon
  rind
4 tablespoons fresh lemon
  juice

½ cup finely chopped
  walnuts (optional)

1. Preheat oven to 350°. Grease and flour two 9-inch cake pans.

2. Sift flour, salt, cloves and cinnamon onto waxed paper and set aside.

3. Combine grated apples and their juice with baking soda in a medium bowl. Set aside.

4. Beat shortening, sugar and eggs in a large bowl with mixer on high speed until well-blended and fluffy. Stir in flour mixture alternately with apple mixture, beating well after each addition. Stir in walnuts. Pour into pans.

5. Bake for 30-35 minutes until centers spring back when lightly touched. Cool in pans on wire racks for 10 minutes; remove from pans and cool completely.

6. Prepare Lemon Butter Frosting: Beat butter in medium bowl until soft. Add powdered sugar alternately with lemon juice and rind and continue beating until frosting is smooth.

7. Frost layers with Lemon Butter Frosting. Pat finely chopped walnuts around sides or on top of cake, if desired.

Chocolate Chip Cupcakes

Perfect for a picnic.

Makes 2 Dozen

1½ cups cake flour
1 cup sugar
1 teaspoon baking soda
½ teaspoon salt
¼ cup unsweetened cocoa
½ cup oil
1 cup water
1 teaspoon vanilla extract
1 tablespoon white
    distilled vinegar

Topping:
8 ounces cream cheese
1 egg
⅓ cup sugar
Dash of salt
6 ounces semi-sweet
    chocolate chips

1. Preheat oven to 350°. In a medium bowl, sift together cake flour, sugar, baking soda, salt and cocoa. Add oil, water, vanilla and vinegar. Mix well.

2. Prepare Topping: In a small bowl, combine cream cheese, egg, sugar and salt. Stir in chocolate chips. Set aside.

3. Place paper baking cups inside muffin tins. Fill each cup ⅓ full with batter, then with a rounded tablespoon of topping. Bake for 18-23 minutes.

Note: May top each cupcake with sliced almonds before baking. These cupcakes freeze well.

Double Chocolate Chip Crater Cake

A superb, densely chocolate cake. The cake sinks in the middle as it cools, leaving a perfect chocolate "crater." True chocoholics will double the frosting recipe and pile a generous amount in the crater .

Serves 10

1¼ cups flour
1½ teaspoons baking powder
¾ teaspoon baking soda
½ teaspoon salt
1 cup unsalted butter or margarine, softened
1¾ cups sugar
¾ cup unsweetened cocoa powder
½ cup hot water
3 eggs
¾ cup light sour cream
2 teaspoons vanilla extract
1½ cups semi-sweet chocolate chips, chopped

Chocolate Chip Frosting:
6 ounces semi-sweet chocolate chips
¼ cup butter
¼ cup light sour cream
Dash of salt

1. Preheat oven to 350°.

2. Generously grease a 10-inch springform pan. Wrap bottom of pan with foil to avoid leakage.

3. Sift together flour, baking powder, baking soda and salt onto waxed paper.

4. Cream butter and sugar in mixer until fluffy. Add cocoa and mix on lowest speed. Still on low speed, slowly add hot water. Mix until smooth and flowing. Increase speed to medium. Add eggs 1 at a time, until well mixed. Add sour cream and vanilla. Mix until smooth. Add reserved sifted dry ingredients, mixing until smooth.

5. Transfer batter to prepared pan. Sprinkle chocolate chips evenly over surface. Use knife to swirl in chips, leaving many on surface.

6. Place cake pan on baking sheet on center rack of oven. Bake until wood pick inserted into center comes out clean, about 55 minutes.

7. Place on rack and let cool completely. Use a knife to separate cake from sides of pan. Remove springform sides.

8. Prepare Chocolate Chip Frosting: Melt chocolate chips and butter together in a double boiler. Stir in sour cream and salt until smooth.

9. Spread Chocolate Chip Frosting over top of cake.

Note: Frosting recipe may be doubled to fill "crater" or sweetened whipped cream may be used as an alternative.

Plum, Pear and Raspberry Streusel Cake

Lovely for a summer dinner party.

Serves 6-8

Streusel Topping:
½ cup flour
⅓ cup light brown sugar, packed
¼ teaspoon cinnamon
¼ teaspoon salt
¼ cup unsalted butter, cold

3 medium firm, ripe pears
6 large firm, ripe plums
1 cup sugar, divided
1 tablespoon quick cooking tapioca
2 tablespoons lemon juice
½ teaspoon cinnamon
2 tablespoons water
⅓ cup sour cream
¼ teaspoon baking soda
¼ cup unsalted butter, softened
1 egg
1½ teaspoons vanilla extract
¾ cup flour
½ teaspoon baking powder
¼ teaspoon salt
⅔ cup raspberries, rinsed and drained

1. Butter an 8-inch square baking pan, preferably glass.

2. Make Streusel Topping: Combine flour, brown sugar, cinnamon and salt in a small bowl. Cut in butter with a pastry blender or 2 knives until butter is the size of small peas. Set aside in refrigerator.

3. Peel and core pears; peel and core plums; cut into 1-inch slices. Combine pears, plums, ½ cup sugar, tapioca, lemon juice, cinnamon and water in a large skillet. Toss gently to combine. Over medium high heat, cook uncovered until pears are tender, yet crisp, about 4-10 minutes depending on pears' ripeness. Stir frequently and add additional water if necessary. Keep warm. Preheat oven to 375°.

4. Mix together sour cream and baking soda. Cream butter, remaining ½ cup sugar and egg in mixer until light and fluffy. Add vanilla and sour cream mixture until well-combined. Gently fold in flour, baking powder and salt until just combined.

5. Spread warm fruit and juices (fruit needs to be warm in order for cake to bake properly) in prepared pan. Sprinkle raspberries over other fruit. Spoon cake batter over fruit and spread in a thin even layer (fruit does not need to be completely covered). Sprinkle Streusel Topping over cake batter and place pan on baking sheet.

6. Bake on center rack of oven for 30 minutes or until surface is deep golden brown and wooden pick inserted in center of cake (not fruit) comes out clean.

Note: Serve warm with ice cream. May be reheated at 300° for 15-20 minutes until warm.

Praline Pumpkin Cheesecake

The praline topping is an inspired accompaniment to this extraordinary cheesecake.

Serves 8

Crust:
1½ cups finely ground
    gingersnap cookies
¾ cup ground pecans
3 tablespoons brown sugar
6 tablespoons unsalted
    butter, melted and
    cooled

Filling:
1½ pounds cream cheese,
    softened
1 cup packed brown sugar
1½ cups canned pumpkin
½ cup whipping cream
⅓ cup pure maple syrup
1 tablespoon vanilla extract
½ teaspoon cinnamon
½ teaspoon allspice
4 large eggs

Praline:
1¼ cups sugar
6 tablespoons water
1 cup coarsely chopped
    pecans

1. Preheat oven to 325°. Prepare Crust: Mix cookie crumbs, pecans and brown sugar in a medium bowl; add butter and combine. Press into 9-inch springform pan on bottom and 2 inches up sides. Bake 8 minutes and cool.

2. Prepare Filling: Beat cream cheese, brown sugar, pumpkin, whipping cream, maple syrup, vanilla, cinnamon and allspice until smooth. Add eggs one at a time, beating until just combined. Pour batter into crust.

3. Bake for 80-90 minutes or until cheesecake is puffed and the center is set. Transfer cake to rack and cool 30 minutes. At the end of that time, run a sharp knife around sides to loosen cheesecake. Cover and refrigerate overnight (may be prepared 2 days ahead).

4. Prepare Praline: Line a cookie sheet with foil and butter the foil. Stir sugar and water in a medium saucepan over low heat until sugar dissolves. Increase heat and boil without stirring until syrup turns a deep golden brown, swirling pan occasionally. Stir in pecans.

5. Immediately pour Praline onto prepared cookie sheet, spreading with the back of a spoon to about ¼-inch thickness. Cool completely. Break or chop Praline into crumbs (can prepare day ahead and refrigerate in airtight container).

6. To assemble, transfer cake to platter. Release pan sides. Arrange Praline on top of cake and slice.

Raspberry Cheesecake

Serves 10-12

3 tablespoons flour

3 tablespoons cornstarch

16 ounces cream cheese, softened

15 ounces whole milk ricotta cheese, liquid drained from top

1½ cups sugar

4 large eggs

1½ tablespoons fresh lemon juice

1 tablespoon vanilla extract

½ cup unsalted butter, melted and cooled

1 pint sour cream

1 cup fresh or defrosted frozen raspberries, pureed

Raspberry Topping:

2 cups fresh or defrosted frozen raspberries, pureed

2 tablespoons fresh lemon juice

4 tablespoons sugar

1½ cups sour cream

1. Preheat oven to 325° and position rack in lower ⅓ of oven. Butter a 9-inch springform pan.

2. Prepare Cheesecake: Sift together flour and cornstarch. Set aside. Beat together cream cheese and ricotta in a large bowl until smooth and no lumps remain. Add sugar in 3 additions, beating until well incorporated. Beat for an additional 30 seconds. Add eggs 1 at a time at 30 second intervals, mixing well after each addition. Mix in flour and cornstarch mixture, lemon juice and vanilla. Add melted butter, sour cream and raspberries and beat well for 30 seconds.

3. Wrap pan snugly in an 18-inch square of heavy aluminum foil to catch any bottom leaks. Pour batter into pan and bake for 1 hour. At the end of 1 hour, turn off oven and without opening the oven door, leave cake in oven for an additional hour.

4. Prepare Raspberry Topping: Mix together raspberries, lemon juice, sugar and sour cream and combine well. Refrigerate until needed.

5. At the end of the second hour, spoon approximately ½ cup of Raspberry Topping over top of cake. Reserve remaining topping in a covered container. Without turning on oven, return cake to oven for 5 minutes. Remove cake from oven and cool completely on rack. Cover and refrigerate overnight.

6. To serve, pour reserved topping in a small pool on individual serving dishes and place slice of cheesecake on top.

Hollywood Black Mint Cheesecake

This luscious cheesecake, laced with subtle chocolate mint flavor, is a real showstopper at the end of an elegant dinner party.

Serves 10-12

Crust:
8½ ounces chocolate
  wafers
⅓ cup unsalted butter,
  melted and cooled

Chocolate:
1½ cups mint chocolate
  chips, divided
3 tablespoons water
1 tablespoon crème de
  menthe

Filling:
1½ pounds cream cheese,
  at room temperature
1¼ cups sugar
4 large eggs
2 teaspoons vanilla extract
2 cups sour cream

1. Prepare Crust: Generously butter a 9-inch springform pan. Break the chocolate wafers into a food processor and pulse until fine crumbs form. Add the melted butter and pulse until just blended. Press the crumb mixture onto the bottom and 2 inches up the sides of the prepared pan. Refrigerate. Can be prepared a day ahead.

2. Preheat oven to 325° and position oven rack in the lower ⅓ of the oven.

3. Place 1¼ cups mint chocolate chips together with the water in a microwave safe bowl and microwave on medium setting until melted, approximately 1½ minutes in 30 second increments. Blend in the crème de menthe. Spoon the chocolate mixture over the bottom of the crust, using the back of a spoon to spread evenly. Set aside.

4. Prepare Filling: Place the cream cheese in a large bowl. Using a mixer, mix for 30 seconds until smooth and creamy. Add sugar in a steady stream, mixing for about 1½ minutes. Mixing on low speed, add the eggs, vanilla and sour cream, blending well.

5. Pour the filling over the chocolate, starting around the sides and then filling in the middle. Bake for 50 minutes.

6. At the end of 50 minutes, turn off oven and leave cake in the oven for an additional hour without opening oven door. Remove from oven.

7. Chop remaining ¼ cup chocolate mint chips and sprinkle evenly on surface of warm cake. Cool on rack for 3 hours, then refrigerate for at least 24 hours before serving. To serve, run a thin knife around edge of pan and carefully remove the rim. Serve in wedges.

Mocha Cheesecake

Serves 10-12

Crust:
6 tablespoons butter or margarine, melted
8½ ounces chocolate wafers, crushed
¼ cup sugar

Filling:
½ cup whipping cream
12 ounces cream cheese, softened
1 cup sugar
3 eggs
⅓ cup unsweetened cocoa
½ teaspoon vanilla extract

Topping:
1 cup sour cream
2 tablespoons sugar
1½ tablespoons instant coffee powder
Chocolate curls (optional)

1. Preheat oven to 325°. Brush bottom and sides of 9-inch spring-form pan with 1 tablespoon of the melted butter.

2. Prepare Crust: Mix the wafer crumbs and ¼ cup sugar until well mixed. Stir remaining butter into crumbs until uniformly moist. Press crumb mixture evenly on bottom and 1 inch up sides of pan, using the back of a spoon to press firmly. Set aside. Can be prepared a day ahead.

3. Prepare Filling: In a small bowl, beat cream until soft peaks form. Set aside.

4. In a large bowl, beat cream cheese until smooth. Blend in sugar gradually. Add eggs 1 at a time at 30 second intervals while beating continuously on low speed. Beat in cocoa and vanilla.

5. Fold in whipped cream until blended. Pour batter into pan and bake for 70 minutes until center is slightly set.

6. Prepare Topping: Stir sour cream, sugar and coffee powder until coffee powder is dissolved. Remove cheesecake from oven and spread top with sour cream mixture. Turn oven off and return cheesecake to oven for 5 minutes. Remove cake to wire rack. Run knife around sides of cake to loosen cake from pan and cool completely. Cover tightly and refrigerate overnight. Before serving let cake stand at room temperature for 30 minutes. Garnish with chocolate curls.

Raspberry Rum Cheesecakes

Especially pretty at Christmas time.

Makes 10 cakes

16 ounces cream cheese,
  softened
¾ cup sugar
2 eggs
1 teaspoon vanilla extract

Raspberry Rum Sauce:
6 ounces frozen
  raspberries, thawed,
  liquid reserved
⅛ cup sugar
2 teaspoons white rum

1. Preheat oven to 350°. Line a muffin tin with 10 paper liners and set aside.

2. Beat cream cheese until creamy. Add sugar and beat until fluffy. Add eggs and vanilla, combining well.

3. Fill prepared cups completely to top with batter. Bake in oven for 25 minutes. Leave cakes in pan to cool.

4. Prepare Raspberry Rum Sauce: Thaw frozen raspberries, but do not drain. Stir in sugar and rum.

5. When cakes are cool, tops will be sunken. Fill each indentation with Raspberry Rum Sauce.

Note: These may be prepared in mini-muffin tins, again using paper liners. Bake for 20 minutes at 350°. Instead of the Raspberry Rum Sauce, substitute any canned fruit pie filling to fill the indentations in the Cheesecakes.

Beverly Hills Chocolate Chip Cheesecake

Serves 8-10

1½ cups finely crushed
  creme-filled chocolate
  sandwich cookies (about
  18)
¼ cup melted butter or
  margarine
24 ounces cream cheese,
  softened
14 ounces sweetened
  condensed milk
3 eggs
2 teaspoons vanilla extract
1 cup mini chocolate chips
1 teaspoon flour

1. Preheat oven to 300°. Combine cookie crumbs and butter; pat firmly on the bottom of a 9-inch springform pan.

2. In a large mixing bowl, beat cream cheese until fluffy. Add sweetened condensed milk and beat until smooth. Add eggs and vanilla.

3. In a small bowl, toss together ½ cup chips with flour to coat. Stir into cheese mixture and pour into prepared pan. Sprinkle remaining chips evenly over top.

4. Bake 1 hour or until cake springs back when lightly touched. Cool to room temperature and refrigerate overnight.

5. To serve, remove sides of pan and cut into wedges. Keep remainder of cake refrigerated.

City of Angels Pie

Sinfully rich layers of meringue, whipping cream and chocolate.

Serves 8

2 eggs, separated
½ teaspoon vinegar
¼ teaspoon salt
¼ teaspoon cinnamon
½ cup sugar
1 9-inch pie shell, baked and cooled
6 ounces chocolate chips
¼ cup water
¼ cup powdered sugar, sifted
⅛ teaspoon cinnamon
1 cup whipping cream, whipped
Grated chocolate for garnish

1. Preheat oven to 325°.

2. Beat egg whites with vinegar, salt and ¼ teaspoon cinnamon. Gradually add sugar and beat until meringue forms stiff peaks. Line cooled pie shell with meringue, making a nest. Bake for 15-18 minutes. Cool.

3. Melt together chocolate chips and water. Mix in egg yolks, combining thoroughly. Spread 3 tablespoons chocolate mixture on meringue. Chill remaining chocolate.

4. Add powdered sugar and ⅛ teaspoon cinnamon to whipped cream. Spread ½ of whipped cream over chocolate layer.

5. Combine remaining whipped cream with chilled chocolate. Spread over whipped-cream layer. Chill at least 4 hours. Garnish with grated chocolate.

French Silk Pie

Serves 6-8

Coconut Pie Shell:
2 cups shredded coconut
½ cup graham cracker crumbs
⅓ cup melted butter

Filling:
½ cup butter
2 squares unsweetened chocolate
¾ cup sugar
¼ cup whipping cream
2 eggs
1 teaspoon vanilla extract
½ cup white corn syrup
¼ cup shredded coconut

1. Preheat oven to 350°.

2. Prepare Coconut Pie Shell: Combine all ingredients and press firmly on bottom and sides of 9-inch pie plate. Set aside.

3. Prepare Filling: In a medium saucepan, over low heat, melt butter and add chocolate, stir until melted. Mix in sugar and whipping cream. Whisk in eggs 1 at a time, beating for at least 2 minutes after each egg. Remove from heat and stir in vanilla and corn syrup, mixing well.

4. Pour filling in Coconut Pie Shell, arranging additional ¼ cup coconut 1 inch around edge of pie. Bake for 35 minutes or until pie is set and coconut is golden brown.

Divine Madness Pie

Guests will rave about this sensational pie. Don't tell anyone how easy it is to make.

Serves 8

1 cup sugar
4 tablespoons cornstarch
2 eggs, lightly beaten
½ cup butter or margarine,
   melted and cooled
3 tablespoons bourbon
6 ounces semi-sweet
   chocolate pieces
1 cup finely chopped
   pecans
1 9-inch unbaked pastry
   shell

Whipped Cream Topping:
½ cup heavy cream
2 tablespoons powdered
   sugar
1 teaspoon bourbon or ½
   teaspoon vanilla extract

1. Preheat oven to 350°.

2. Combine sugar and cornstarch in a medium bowl. Beat in eggs. Mix in cooled butter, bourbon, chocolate pieces and pecans. Pour into pastry shell.

3. Bake for 35-40 minutes or until puffy and lightly browned. Cool pie completely on wire rack. Cut pie into slim wedges and top individual slices with Whipped Cream Topping.

4. Prepare Whipped Cream Topping: Beat heavy cream with powdered sugar in a small bowl to soft peaks. Add bourbon or vanilla and beat to stiff peaks.

Note: Pie freezes well. Bake and cool pie and wrap it in foil and freeze. When ready to serve, set unwrapped, but still solidly frozen pie in 300° oven and warm gently for 35-40 minutes.

Dutch Crumble Apple Pie

An easy variation of a classic American pie.

Serves 6

5-6 tart apples, peeled and
   sliced
½ cup sugar
1½ teaspoons cinnamon
1 9-inch pie shell, unbaked
⅔ cup flour
½ cup packed brown sugar
⅓ cup cold margarine, cut
   into small pieces

1. Preheat oven to 425°.

2. Combine apples, sugar and cinnamon. Mix until apples are well-coated with sugar and cinnamon. Place in pie shell.

3. Mix flour and brown sugar. With pastry blender or 2 knives, cut in margarine until coarse crumbs form. Sprinkle over apples.

4. Bake for 15 minutes. Reduce heat to 375° and bake an additional 35 minutes.

Refreshing Custard Pie

Serves 6-8

4 eggs
6 tablespoons butter or
  margarine, melted and
  cooled
2 cups milk
¾ cup sugar
1 teaspoon vanilla extract
½ cup flour
½ teaspoon nutmeg or to
  taste
2 cups fresh or frozen
  raspberries, blackberries
  or peaches
Whipped cream for
  garnish

1. Preheat oven to 350°.

2. Mix eggs, cooled butter, milk, sugar, vanilla and flour at high speed in food processor, blender or mixer until well-blended. Pour into greased 9-inch glass pie plate. Sprinkle nutmeg on top. Bake for 45-55 minutes, until puffy and golden. Serve with fruit and whipped cream.

Fresh Strawberry Pie

Serves 6-8

5 pints fresh strawberries
1 cup sugar
¼ cup cornstarch
¾ cup water
1 tablespoon lemon juice
  or Grand Marnier
1 tablespoon cherry or
  strawberry gelatin
1 9-inch pie crust, baked

1. Wash and hull strawberries. Set aside 1 rounded cup of the less-than-perfect berries. Let berries dry on paper towels.

2. Prepare glaze: In a small bowl, mix together the sugar and cornstarch. In a blender, puree the cup of set aside berries. Add the cornstarch mixture and the water to the berry puree and blend.

3. Pour into a microwave safe bowl and cook at high setting in the microwave for 4-5 minutes until clear, stirring once. Add lemon juice or liqueur and gelatin. Cool to lukewarm.

4. Brush the baked pie crust with some of the glaze. Toss the berries gently in the remaining glaze and pour into crust. Chill.

Note: Serve pie topped with whipped cream.

Double Delight Lemon Pie

Our tasters say this is the best lemon pie ever created.

Serves 8-10

Crust:
2 cups flour
1 teaspoon salt
⅔ cup shortening
1 tablespoon lemon juice
3-6 tablespoons cold water
(1 9-inch ready made pie
  shell may be substituted)

Clear Filling:
1½ cups sugar
½ cup cornstarch
1¾ cups water
4 large egg yolks
½ cup fresh lemon juice
  (3-4 lemons)
1 tablespoon butter or
  margarine
1 teaspoon grated lemon
  peel

Creamy Filling:
1 cup whipping cream
8 ounces cream cheese,
  softened
14 ounces sweetened
  condensed milk
6 ounces frozen lemonade
  concentrate, thawed
3.4 ounces lemon flavor
  instant pudding

Topping:
1 cup whipping cream
3 tablespoons powdered
  sugar (optional)

1. Preheat oven to 450°. Make Crust: Mix together flour and salt. Cut in shortening with 2 knives or pastry cutter until fine crumbs form. Sprinkle lemon juice and enough cold water over mixture so that when it is stirred, it forms a ball. Do not overwork dough. Roll out and fit into a 9½-inch deep dish or 10-inch regular pie plate. Prick bottom and sides of crust with a fork. Bake for 9-11 minutes. Cool.

2. Prepare Clear Filling: In a medium saucepan, mix sugar and cornstarch. Gradually stir in water. Cook over medium heat, stirring constantly, until mixture thickens and boils. Boil 1 minute and remove from heat. In a small bowl, beat egg yolks and lemon juice with a fork. Stir egg yolk mixture into cornstarch mixture, stirring rapidly to prevent lumping. Return saucepan to heat. Cook, stirring, until filling is very thick, 1-2 minutes longer. Remove from heat. Stir in butter or margarine and lemon peel. Refrigerate Clear Filling while preparing Creamy Filling (refrigerate no longer than 1 hour).

3. Prepare Creamy Filling: Whip cream until stiff peaks form. In a large bowl, beat cream cheese and sweetened condensed milk until smooth. Add lemonade concentrate and pudding mix and beat until blended. Fold whipped cream into pudding mixture.

4. Spoon Creamy Filling into cooled pie shell. Refrigerate for 15-20 minutes. Remove and with a spoon make a shallow depression in the filling center to 1-inch from edge (spoon center contents around edge of pie). Refrigerate until Creamy Filling is set; then spoon Clear Filling in depression of Creamy Filling. Gently spread just until smooth. Refrigerate at least 2 hours until fillings are set. To serve, top individual portions with whipped cream sweetened with powdered sugar, if desired.

Country Sour Cherry Pie

Serves 10

Filling:
32 ounces pitted tart cherries, drained and ½ cup liquid reserved
1 cup sugar
¼ cup cornstarch
¾ teaspoon vanilla extract
½ teaspoon almond extract
2 tablespoons margarine or butter
5-6 drops red food coloring

Crust:
3 cups all purpose flour
1 tablespoon sugar
1 teaspoon salt
1 cup plus 2 tablespoons shortening
¼ cup cold water
1 tablespoon white vinegar
1 large egg

1. Preheat oven to 375°. Prepare Filling: In a 3-quart saucepan over medium-high heat, cook cherries, sugar, liquid from cherries and cornstarch, stirring occasionally, until mixture boils and thickens. Boil 1 minute. Remove saucepan from heat. Stir in vanilla and almond extracts, margarine or butter and food coloring. Cool 1 hour.

2. Prepare Crust while filling is cooling: In a large bowl, mix flour, sugar and salt. Cut in shortening until mixture resembles coarse crumbs. In a cup, mix water, vinegar and egg. Stir this into flour mixture, 1 tablespoon at a time, until mixture forms a ball. Divide in half. Roll dough 1 inch larger than inverted 9-inch pie plate. Ease dough into pie plate. Trim edge even with pie plate. Spoon cherry filling into pie shell. Roll remaining half of dough. Lift top crust onto filled pie. Turn overhang under bottom crust. Flute edge.

3. Bake for 35-40 minutes until crust is golden brown and filling is bubbling. Cool.

Pecan-Pumpkin Pie

So delicious it may replace your traditional pumpkin pie.

Pumpkin Filling:
½ cup light brown sugar,
  firmly packed
1 tablespoon flour
1 teaspoon cinnamon
½ teaspoon salt
½ teaspoon ginger
½ teaspoon nutmeg
Pinch of cloves
16 ounces pumpkin
2 eggs
1 cup evaporated milk
2 teaspoons vanilla extract
1 9-inch pie shell, unbaked

Pecan Topping:
¼ cup firmly packed
  brown sugar
¼ cup butter or margarine
1 cup pecans, finely
  chopped

Whipped cream
Pecans for garnish

1. Preheat oven to 425° and place oven rack in lowest position.

2. Prepare Pumpkin Filling: Mix together ½ cup brown sugar, flour, cinnamon, salt, ginger, nutmeg and cloves in a large bowl until well mixed. Add pumpkin, eggs, evaporated milk and vanilla; stir with whisk or beater until smooth. Pour into pie shell.

3. Bake 15 minutes. Reduce to 350° and bake 10 minutes longer.

4. Prepare Pecan Topping: Beat together the ¼ cup brown sugar and butter in a small bowl until well mixed. Stir in pecans.

5. After pie has baked at 350° for 10 minutes, sprinkle Pecan Topping evenly over top of pie. Continue baking at 350° for 30-35 minutes, until knife inserted in center comes out clean. Cool on a wire rack. Serve at room temperature with whipped cream and pecans for garnish.

Easy Pecan Pie

Serves 6-8

1 cup white corn syrup
1 cup brown sugar, packed
3 eggs
1 teaspoon vanilla extract
Pinch of salt
1 9-inch pie shell, unbaked
1½ cups shelled pecan
  halves

1. Preheat oven to 350°.

2. Mix together corn syrup, brown sugar, eggs, vanilla and salt until well combined. Pour into pie shell.

3. Arrange pecan halves in concentric circles on top. Bake until firm, approximately 45 minutes.

Blueberry Crumb Pie

Serves 6

1 9-inch pie shell, unbaked

Filling:
⅔ cup sugar
4 tablespoons flour
¼ teaspoon nutmeg
1½ tablespoons butter,
  softened
3 cups fresh or frozen
  blueberries
1 teaspoon lemon juice

Crumb Topping:
¾ cup flour
¼ cup sugar
¼ cup butter, cut into
  small pieces
⅛ teaspoon salt

1. Preheat oven to 350°. Bake pie shell for 10 minutes until the dough begins to puff. Remove and set aside (this will prevent dough from becoming soggy when baked). Increase oven heat to 375°.

2. Prepare Filling: In a large bowl, combine the sugar, flour, nutmeg and butter. Stir in the blueberries and add the lemon juice. Pour into the pie shell.

3. Prepare Crumb Topping: Combine flour, sugar, butter and salt in a medium bowl. Using a pastry cutter or 2 knives, cut butter into mixture until fine crumbs form. Sprinkle evenly on top of filling.

4. Bake for 10 minutes. Reduce heat to 350° and bake for 35 minutes more until fruit bubbles around edges of pie plate.

Brandy Alexander Pie

Serves 8

1 envelope unflavored
  gelatin
½ cup cold water
⅔ cup sugar, divided
Pinch of salt
3 eggs, separated
¼ cup cognac
¼ cup crème de cacao,
  brown
1 cup heavy cream,
  whipped
1 9-inch graham cracker
  crust
Chocolate shavings for
  garnish (optional)

1. In a medium saucepan, sprinkle gelatin over cold water. Add ⅓ cup sugar, salt and 3 egg yolks. Stir by hand until well-blended. Place over low heat and stir constantly until mixture has thickened and gelatin has dissolved. Do not allow to boil. Remove from heat.

2. Stir in cognac and crème de cacao. Place in refrigerator until mixture begins to mound.

3. In a medium bowl, beat 3 egg whites until stiff peaks form. Gradually beat in remaining ⅓ cup sugar. Fold into chilled gelatin mixture. Fold in whipped cream.

4. Pour mixture into pie crust and refrigerate overnight. Decorate with chocolate shavings, if desired.

Pecan Bourbon Pie

3 large eggs
½ cup brown sugar, packed
1 cup dark corn syrup
3 tablespoons bourbon or
   ½ teaspoon vanilla
   extract
2 tablespoons margarine or
   butter, melted
¼ teaspoon salt
1 cup pecans, finely
   chopped
1 9-inch pie shell, unbaked
1 cup whipped cream
3 tablespoons powdered
   sugar

1. Preheat oven to 350°.

2. In a large bowl, beat eggs and brown sugar with wire whisk or fork until well blended. Beat in corn syrup, bourbon or vanilla, margarine or butter, salt and pecans. Pour filling into unbaked pie shell.

3. Bake for 30 minutes. Cool. To serve, top individual slices with whipped cream sweetened with powdered sugar.

Sunny Lemon Pie with Meringue Topping

Serves 6-8

Filling:
1¼ cups sugar
6 tablespoons cornstarch
¼ teaspoon salt
½ cup cold water
½ cup fresh lemon juice
3 egg yolks, well beaten
2 tablespoons butter
1½ cups boiling water
1 teaspoon lemon peel,
   grated
3-4 drops yellow food
   coloring
1 9-inch pie shell, baked

Meringue:
2 egg whites
¼ teaspoon cream of tartar
3 tablespoons sugar
½ teaspoon vanilla extract

1. Preheat oven to 325°.

2. Prepare Filling: Sift sugar, cornstarch and salt into a 2-quart saucepan. Gradually blend in water and lemon juice. When smooth, add egg yolks and butter, blending thoroughly. While stirring constantly, gradually add the boiling water. Bring the mixture to a full boil, stirring gently. As it begins to thicken, reduce the heat and allow it to simmer slowly for 1 minute. Remove from heat and stir in lemon peel and food coloring. Pour into pie shell and cool.

3. Prepare Meringue: Whip egg whites until frothy. Add cream of tartar. Continue whipping until soft peaks form. Beat in sugar, 1 tablespoon at a time, being careful not to overbeat. Add vanilla and blend well. Spread on pie and bake for 10-15 minutes or until Meringue is lightly golden.

Millionaire's Pie

Serves 6-8

4 eggs, beaten
½ cup melted butter
1 cup white corn syrup
1 cup sugar
1 teaspoon vanilla extract
1 cup pecans, chopped
½ cup semi-sweet
   chocolate chips
1 9-inch pie shell, unbaked
Whipped cream

1. Preheat oven to 350°.

2. Mix together the eggs, butter and corn syrup. Add the sugar and blend well. Stir in vanilla, pecans and chocolate chips. Pour into pie shell.

3. Bake for 45-55 minutes or until softly set in the middle. Serve with whipped cream.

Pear Torte

Serves 6-8

Crust:
½ cup butter, softened
⅓ cup sugar
¼ teaspoon vanilla extract
¾ cup flour
⅔ cup chopped walnuts or
   pecans

Filling:
8 ounces cream cheese,
   softened
1 egg
¼ cup sugar
½ teaspoon vanilla

Topping:
16 ounces canned Bartlett
   pears, drained and sliced
1 teaspoon sugar
½ teaspoon cinnamon

1. Preheat oven to 350°. Spray an 8x8-inch pan with vegetable spray. Set aside.

2. Prepare Crust: Cream together butter and sugar. Add vanilla, flour and chopped nuts; blend well. Press mixture into prepared pan. Prick bottom and sides of mixture with a fork. Bake in oven for 8-10 minutes. Remove and cool.

3. Prepare Filling: Beat cream cheese, egg, sugar and vanilla until smooth. Spread over the cooled crust.

4. Prepare Topping: Lay the pear slices over the Filling. Mix the sugar and cinnamon and sprinkle over the pears and Filling.

5. Increase the oven temperature to 375°. Bake for 25 minutes. Cool on rack, then chill and store in refrigerator.

Fudge Crackles

Soft, chewy and very fudgy.

Makes 3½ dozen cookies

7 ounces semi-sweet
  chocolate, chopped
2 ounces unsweetened
  chocolate, chopped
3 tablespoons unsalted
  butter
1 cup sugar
3 eggs
1 teaspoon vanilla extract
¾ cup all purpose flour
½ teaspoon baking powder
¾ teaspoon salt
1 cup semi-sweet chocolate
  chips
½ cup chopped walnuts
Powdered sugar

1. Preheat oven to 350°. Line baking sheet with foil. Set aside.

2. In a double boiler or in microwave, melt chopped semi-sweet and unsweetened chocolate with the butter. Remove from heat and stir until smooth.

3. Beat sugar and eggs to ribbon stage, 3-5 minutes. Add vanilla and chocolate mixture. Sift dry ingredients together and stir in. Stir in chocolate chips and nuts. Drop by rounded spoonfuls onto prepared cookie sheet. Bake for 8 minutes. Remove immediately to racks. Cool completely and sift powdered sugar over tops.

Soft Ginger Cookies

Moist and spicy, these travel well.

Makes 5 dozen

1½ cups vegetable oil or ¾
  cup butter or margarine,
  softened
2 cups sugar
2 eggs
½ cup light molasses
4 cups flour
4 teaspoons baking soda
1 teaspoon salt
1 tablespoon ginger
2¼ teaspoons cinnamon
Granulated sugar for
  coating

1. In a large mixing bowl, beat oil or butter, sugar, eggs and molasses.

2. Sift dry ingredients and add to molasses mixture until blended. Refrigerate dough for 2 hours.

3. Preheat oven to 350°. Form dough into balls, using 1 heaping teaspoonful for each ball. Roll each ball in granulated sugar.

4. Bake on ungreased baking sheet for 7 to 9 minutes or until cookies are puffed and tops are cracked. Do not overbake. Cookies will be puffy when removed from oven, but will flatten as they cool. Cool on rack.

Golden Maple Cookies

Makes 4½ dozen

½ cup butter or margarine,
   softened
1½ cups packed brown
   sugar
2 eggs
1 cup sour cream
1 tablespoon maple
   flavoring
2¾ cups flour
½ teaspoon baking soda
1 teaspoon salt
1 cup chopped nuts

Maple Butter Glaze:
½ cup butter
2 cups sifted powdered
   sugar
2 teaspoons maple
   flavoring
2-4 tablespoons hot water

1. Preheat oven to 375°.

2. Mix ½ cup butter or margarine, sugar and eggs thoroughly. Stir in
   sour cream and maple flavoring. Stir together flour, soda and salt;
   blend in. Mix in nuts. Chill dough if soft.

3. Drop rounded tablespoons of dough about 2 inches apart on a
   greased cookie sheet. Bake about 10 minutes or until almost no
   imprint remains when touched lightly. Cookies will be slightly
   browned. Cool.

4. Prepare Maple Butter Glaze: Heat ½ cup butter until golden
   brown. Blend in sifted powdered sugar and maple flavoring. Stir
   in 2 to 4 tablespoons hot water until spreadable. Spread on cooled
   cookies.

Rodeo Drive Cookies

Rich and irresistible.

Makes 5 dozen cookies.

1 cup butter, softened
·1 cup sugar
1 cup brown sugar
2 eggs
1 teaspoon vanilla extract
2 cups flour
2½ cups blended oatmeal
½ teaspoon salt
1 teaspoon baking powder
1 teaspoon baking soda
12 ounces semi-sweet
    chocolate chips
7 ounces semi-sweet
    chocolate, grated
1½ cups chopped walnuts

1. Preheat oven to 375°.

2. Cream together butter and sugars until well combined. Add eggs and vanilla and mix until fluffy.

3. In a medium bowl, stir together the flour, oatmeal, salt, baking powder and baking soda. Gradually add to creamed mixture. Stir in chocolate chips, grated chocolate and walnuts.

4. Roll dough into 1-inch balls and bake 2 inches apart on an ungreased cookie sheet. Bake for 9-10 minutes.

Note: To make blended oatmeal, place oatmeal in a blender and blend to a fine powder.

Tea Time Tassies

Makes 24

Pastry:
½ cup margarine, softened
3 ounces cream cheese,
    softened
1 cup flour

Filling:
1½ cups brown sugar
2 teaspoons butter, melted
1 teaspoon vanilla extract
2 eggs
¾ cup chopped pecans

1. Prepare Pastry: Mix Pastry ingredients together well and place in refrigerator for 30 minutes. When chilled, form mixture into 1½-inch balls. Dip the bottom of a glass or measuring cup into flour and flatten the ball. Fit the dough into bottom and sides of a mini muffin tin.

2. Preheat oven to 350°.

3. Prepare Filling: In a medium bowl, mix together all Filling ingredients, except pecans, until well combined. Place a teaspoon of pecans in each pastry shell. Fill the shell with the Filling mixture and top with another teaspoon of pecans.

4. Bake for 30 minutes. Remove tarts from pan to rack and cool completely.

Note: These may be made ahead and frozen.

Glazed Fresh Apple Cookies

The glaze makes these truly exceptional.

Makes 5 dozen

½ cup butter
1⅓ cups brown sugar
1 egg
2 cups flour
½ teaspoon baking soda
1 teaspoon baking powder
½ teaspoon salt
1½ teaspoons cinnamon
½ teaspoon nutmeg
¼ cup apple juice
1 cup chopped walnuts
1 cup raisins
1 cup finely chopped
    unpeeled tart apple

Apple Glaze:
1 tablespoon butter
1½ cups powdered sugar
⅛ teaspoon salt
2½ tablespoons apple juice
¼ teaspoon vanilla extract

1. Preheat oven to 400°.

2. Cream butter and sugar until well combined. Add egg and beat well. Sift together flour, baking soda, baking powder, salt, cinnamon and nutmeg. Add to creamed mixture alternately with apple juice, beginning and ending with flour mixture. Stir in nuts, raisins and apple.

3. Drop by teaspoons on greased cookie sheets about 2 inches apart. Bake for 9-12 minutes.

4. Prepare Apple Glaze: Cream butter, sugar and salt. Stir in apple juice and vanilla.

5. After baking, remove cookies immediately from baking sheet. Glaze cookies while still hot.

Toffee Butter Bars

These are extremely easy to make yet earn rave reviews everywhere!

Makes 24 bars

1 cup butter
1 cup sugar
1 egg
1 teaspoon vanilla extract
2 cups flour
1½-2 7-ounce bars
    Hershey Special Dark
    Chocolate, broken into
    squares
½ cup walnuts or pecans,
    finely chopped

1. Preheat oven to 350°. Grease a 9x13-inch baking pan.

2. Cream butter and sugar until fluffy. Beat in egg and vanilla. Add flour gradually, mixing well.

3. Spread mixture in prepared pan. Bake for 20 minutes (cookie bottom may not appear done, but is fully baked).

4. Place chocolate squares on top of cookie bottom immediately after removing from oven. When chocolate is melted, spread evenly with spatula. Sprinkle on nuts. Cut into bars immediately.

Tin Roof Morsels

Any child will tell you that peanut butter and chocolate are a divine combination, but the chocolate chips can be omitted if you prefer.

Makes 4-5 dozen cookies

½ cup butter or shortening
½ cup firmly packed
  brown sugar
½ cup sugar
1 egg
1 cup chunky peanut
  butter
½ teaspoon salt
½ teaspoon baking soda
½ teaspoon vanilla extract
1 to 1½ cups all purpose
  flour
6 ounces semi-sweet
  chocolate chips

1. Preheat oven to 375°.

2. Beat butter or shortening until soft. Add brown sugar and sugar, blend until creamy. Beat in egg, peanut butter, salt, baking soda and vanilla.

3. Sift the flour before measuring. Use the greater amount of flour if peanut butter is heavy in oil. Add flour to creamed mixture and blend thoroughly. Stir in chocolate chips.

4. Using a small ice cream scoop, drop dough onto a greased cookie sheet. Bake 10-12 minutes. Cool on a wire rack.

Note: If you are omitting the chocolate chips, press dough flat with a fork in a criss-cross design and sprinkle a small amount of sugar on top.

Almond Oatmeal Cookies

A crispy, chewy cookie with a subtle almond flavor.

Makes 3 dozen

½ cup butter or margarine, softened
½ cup sugar
½ cup firmly packed brown sugar
1 egg
⅛ teaspoon almond extract
½ teaspoon vanilla extract
¾ cup flour
½ teaspoon baking soda
½ teaspoon salt
1½ cups rolled oats

Almond Topping:
⅓ cup sugar
¼ cup butter or margarine
1 tablespoon light corn syrup
⅛ teaspoon almond extract
⅓ cup chopped sliced almonds

1. Preheat oven to 350°.

2. In a large bowl, cream together butter or margarine and sugars. Add egg and extracts and beat until fluffy.

3. In a separate bowl, stir together flour, baking soda and salt. Add to creamed mixture and beat until smooth. Stir in rolled oats.

4. Drop by teaspoons on lightly greased baking sheet. Bake for 12-14 minutes or until golden brown.

5. Prepare Almond Topping: Mix together sugar, butter or margarine, corn syrup and almond extract. Stir in chopped almonds.

6. With a knife, spread about ½ teaspoon Almond Topping on each cookie after cookies have been removed from oven. Transfer cookies to a rack to cool.

Mocha Mocha Cookies

Three kinds of chocolate and a rich mocha flavor!

Makes 3 dozen cookies

2 squares unsweetened
  chocolate
6 squares semi-sweet
  chocolate
2 tablespoons butter
¼ cup sifted all purpose
  flour
¼ teaspoon baking powder
⅛ teaspoon salt
2 eggs
¾ cup sugar
2¼ teaspoons instant
  coffee powder
1 teaspoon vanilla extract
1 cup semi-sweet chocolate
  pieces
2 cups chopped pecans

1. Preheat oven to 350° and place oven rack ⅓ down from top of oven. Line cookie sheets with aluminium foil.

2. Melt the unsweetened and semi-sweet chocolates together with the butter in the top of a double boiler, stirring until smooth. Remove from heat and cool completely.

3. Sift together the flour, baking powder and salt. Set aside.

4. Beat eggs, sugar, coffee powder and vanilla with an electric mixer at high speed until thick and fluffy, about 3 minutes. Beat in cooled chocolate. Add dry ingredients and blend well. Stir in chocolate pieces and pecans.

5. Drop mixture by teaspoons 1 inch apart on aluminum foil. Bake for 10 minutes or until cookies appear set (centers should remain chewy and soft). Do not overbake. Remove cookies to wire rack to cool.

Chocolate Nut Meringue Cookies

Makes 6 dozen cookies

6 egg whites
¼ teaspoon salt
¼ teaspoon cream of tartar
1½ cups sugar
1 teaspoon vanilla extract
¾ cup chopped walnuts or
  pecans
1½ cups semi-sweet
  chocolate chips, chopped

1. Preheat oven to 275°. Cover 2 baking sheets with aluminium foil; butter the foil and set aside.

2. Place egg whites in a large bowl and sprinkle salt and cream of tartar over them. Beat whites until foamy. Gradually beat in sugar a few tablespoons at a time. Continue to beat until whites are stiff but not dry. Add vanilla extract. Gently stir in nuts and chocolate chips.

3. With a teaspoon, drop mixture onto baking sheets 1 inch apart and shape into small mounds. Bake for 35-40 minutes, or until cookies are set. Remove from the foil using a wide spatula while cookies are warm.

Note: To save time use 2 baking sheets and 2 ovens simultaneously.

Applesauce Cookies

Makes 4-5 dozen cookies

½ cup butter or margarine
1 cup sugar
1 egg
1 teaspoon vanilla extract
1 cup unsweetened
   applesauce
2 cups flour
1 teaspoon baking soda
½ teaspoon baking powder
½ teaspoon salt
1 teaspoon cinnamon
½ teaspoon nutmeg
½ teaspoon cloves
½ cup walnuts, chopped

Frosting:
3 tablespoons brown sugar
3 tablespoons whipping
   cream or milk
3 tablespoons butter
1 teaspoon vanilla extract
2 cups sifted powdered
   sugar

1. Preheat oven to 375°.

2. Cream together butter and sugar until fluffy. Add egg and vanilla and beat until well combined. Add applesauce and mix well.

3. Sift together flour, baking soda, baking powder, salt, cinnamon, nutmeg and cloves. Gradually add to creamed mixture. Stir in walnuts.

4. Drop teaspoons of dough onto lightly greased baking sheet about 1 inch apart. Bake for 8-10 minutes or until golden. Cool.

5. Prepare Frosting: Combine brown sugar, whipping cream or milk and butter in medium saucepan. Boil over low heat until sugar is dissolved. Add vanilla. Remove from heat and mix in powdered sugar. Additional milk may be needed for spreadability.

6. Frost cookies lightly when cool.

Great Pumpkin Cookies

Makes 6 dozen cookies

2 cups flour
1 cup rolled oats
1 teaspoon baking soda
1½ teaspoons ground
   cinnamon
½ teaspoon salt
1 cup butter or margarine,
   softened
1 cup firmly packed brown
   sugar
¾ cup sugar
1 egg, slightly beaten
1 teaspoon vanilla extract
1 cup solid pack pumpkin
1 cup semi-sweet chocolate
   chips
½-1 cup chopped walnuts
   or pecans

1. Preheat oven to 350°.

2. Combine flour, oats, baking soda, cinnamon and salt. Set aside.

3. Cream butter; gradually add sugars, beating until light and fluffy. Add egg and vanilla. Mix well.

4. Alternate additions of dry ingredients and pumpkin, mixing well after each addition. Stir in chocolate chips and nuts.

5. Using a teaspoon or small ice cream scoop, drop onto greased cookie sheet.

6. Bake 15 minutes until cookies are firm and lightly browned. Remove from cookie sheets and cool on racks.

Note: Decorate cookies with a vanilla icing drizzled on top, if desired. One cup raisins may be substituted for the chocolate chips.

Peanut Butter Incredibles

You guessed it: incredibly easy and incredibly good.

Makes 36 bars

⅔ cup butter or margarine
1 cup chunky peanut
   butter
2 cups powdered sugar
1½ cups fine graham
   cracker crumbs
1¼ cups semi-sweet
   chocolate chips
1 cup butterscotch morsels

1. Over low heat, melt butter or margarine in a medium saucepan and add peanut butter. Stir until smooth. Add sugar and graham cracker crumbs. Stir until well blended. Press crumbs into a buttered 9x13-inch baking pan.

2. Melt the chocolate chips and butterscotch morsels in microwave for a total of 2½ minutes on high, stirring after each 30 seconds. Pour over crumb mixture.

3. Refrigerate until chocolate is set. Remove and cut into bars. Store at room temperature.

Iced Cinnamon Raisin Bars

Always a hit!

Makes 24 bars

½ cup sugar
1 tablespoon cornstarch
1 cup water
2 cups raisins
½ cup butter or margarine
1 cup brown sugar
1½ cups flour, sifted
½ teaspoon baking soda
½ teaspoon salt
1½ cups rolled oats, quick
   cooking
3 tablespoons water,
   divided
1 teaspoon vanilla

Cinnamon Icing:
1 cup powdered sugar
¼ teaspoon cinnamon
1½ tablespoons milk

1. Preheat oven to 350°.

2. Mix the sugar and cornstarch together in a saucepan. Add the water and raisins and cook over medium heat until the sauce is thick and clear. Remove from heat and set aside.

3. Cream together butter and brown sugar. Sift together the flour, soda and salt; add to butter mixture along with oats, 1 tablespoon water and vanilla. Mix until crumbly. Firmly press ½ of this mixture into a lightly greased 9x13-inch pan. Top with raisin mixture.

4. Stir 2 tablespoons water into remaining ½ of crumbs and spoon onto the filling. Spread smooth. Bake for 35 minutes. Cut into bars while still warm.

5. Prepare Cinnamon Icing: Mix together powdered sugar, cinnamon and milk. Drizzle over warm bars.

Chocolate Rum Cream Cheese Bars

Makes 36 bars

Crust:
1 cup flour
¼ cup brown sugar, packed
½ cup butter or margarine,
  softened
¾ cup semi-sweet
  chocolate chips, melted

Filling:
½ cup sugar
½ cup brown sugar, packed
⅓ cup butter or margarine,
  softened
8 ounces cream cheese,
  softened
½ cup flour
½ teaspoon baking powder
¼ teaspoon salt
1 tablespoon rum
1 tablespoon vanilla extract

Glaze:
½ cup semi-sweet
  chocolate chips
1 tablespoon rum
1-2 teaspoons water

1. Preheat oven to 325°. Prepare Crust: In a large bowl, combine ingredients, mixing well. Press mixture firmly into the bottom of an 11x7-inch pan. Set aside.

2. Prepare Filling: In a large bowl, beat granulated sugar, brown sugar, butter and cream cheese until smooth. Add flour, baking powder, salt, rum and vanilla, blending well. Spread mixture over crust. Bake for 38-43 minutes or until edges are light golden brown and set. Cool 30 minutes on rack.

3. Prepare Glaze: In a small saucepan, combine ingredients. Stir constantly over low heat until chocolate chips are melted. Spread over warm bars. Chill at least 1 hour before cutting into bars and serving.

Graham Cracker Squares

Crispy on the outside and chewy on the inside - addictive!

Makes 15 squares

Squares:
30 graham cracker squares,
  divided
1 cup butter or margarine
1 cup sugar
1 egg, slightly beaten
½ cup milk
¾ cup coconut
1¾ cups chopped walnuts,
  divided
1 cup graham cracker
  crumbs

Frosting:
½ cup butter, softened
2 cups powdered sugar
1 teaspoon vanilla extract
3 tablespoons milk

1. Place a layer of graham cracker squares (15 squares) on the bottom of a 9x13-inch pan.

2. Melt butter in saucepan. Add the sugar, egg and milk. Cook over moderate heat until mixture comes to a full boil. Boil 1 minute. Remove from heat.

3. Add the coconut, 1 cup of walnuts and the graham cracker crumbs to the warm butter mixture. Mix well. Pour over graham cracker layer. Place another layer of graham cracker squares (15 squares) on top of the mixture.

4. Prepare Frosting: Combine butter, powdered sugar, vanilla and milk and mix until smooth. Spread over graham cracker layer. Sprinkle ¾ cup chopped walnuts over frosting. Refrigerate until cool and cut into squares.

California Dreams

This divine combination of caramel and chocolate is almost like candy.

Makes 16 squares

32 caramel candies
⅓ cup evaporated milk
½ cup flour
½ teaspoon baking soda
¼ teaspoon salt
½ cup dark brown sugar,
 packed
½ cup rolled oats
4 tablespoons butter or
 margarine, softened
6 ounces semi-sweet
 chocolate chips
½ cup chopped pecans

1. Preheat oven to 350°.

2. In the top of a double boiler, combine caramels and milk. Heat over simmering water until melted, stirring occasionally. Remove from heat and set aside.

3. Sift together flour, baking soda and salt in a medium bowl. Stir in brown sugar and oats. Mix in butter until mixture forms coarse crumbs.

4. Press ½ of the flour mixture evenly into a buttered 8-inch square pan. The layer will be fairly thin. Sprinkle chocolate chips and pecans over surface evenly. Pour caramel mixture over chocolate chips and nuts. Sprinkle with remaining flour mixture.

5. Bake for 20 minutes or until lightly browned. Cool. Refrigerate until set, then cut into squares.

Cheesecake Bars

Makes 24 bars

½ cup butter, softened
⅓ cup brown sugar
1 cup flour
½ cup finely chopped
 walnuts or pecans
¼ cup sugar
8 ounces cream cheese,
 softened
1 egg
2 tablespoons milk
½ teaspoon vanilla extract
1 tablespoon fresh lemon
 juice

1. Preheat oven to 350°. Spray an 8-inch square baking pan with vegetable spray and set aside.

2. Blend butter and brown sugar until well combined. With a pastry blender or 2 knives, cut in flour until mixture resembles coarse crumbs. Mix in chopped nuts.

3. Set aside 1 cup of the mixture. Press remaining mixture into prepared pan. Bake for 8 minutes. Cool.

4. With an electric mixer, combine granulated sugar and cream cheese, beating well until smooth and fluffy. Add egg, milk, vanilla and lemon juice and beat well. Spread cream cheese mixture over cooled crust. Sprinkle reserved brown sugar crumb mixture over top and bake for an additional 20-25 minutes. Remove and cool, then refrigerate.

Butter Lemon Bars

The lemon flavor is a great inspiration in this wonderfully buttery bar.

Makes 48 bars

Crust:
2½ cups flour
⅔ cup powdered sugar
1 cup butter, chilled and
   cut into small pieces.
¼ cup margarine, chilled
   and cut into small pieces

Filling:
5 eggs
2½ cups sugar
6 tablespoons lemon juice
½ cup flour
¾ teaspoon baking soda

1. Preheat oven to 350°.

2. Prepare Crust: In a large bowl, combine flour, powdered sugar, butter and margarine. Beat at low speed about 1 minute, then at medium speed until crumbly. Press dough into a greased 10x15x1-inch jellyroll pan.

3. Bake for 15-20 minutes until Crust is firm, but not brown. Remove from oven.

4. Prepare Filling: Combine eggs, sugar and lemon juice in a small bowl. Mix the flour with the baking soda and add to egg mixture, beating at low speed just until blended. Pour over hot baked Crust.

5. Bake for 25 minutes or until set, lightly brown and pulled away from edges. Let cool on rack, then sprinkle with additional powdered sugar. Cut diagonally or in small squares.

Chocolate Mint Bars

These brownies burst with a fudgy mint flavor.

Serves 8

Brownies:
2 squares unsweetened
  chocolate
½ cup butter
2 eggs, beaten
1 cup sugar
1 teaspoon salt
¼ teaspoon peppermint
  extract
1 teaspoon vanilla extract
½ cup flour
½ cup chopped nuts
  (optional)

Frosting:
2 tablespoons butter
2 tablespoons heavy cream
1½ cups powdered sugar
½ teaspoon peppermint
  extract

Glaze:
2 squares semi-sweet
  chocolate
2 tablespoons butter

1. Preheat oven to 350°.

2. Prepare Brownies: Melt unsweetened chocolate and butter together over low heat in a saucepan. Set aside.

3. Mix together eggs, sugar, salt, peppermint and vanilla until well combined. Mix in flour. Add chocolate mixture and nuts.

4. Bake in greased 9-inch square pan for 20-25 minutes. Remove and cool thoroughly.

5. Prepare Frosting: Combine ingredients until smooth. Spread on cooled Brownies, then refrigerate for 5 minutes.

6. Prepare Glaze: Melt ingredients together and spread over set Frosting. Cut into squares.

Chocolate Macaroons

Makes 2 dozen cookies

6 ounces semi-sweet
    chocolate chips
7 ounces shredded coconut
¼ teaspoon salt
1 teaspoon vanilla extract
2 egg whites
½ cup sugar

1. Preheat oven to 350°.

2. In a double boiler over simmering water, melt the chocolate chips. Add the coconut, salt and vanilla, mixing well.

3. Beat the egg whites until soft peaks form. Gradually add the sugar, beating until stiff, but not dry. Fold egg whites into chocolate mixture.

4. Drop by teaspoons onto greased cookie sheet. Bake for 12 minutes; cookies will be set, but not brown. Immediately remove from cookie sheet to rack.

Double Frosted Kahlúa Brownies

Makes 24 brownies

Brownie Base:
2 squares unsweetened
    chocolate
½ cup butter or margarine
1 cup sugar
2 eggs
1 teaspoon vanilla extract
½ cup flour
½ cup chopped nuts
1½ tablespoons Kahlúa

White Frosting:
1½ cups powdered sugar
¼ cup butter or margarine,
    softened
1 teaspoon vanilla extract
1 tablespoon milk

Chocolate Glaze:
6 ounces semi-sweet
    chocolate chips
1 tablespoon butter or
    margarine

1. Preheat oven to 300°. Butter an 8-inch square baking pan. Set aside.

2. Prepare Brownie Base: Melt chocolate and butter together in a medium saucepan over low heat, stirring constantly to avoid scorching. Remove from heat and slowly stir in sugar. Add eggs and vanilla, stirring well. Gradually stir in flour, then add nuts.

3. Spread Brownie Base into prepared pan. Bake for 30 minutes. Remove from oven and immediately sprinkle Kahlúa over brownie surface. Cool to room temperature.

4. Prepare White Frosting: Beat together powdered sugar, butter, vanilla and milk until smooth and spreadable. Spread evenly over surface of cooled brownies. Refrigerate.

5. Prepare Chocolate Glaze: Microwave chocolate chips and butter on high for 60 seconds, stirring after 30 seconds. Stir, then spread over White Frosting. Refrigerate until glaze has hardened, then cut into squares. Brownies may be stored at room temperature.

Black Walnut Fudge Brownies

One bite sends you into a chocolate lover's paradise.

Makes 16 brownies

¾ cup flour
¼ teaspoon salt
½ teaspoon baking soda
½ cup butter
¾ cup light brown sugar,
    packed
1 egg
½ teaspoon butter
    flavoring
1½ teaspoons vanilla
    extract
2 cups quick cooking oats
14 ounces sweetened
    condensed milk
1 tablespoon vegetable
    shortening
4 squares semi-sweet
    chocolate
2 squares unsweetened
    chocolate
¼ teaspoon black walnut
    extract
½ cup chopped walnuts

1. Preheat oven to 350°.

2. Sift together flour, salt and baking soda. Set aside.

3. Combine butter, sugar, egg, butter flavoring and ½ teaspoon of the vanilla. Add flour mixture and oats. Reserving half of the mixture, press remaining half into greased 8-inch square pan. Set aside.

4. Heat milk, shortening and chocolate over low heat until chocolate is melted. Remove from heat and stir in remaining teaspoon vanilla, black walnut extract and walnuts. Spread over oat mixture in pan. Place small spoonfuls of reserved oat mixture over chocolate layer and smooth together to cover.

5. Bake for 20-25 minutes. Cool completely and cut into 2-inch squares.

Brownie Bites

Soft, chewy and delightfully chocolaty.

Makes 24 squares

½ cup unsalted butter
2 ounces unsweetened
  chocolate
1 cup sugar
½ cup flour, sifted
½ teaspoon baking powder
½ teaspoon vanilla extract
2 eggs, slightly beaten
6 ounces semi-sweet
  chocolate chips
½ cup chopped walnuts
¼ cup sifted powdered
  sugar
2 tablespoons cocoa
  powder

1. Preheat oven to 350°. Butter an 8-inch square glass baking pan.

2. Melt the butter and chocolate together in a double boiler or in microwave. Cool ten minutes. Add sugar, flour, baking powder and vanilla. Stir until well combined. Add eggs and mix well. Stir in chocolate chips and walnuts.

3. Spread batter into prepared pan. Bake for 30 minutes.

4. Combine powdered sugar and cocoa powder. Sprinkle over brownies and cut into squares.

Note: Brownie Bites freeze well. Wrap in plastic wrap. Thaw completely while still wrapped.

Colorado Boulevard Brownies

The mixture of three types of chips makes this brownie unique and sensational.

Makes 16 brownies

¾ cup flour
¼ teaspoon baking soda
¼ teaspoon salt
⅓ cup butter
¾ cup sugar
2 tablespoons water
6 ounces semi-sweet
  chocolate, chopped
2 eggs
½ cup vanilla milk chips
½ cup semi-sweet
  chocolate chips
¼ cup butterscotch chips
½ cup chopped walnuts

1. Preheat oven to 325°. Sift together flour, baking soda and salt. Set aside.

2. In a saucepan, combine butter, sugar and water. Heat just to a boil. Remove from heat and add semi-sweet chocolate. Stir until chocolate is melted and mixture is smooth.

3. Add eggs, 1 at a time, beating after each addition. Gradually blend in flour mixture.

4. Stir in vanilla milk chips, semi-sweet chocolate chips, butterscotch chips and walnuts.

5. Spread into greased 8-inch square pan. Bake for 30-35 minutes. Cool and cut into 2-inch squares.

Chocolate-Caramel Brownie Heaven

Divine!

Makes 24 brownies

14 ounces caramels
14 ounces sweetened
   condensed milk
1 cup shortening
2 cups sugar
3 eggs
⅔ cup cocoa
⅓ cup milk
1 teaspoon vanilla extract
1½ cups flour
½ teaspoon salt
1 teaspoon baking powder
1½ cups semi-sweet
   chocolate chips
1 cup chopped pecans,
   divided

1. Preheat oven to 350°.

2. Place caramels and sweetened condensed milk in a double boiler and cook over low heat until caramels are melted. Stir often and blend well. As caramels are melting, place shortening in another saucepan and melt over low heat. Remove from heat and cool.

3. Beat sugar and eggs until well combined. Add cocoa, milk, vanilla and cooled shortening. Sift flour, salt and baking powder and add to chocolate mixture, beating well. Stir in chocolate chips and ½ cup pecans.

4. Spread ⅔ of the batter into a greased 9x13-inch pan and bake 12 minutes. Remove brownies from the oven and pour melted caramels evenly over surface. If caramel mixture has stiffened, reheat briefly to liquefy. Sprinkle remaining ½ cup pecans over caramels. Drop remaining ⅓ of chocolate batter by tablespoonful and spread over surface with knife or spatula as evenly as possible. Using a knife, cut through brownie batter to marbleize.

5. Return pan to oven and bake for an additional 25-30 minutes. Remove from oven and cover with foil for 1 hour. Refrigerate foil-covered pan for an additional hour or until cooled. Cut into 2x3-inch bars and store at room temperature.

Double Chocolate Walnut Brownies

This is an intensely fudgy brownie adored by chocolate lovers everywhere.

Makes 28 brownies

1 cup butter
4 squares unsweetened
   chocolate
2 cups sugar
3 eggs
1 teaspoon vanilla extract
1 cup all purpose flour,
   sifted
1½ cups walnuts, coarsely
   chopped and divided
6 ounces semi-sweet
   chocolate pieces

1. Preheat oven to 350°.

2. Melt butter and chocolate in a medium pan over low heat until melted.

3. Beat in sugar gradually with a wooden spoon until thoroughly combined. Add eggs 1 at a time, beating well after each. Stir in vanilla. Stir in flour until thoroughly combined. Add 1 cup walnuts.

4. Spread into buttered 9x11-inch pan. Combine remaining ½ cup walnuts with chocolate pieces; sprinkle over top of brownie mixture, pressing down lightly.

5. Bake for 35 minutes. Cool completely in pan. Cut into bars.

Double Feature Brownies

The unsweetened chocolate topping gives an unexpected bittersweet flavor to these superb brownies.

Makes 24 brownies

Brownies:
2 squares unsweetened
   chocolate
½ cup butter
2 eggs
1 cup sugar
½ cup flour
¼ teaspoon salt
1 teaspoon vanilla extract

Frosting:
1½ cups sugar
½ cup half and half
⅓ cup butter
1 teaspoon vanilla extract
3 squares unsweetened
   chocolate

1. Preheat oven to 350°. In a medium saucepan, over low heat, melt chocolate with butter. Remove from heat and cool slightly.

2. Beat eggs; add sugar and mix well. Stir into chocolate mixture.

3. Mix flour and salt. Blend into the egg and chocolate mixture. Add vanilla.

4. Spread onto a greased 7x11x1½-inch pan. Bake for 20 minutes.

5. While brownies are cooling, prepare Frosting: In a heavy saucepan, mix sugar, half and half and butter. Bring to a boil, stirring constantly, and cook to 236° or soft ball stage (boiling time is approximately 5 minutes). Cool slightly. Add vanilla and beat until creamy. Immediately spread on brownie mixture.

6. Melt 3 squares of unsweetened chocolate and quickly spread on frosting. Refrigerate until firm. Cut into bars.

Espresso Brownies

These wonderful brownies are a perfect balance of chocolate and coffee flavors. Very sophisticated!

Makes 24 brownies

Brownies:
½ cup butter or margarine
6 1-ounce squares
    unsweetened chocolate
1½ cups sugar
2½ tablespoons instant
    espresso coffee powder
1 teaspoon vanilla extract
3 large eggs, lightly beaten
¼ teaspoon salt
1 cup flour

Espresso Topping:
½ cup margarine, softened
1½ cups powdered sugar
1 teaspoon vanilla extract
1 tablespoon milk
1 tablespoon instant
    espresso coffee powder

1. Preheat oven to 350°. Butter an 8-inch square baking pan. Set aside.

2. In a medium saucepan, over low heat, melt butter and chocolate, stirring until smooth. Remove from heat, stir in sugar, espresso powder and vanilla. Add eggs and salt, blending well. Gradually stir in flour, mixing until smooth.

3. Spread batter evenly in prepared pan. Bake 25-30 minutes or until wooden pick inserted in center comes out clean. Cool completely in pan on wire rack.

4. When cool, make Espresso Topping: Mix all ingredients in medium bowl until smooth. Add a little more milk if mixture is too stiff. Spread on cooled brownie base.

Cocoa Butterscotch Brownies

The combination of chocolate and butterscotch makes this a dense brownie with a superb flavor.

Chocolate Layer:
2 eggs
¾ cup sugar
¾ cup all purpose flour
Dash of salt
¼ cup cocoa powder
½ cup butter
½ cup chopped pecans
1 cup semi-sweet chocolate
  chips

Butterscotch Layer:
½ cup butter, softened
1½ cups brown sugar
2 eggs, beaten
2 tablespoons vanilla
  extract
1 cup all purpose flour
Dash of salt
½ cup pecans, chopped
1 cup butterscotch chips

1. Preheat oven to 350°.

2. Prepare Chocolate Layer: Beat eggs until foamy. Stir in sugar and combine well. Add flour and salt, combining well.

3. In a small saucepan, combine cocoa powder and butter and stir over low heat until butter is melted. Add to egg mixture, combining well. Stir in chopped pecans and chocolate chips. Spread batter evenly in a greased 9x13-inch glass pan. Set aside.

4. Prepare Butterscotch Layer: Cream butter and sugar. Add eggs and vanilla, beating until well mixed. Mix in flour and salt. Add pecans and butterscotch chips. Spoon over Chocolate Layer in small spoonfuls, spreading as evenly as possible.

5. Bake for 25-30 minutes. Remove from oven and cool completely before cutting.

Summer Fruit Crisp

An exceptional dessert that is both tangy and sweet. Top it with whipped cream or vanilla ice cream to make it an event.

Serves 6-8

Filling:
1 cup sugar
1 cup water
4 tablespoons cornstarch
2 teaspoons fresh lemon juice
1 teaspoon vanilla extract
4 cups rhubarb, diced (fresh or frozen, then thawed)
1 cup strawberries, hulled and quartered
¾ cup blueberries
1½ teaspoons grated orange rind

Topping:
½ cup rolled oats
¾ cup flour
¾ cup light brown sugar, packed
6 tablespoons melted butter
1 teaspoon cinnamon

Whipped cream or vanilla ice cream (optional)

1. Preheat oven to 350°.

2. Make Filling: In a medium saucepan, combine sugar, water and cornstarch. Place over moderate heat and cook until thick and clear, stirring constantly. Remove from heat and stir in lemon juice and vanilla. Add remaining filling ingredients and mix well. Turn into an 8-inch or 9-inch square buttered baking dish.

3. Prepare Topping: In a small bowl, mix together Topping ingredients and sprinkle evenly over filling. Bake in oven for 45-55 minutes or until filling bubbles. Serve warm with whipped cream or vanilla ice cream.

Old Fashioned Apple Crisp

All of the flavor of a homemade apple pie with much less effort. Our favorite fall dessert.

Serves 6-8

5½ cups Granny Smith or
  Pippin apples, peeled
  and sliced
¼ cup water
¼ cup sugar
½ cup light brown sugar,
  firmly packed
½ teaspoon nutmeg
1 teaspoon cinnamon
¼ teaspoon salt
¾ cup flour
½ cup butter, cold
⅓ cup pecans, chopped

Vanilla ice cream
  (optional)

1. Preheat oven to 350°.

2. Place apples in an ungreased 8½ x11-inch casserole and pour water over them. Set aside.

3. Combine sugars, nutmeg, cinnamon, salt and flour. Cut in butter with a pastry blender until fine crumbs form. Stir in pecans.

4. Spoon sugar mixture evenly over apples. Cover casserole and bake 30 minutes. Uncover and bake 30 minutes longer. Serve warm with vanilla ice cream.

Fresh Peach Cobbler

A sumptuous welcome to summer!

Serves 8

2 tablespoons cornstarch
¼ cup brown sugar, packed
¼ cup honey
½ cup water
6 cups peaches, sliced
4 tablespoons butter,
   softened and divided
1½ tablespoons lemon
   juice
1 cup flour
1 cup sugar
1 teaspoon baking powder
½ teaspoon salt
1 extra large egg, slightly
   beaten
1-2 tablespoons milk
   (optional)

Whipped cream

1. Preheat oven to 375°.

2. Place cornstarch, brown sugar and honey in a medium saucepan. Gradually add water, stirring constantly until smooth. Cook over moderate heat until thickened, stirring constantly. Add peaches and boil 1 minute.

3. Remove from heat and add 2 tablespoons of the butter and the lemon juice. Stir until butter is melted. Pour mixture into a buttered 9x13-inch baking dish.

4. Combine flour, sugar, baking powder, salt, remaining 2 tablespoons butter and egg, beating until well mixed and smooth. (If mixture is too dry, add 1-2 tablespoons of milk to obtain desired consistency.) Drop by tablespoons over the hot peach mixture.

5. Bake for 60 minutes. Serve warm with whipped cream.

Strawberry Rhubarb Crunch

Sweet, tangy and crunchy all at once, this is truly an exceptional dessert.

Serves 8

1 cup flour
¾ cup rolled oats
1 cup brown sugar, packed
½ cup butter, melted
1 teaspoon cinnamon
1 cup sugar
2 tablespoons cornstarch
1 cup water
1 teaspoon vanilla extract
3 cups fresh or frozen
  defrosted rhubarb,
  chopped
1 cup frozen strawberries,
  thawed

Whipped cream

1. Preheat oven to 350°.

2. Mix flour, oats, brown sugar, butter and cinnamon together until crumbly. Press ½ of mixture into bottom of a 9-inch square baking pan.

3. Mix sugar, cornstarch, water and vanilla extract in a medium saucepan. Cook over medium heat, stirring constantly, until thick and clear, about 5 minutes. Set aside.

4. Toss rhubarb and strawberries together gently. Place tossed fruit over the crumb mixture in the prepared pan. Pour cornstarch mixture over fruit and top with remaining crumbs.

5. Bake approximately 1 hour or until crisp. Serve with whipped cream.

Blackberry Peach Crisp

The combination of blackberries and peaches makes a delightfully old fashioned summer dessert. A real favorite!

2 cups blackberries, picked over and rinsed

1½ pounds peaches, peeled, pitted and cut into ½-inch wedges

1 tablespoon cornstarch

2 tablespoons fresh lemon juice

⅓ cup sugar

⅔ cup all purpose flour

¾ cup light brown sugar, firmly packed

½ cup rolled oats

½ teaspoon salt

1¼ teaspoons cinnamon

½ teaspoon nutmeg

6 tablespoons unsalted butter, cold and cut into bits

¾ cup pecans, lightly toasted and coarsely chopped

Vanilla ice cream

1. Preheat oven to 375°.

2. In a large bowl, toss the blackberries and peaches gently with cornstarch, lemon juice and sugar until the mixture is combined well.

3. In a small bowl, stir together the flour, brown sugar, oats, salt, cinnamon and nutmeg. Cut in butter, blending the mixture until it resembles coarse meal. Stir in the pecans.

4. Spread the peach mixture in a 9x13-inch baking dish. Sprinkle the pecan mixture evenly over peaches, and bake the crisp in the middle of the oven for 40-45 minutes or until the top is golden. Serve the crisp warm with vanilla ice cream. May also be served at room temperature.

Maple-Topped Apple Cranberry Crisp

The tangy cranberries together with the maple whipped cream is a delightful departure from the usual apple crisp.

Serves 8-10

Crisp:
1 cup rolled oats
¾ cup unbleached all-purpose flour
¾ cup dark brown sugar, firmly packed
1 teaspoon cinnamon
½ teaspoon salt
¼ teaspoon nutmeg
½ cup cold unsalted butter, cut into pieces
¾ cup walnuts, chopped

Filling:
8 large tart green apples, peeled, cored and cut into ¼-inch slices
1⅓ cups cranberries
⅓ cup sugar
2 tablespoons fresh lemon juice

Maple Whipped Cream:
1 cup whipping cream
1 tablespoon pure maple syrup

1. Preheat oven to 375°. Butter a 9x13-inch pan.

2. Mix first 6 ingredients in a small bowl. Cut in butter until mixture resembles coarse meal. Stir in walnuts. Cover and refrigerate. (Mixture may be prepared 1 day ahead.)

3. Combine apples, cranberries, sugar and lemon juice in a large bowl; toss gently. Transfer fruit to prepared dish. Sprinkle refrigerated topping over fruit.

4. Cover with foil and bake 20 minutes. Uncover and continue baking until apples are tender and topping browns, about 40 minutes. Cool slightly.

5. Prepare Maple Whipped Cream: In a large bowl, whip cream to soft peaks. Beat in 1 tablespoon of syrup. Taste, adding more maple syrup if sweeter flavor is desired. Continue whipping to firm peaks.

6. Spoon crisp into bowls. Top each with a dollop of Maple Whipped Cream and serve.

Cherry Cobbler

Guaranteed to please your guests.

Serves 6

3 16-ounce cans tart pie
  cherries, drained
1 cup plus 2 tablespoons
  sugar, divided
¼ cup brown sugar, packed
2 tablespoons minute
  tapioca
½ teaspoon almond extract
1½ cups all-purpose flour,
  sifted
2 teaspoons baking powder
½ teaspoon salt
6 tablespoons butter, cold
  and divided
1 egg
⅓ cup milk
½ teaspoon nutmeg

Vanilla ice cream
  (optional)

1. Preheat oven to 400°.

2. Combine cherries, 1 cup granulated sugar, brown sugar, tapioca and almond extract. Allow this to stand while preparing batter.

3. In a medium bowl, mix together flour, baking powder and salt. Cut 4 tablespoons of the butter into small pieces and add to flour mixture. Using a pastry blender or 2 knives, blend the butter into the flour until fine crumbs form.

4. In a small bowl, beat the egg and add the milk. Make a well in the flour mixture and add the egg mixture. Stir just until blended and a soft dough forms.

5. Pour the cherry mixture into a 9x9-inch pan. Dot with the 2 remaining tablespoons of butter. Drop the batter on top of the cherries in 6 equal mounds.

6. In a small bowl, combine the 2 remaining tablespoons of granulated sugar with the nutmeg. Sprinkle on top of batter and cherries.

7. Bake for 25-30 minutes or until the fruit is bubbling up around the middle and edges of the pan and the dumplings are golden brown. Serve warm or at room temperature accompanied by vanilla ice cream, if desired.

Malibu Mud Pie

The fudge sauce makes this mud pie rival any found in the best ice cream parlors.

Serves 8

Pie:
¼ cup melted butter
1 cup chocolate wafer
   cookies, crushed
½ gallon high quality
   coffee ice cream,
   softened or 1 quart
   coffee ice cream and 1
   quart vanilla Swiss
   almond, layered,
   softened

Fudge Sauce:
½ cup unsalted butter
1⅔ cups powdered sugar
6 ounces semi-sweet
   chocolate chips
⅓ cup evaporated milk
¼ teaspoon salt
⅛ cup coffee liqueur

Whipped cream
Sliced almonds

1. Mix together butter and cookie crumbs and press into a 9-inch pie plate. Cover with ice cream and freeze until ice cream is firm.

2. Prepare Fudge Sauce: Heat water in a double boiler until boiling. Place top of double boiler over water. Melt the butter and sugar in the top of the double boiler. Add the chocolate chips and milk; it is not necessary to mix them in. Cover tightly and continue to cook over boiling water for exactly 30 minutes, leaving the lid in place during the whole time. Remove from heat, stir until smooth and add salt and liqueur. Refrigerate until cold.

3. Spread Fudge Sauce on top of firm ice cream. Freeze pie for 10-12 hours and top with whipped cream and sliced almonds for garnish.

Note: Fudge Sauce is an excellent accompaniment for other ice cream dishes or may be packaged for gifts. This recipe makes 1½ cups. Store in refrigerator.

Frozen Almond Butterscotch Balls

This is a delicious "make ahead" dessert. The butterscotch sauce is wonderful with other ice cream desserts as well.

Serves 8

Ice Cream Balls:
1 quart vanilla ice cream
1 cup almonds, toasted
 and chopped

Butterscotch Sauce:
1 pound light brown sugar
2 cups white corn syrup
1 cup butter
1 cup whipping cream

1. Make balls of ice cream with a scoop. Quickly roll them in almonds. Place them in muffin tins or pie plate and freeze.

2. Prepare Butterscotch Sauce: Mix brown sugar and corn syrup in a large saucepan. Over medium heat, bring to boil and boil 5 minutes. Remove from heat. Add butter. Stir occasionally while cooling to keep crust from forming. When cool, add whipping cream.

3. To serve, place 2 or 3 ice cream rounds in each individual dessert dish and top with Butterscotch Sauce.

Celebrity Mocha Freeze

Easy, yet sophisticated.

Serves 8-10

6 ounces semi-sweet
 chocolate chips
¾ cup almonds
1 pint whipping cream
⅓ cup brandy
⅔ cup chocolate syrup
1 quart coffee ice cream,
 softened

Whipped cream and
 chocolate shavings for
 garnish (optional)

1. In a blender or food processor, coarsely chop chocolate chips and almonds.

2. In a large bowl, mix whipping cream, brandy and chocolate syrup. Beat until thickened but not stiff. Fold in ice cream, chopped chocolate and almonds.

3. Freeze, uncovered, until solid on top but still soft inside. Remove from freezer. Stir well to bring chips and almonds up from bottom of bowl. Cover and freeze until solid. Mixture will keep in the freezer for several months..

4. To serve, spoon frozen mixture into individual serving dishes and garnish with whipped cream and chocolate shavings, if desired.

Frozen Lemon Cream with Raspberry Puree

Serves 10-12

Crust:
1 package graham cracker crumbs
6 tablespoons butter, melted

Lemon Cream:
3 cups whipping cream
½ cup fresh lemon juice
1¼ cups sugar
3 tablespoons lemon peel, grated

Topping:
6 ounces frozen raspberries
¾ cup water
½ cup sugar

Whipped Cream (optional)

1. Preheat oven to 350°.

2. Prepare Crust: Combine graham cracker crumbs and melted butter. Pat onto bottom and 1 inch up sides of a 10-inch springform pan. Bake for 10 minutes. Cool.

3. Prepare Lemon Cream: Mix whipping cream, lemon juice, sugar and lemon peel until blended and slightly thickened. Pour into springform pan and cover with foil. Freeze overnight or up to 1 month. Do not thaw before serving.

4. To serve, remove sides of springform pan. Make Topping: Puree raspberries together with water and sugar. Spread Topping over center of pie or cut individual slices and spoon over each slice. Garnish with whipped cream, if desired.

Crunchy Chocolate Tortoni

Serves 12

8 ounces semi-sweet
   chocolate squares
⅔ cup light or dark corn
   syrup
2 cups whipping cream,
   divided
1½ cups chocolate wafers,
   broken
1 cup walnuts, coarsely
   chopped

Chopped walnuts or
   shaved chocolate for
   garnish

1. Line 12 2½-inch muffin cups with foil liners. Set aside.

2. In a 3-quart saucepan, stir chocolate and corn syrup over low heat until chocolate melts. Stir in ½ cup whipping cream until blended. Refrigerate for 15 minutes or until cool.

3. Beat remaining cream until soft peaks form. Gently stir into chocolate mixture. Stir in wafers and nuts. Spoon into prepared muffin cups or ramekins, mounding mixture high.

4. Freeze 4-6 hours, or until firm. May be garnished with chopped walnuts or shaved chocolate. Let stand at room temperature a few minutes before serving. May be stored, covered, in a freezer for up to 1 month.

Cafe Tortoni

Little frozen treats with an excellent coffee flavor.

Makes 24

2 egg whites
2¼ teaspoons instant
   coffee
¾ cup sugar plus 1
   tablespoon sugar,
   divided
1½ cups whipping cream
1½ teaspoons vanilla
   extract
⅛ teaspoon almond extract

Toasted sliced almonds for
   garnish

1. Place paper liners in two 12-cup muffin tins. Set aside. Combine egg whites, instant coffee and 1 tablespoon sugar in a mixing bowl and whip together until stiff.

2. In another mixing bowl, whip cream until it begins to thicken. Continue whipping and gradually add ¾ cup sugar, vanilla and almond extracts. Whip until mixture is stiff. Fold whipped cream mixture into egg mixture.

3. Spoon into prepared paper liners and sprinkle with toasted almonds. Freeze and store in freezer. May also be frozen and served in small custard dishes.

Raspberry Cognac Cream Parfaits

A spectacular company dessert that is a snap to prepare.

Serves 4

8 ounces cream cheese,
  softened
⅛ teaspoon salt
4 egg yolks
½ cup sugar
2 tablespoons cognac
2 tablespoons sour cream
1 pint fresh raspberries or
  16 ounces frozen
  raspberries, defrosted

1. With a mixer or food processor, combine cream cheese and salt until smooth. Add egg yolks, 1 at a time, blending after each until mixture is smooth and creamy. Add sugar, cognac and sour cream and beat until thick and creamy. Store in refrigerator until serving time.

2. To serve, place raspberries in parfait glasses until glasses are ¼ filled. Top with cream sauce. Layer raspberries and cream sauce until glasses are full.

Note: Other fresh fruit may be substituted.

Old Fashioned Fudge

Handed down by at least two generations of a Southern California family, this is a heavenly fudge recipe that is quick and almost foolproof. It makes a great gift!

Makes 2½ pounds

12 ounces semi-sweet
  chocolate chips
1 cup margarine
7 ounces marshmallow
  creme
4½ cups sugar
12 ounces evaporated milk
2 cups walnuts, chopped
1 teaspoon vanilla extract

1. Place the chocolate chips, margarine and marshmallow creme in a large bowl. Set aside.

2. In a large heavy saucepan or Dutch oven, cook the sugar and milk over moderate heat, stirring constantly until a candy thermometer reaches 237° (soft ball stage). It will need to be at a rolling boil for about 5 minutes. Remove from heat.

3. Pour the hot milk mixture over the chocolate mixture. Stir until fudge is well combined and has lost its initial sheen. Add the nuts and vanilla.

4. Pour into a 9x13-inch pan and let cool at room temperature. Cut into cubes and refrigerate until ready to serve.

German Chocolate Fudge

Makes 5 pounds

12 ounces semi-sweet
    chocolate chips
12 ounces sweet German
    chocolate, broken into
    pieces
7 ounces marshmallow
    creme
4 cups sugar
2 tablespoons butter or
    margarine
13 ounces evaporated milk
Pinch of salt
1 teaspoon vanilla extract
2 cups chopped pecans

1. Combine chocolate chips, German chocolate and marshmallow creme in a large bowl; set aside.

2. Combine sugar, butter, milk and salt in a heavy skillet. Bring to a rapid boil, then boil 6 minutes, stirring constantly. Add vanilla.

3. Pour hot butter mixture over chocolate mixture in a large bowl. Stir with a wooden spoon until smooth. Add nuts and mix well. Spread fudge in a 15½x10½x2-inch jellyroll pan. When cool, cut into squares

Anna's Chocolate Bark

One bite and you're hooked!

1 package graham crackers
    (40 unsalted saltines
    may be substituted)
2 cups butter
1 cup brown sugar, packed
12 ounces semi-sweet
    chocolate chips
1 cup pecans, coarsely
    chopped

1. Preheat oven to 400°. Line a 17x11x1-inch cookie pan with heavy duty foil; butter foil.

2. Place crackers in a single layer to cover bottom of pan.

3. Melt together butter and brown sugar in a heavy saucepan over moderate heat; bring to a boil. Boil for 3 minutes, stirring constantly. Remove from heat and pour over crackers, covering evenly. Bake for 3 minutes. Mixture will be hot and bubbling.

4. Remove from oven and sprinkle chocolate chips evenly over top. Let melt and spread to cover crackers. Sprinkle pecans over chocolate and press in gently. Refrigerate until solid. Break into pieces.

Tinseltown Toffee

Outstanding!

Makes 1½ pounds

1 cup sugar
1 cup butter
3 tablespoons water
1 teaspoon vanilla extract
7 ounces Hershey Special
    Dark chocolate candy
    bar
1 cup pecans, finely
    chopped

1. Line a baking sheet with foil measuring approximately 13x17-inches.

2. Combine sugar, butter, water and vanilla in a heavy saucepan. Cook over low heat, stirring constantly until light brown and hard crack stage (290-300° on a candy thermometer.) Pour toffee onto foil, spreading smoothly and quickly into a 6x12-inch rectangle. Cool. Carefully transfer candy to waxed paper. It breaks easily.

3. Melt half of the candy bar and spread on top of the toffee. Sprinkle with ½ cup pecans, pressing into chocolate firmly. Refrigerate until set. Melt the other half of the candy bar. Turn toffee over and spread remaining chocolate over surface. Sprinkle with remaining pecans, pressing into chocolate firmly. Cool and break into pieces.

Note: Recipe is easily doubled and may be packaged for gifts.

Double Chocolate Pecan Clusters

Makes 3 dozen

⅓ cup butter or margarine
6 ounces semi-sweet
    chocolate chips
4 ounces large
    marshmallows, about 16
1 tablespoon cocoa powder
2 cups coarsely chopped
    pecans

1. In the top of a double boiler set over simmering water, melt butter, chocolate and marshmallows. Cook, stirring occasionally, until chocolate and marshmallows are well blended; stir in cocoa powder. Remove pan from heat; stir in pecans.

2. Line 2 cookie sheets with wax paper. Drop pecan mixture by rounded teaspoonsful onto wax paper. Refrigerate about 2 hours until very firm. Store in a covered container.

Pecan Penuche

A creamy candy full of crunchy pecans.

2 cups dark brown sugar,
  firmly packed
¾ cup milk
⅛ teaspoon salt
¼ cup unsalted butter, at
  room temperature
2 teaspoons vanilla extract
1½ cups pecans, coarsely
  chopped

1. Butter an 8-inch square pan. Set aside. In a large, heavy saucepan, combine sugar, milk and salt. Cook over moderate heat, stirring constantly, until the mixture comes to a boil. Continue cooking, without stirring, until mixture reaches soft ball stage (236° on a candy thermometer). Remove the pan from heat and stir in butter and vanilla. Cool candy to lukewarm (110°).

2. With a wooden spoon, beat the candy until it becomes thick and begins to lose its gloss. Quickly stir in pecans. Pour the candy into prepared pan and cool on a wire rack. Cut into squares when firm and completely cool.

Note: Candy is best made on a day that is not damp or raining. If dampness is unavoidable, cook candy to 240° and refrigerate after cooling on a wire rack if candy does not become firm.

Individual Chocolate Soufflés with Chocolate Kahlúa Sauce

Impressive to even the most discriminating guest. These can be made a day ahead.

Serves 8

Soufflés:
8 ounces semi-sweet
  chocolate, chopped
1 tablespoon unsalted
  butter
1 tablespoon all purpose
  flour
½ cup milk
3 egg yolks
1 teaspoon vanilla extract
4 egg whites
⅛ teaspoon cream of tartar
¼ cup sugar
2 to 3 tablespoons
  powdered sugar for
  dusting

Chocolate Kahlúa Sauce:
4 squares unsweetened
  chocolate
1 cup water
½ cup sugar
2 tablespoons Kahlúa

1 cup whipping cream,
  sweetened and whipped

1. Preheat oven to 375°. Lightly butter eight 6-ounce ramekins or custard cups and dust with granulated sugar. Place on a baking sheet and set aside.

2. Melt the chocolate in a double boiler or in a microwave. Stir until smooth. Set aside and cool.

3. In a small saucepan, melt the butter over low heat. Stir in the flour and cook until thickened, but not browned, 1 to 2 minutes. Add the milk and whisk until smooth and thick, about 3 minutes. Remove from heat and add the melted chocolate, whisking until smooth. Whisk in egg yolks and vanilla and set aside.

4. In a medium bowl, beat egg whites and cream of tartar until soft peaks form. Gradually sprinkle the sugar on top and beat at high speed until egg whites are stiff but not dry. With a spatula, fold ¼ of egg white mixture into chocolate mixture to lighten it, then fold in remaining whites. Spoon mixture into prepared ramekins, filling them about ¾ full (Soufflés can be prepared to this point up to 1 day ahead; cover and refrigerate.)

5. Bake the soufflés 15-17 minutes until puffed and slightly cracked and a tester inserted in the middle indicates soufflés are moist but not runny.

6. Prepare Chocolate Kahlúa Sauce: Melt the chocolate with the water over low heat. Add the sugar and stir until it is dissolved. Bring the sauce to a simmer and stir continuously for 2 minutes.

7. Remove pan from heat and let sauce cool briefly. Add Kahlúa and stir well.

8. Dust soufflés with powdered sugar. After dusting, make a hole in the middle of each soufflé with the end of a wooden spoon. Spoon in a small amount of the sweetened whipped cream, top with Chocolate Kahlúa Sauce, then more whipped cream.

Classic Cream Puffs

These require a little extra effort, but the end result is worth it!

Makes 18 cream puffs

Cream Puff Dough:
½ cup butter
1 cup boiling water
1 cup flour
½ teaspoon salt
4 eggs

Cream Filling:
1 cup sugar
⅓ cup flour
⅛ teaspoon salt
2 eggs, lightly beaten
2 cups milk
1 teaspoon vanilla extract
1 tablespoon butter

Cream Puff Frosting:
1 square unsweetened
   chocolate (or 2
   tablespoons cocoa)
1½ tablespoons butter
1 cup powdered sugar,
   sifted
2-3 tablespoons boiling
   water

1. Preheat oven to 375°.

2. Combine butter with boiling water in a medium saucepan and bring to a boil. When mixture reaches a full boil, add the flour and salt all at once. Beat vigorously with a spoon until the dough is smooth. Remove from heat and add the eggs 1 at a time, stirring well after each addition.

3. Drop by teaspoonfuls onto greased cookie sheets approximately 2 inches apart. Shape the dough into peaks in the center and round at the bottom. Bake for 10 minutes. Reduce heat to 350° and bake 25 minutes more. Remove to rack and cool.

4. Meanwhile, prepare Cream Filling: Use a double boiler to combine sugar, flour and salt. Gradually add the eggs and milk. Place over boiling water and cook for approximately 15 minutes, stirring constantly until thickened. Remove from heat and stir in vanilla and butter. Cool.

5. Prepare Cream Puff Frosting: Melt chocolate and butter in a small saucepan, stirring constantly until smooth.

6. With a wire whisk, blend in the powdered sugar and water, whisking until smooth. Add additional water if thinner consistency is desired.

7. To assemble, cut top off cream puff and fill with 2 tablespoons of Cream Filling. Replace top and frost with Cream Puff Frosting.

Note: This is also an excellent frosting or topping on a bundt or tube cake.

Coconut Cracker Pudding

This unusual dessert is especially good sprinkled with nutmeg or sliced ripe bananas.

Serves 6-8

1 quart of milk
2 egg yolks
⅔ cup sugar
2 cups broken saltine
   crackers (not crumbs)
1 cup flaked coconut
1 teaspoon vanilla extract
2 egg whites, stiffly beaten

Nutmeg or sliced bananas
   (optional)

1. Prepare and assemble all ingredients so that they are close at hand.

2. In a Dutch oven or 5-quart pan, heat the milk over high heat until almost to the boiling point.

3. In a separate bowl, beat the egg yolks and sugar together until light in color. Gradually add to the hot milk. Reduce heat to medium. Add the crackers to the milk and stir constantly until the mixture comes to a boil. Add the coconut and stir until the pudding thickens and bubbles (about 3 minutes). Remove from heat and add vanilla. Fold in the egg whites.

4. To serve, spoon into individual dessert dishes. Top with a sprinkle of nutmeg or sliced ripe bananas, if desired.

Mexican Pears

Serves 4-6

5 cups fresh ripe pears,
   peeled and sliced (about
   5 whole pears)
½ cup brown sugar, lightly
   packed, divided
¾ cup unsalted soda
   cracker crumbs
1 teaspoon cinnamon
¼ cup chopped walnuts
¼ cup melted butter or
   margarine
3 tablespoons Kahlúa

1. Place sliced pears in an 8-inch microwave safe dish. Sprinkle ¼ cup brown sugar evenly over pears.

2. Combine cracker crumbs, cinnamon, walnuts and remaining ¼ cup brown sugar. Add butter and toss lightly to mix. Sprinkle mixture over pears.

3. Microwave on high for 10-12 minutes or until pears are tender. Turn dish after 5 minutes if microwave does not have a revolving shelf.

4. Sprinkle Kahlúa over surface and serve warm. May also be served at room temperature.

Double Baked Caramel Pears

Serves 4

3 large ripe firm Bartlett
  pears, peeled, cored and
  split lengthwise
2 tablespoons brown sugar
2 tablespoons dark rum
½ teaspoon lemon juice
1 tablespoon unsalted
  butter
13 square caramels
1 teaspoon dark rum
Cooking juices from pears
Vanilla ice cream

1. Preheat oven to 400°. In an 8-inch square baking pan, arrange pears, cut side down with tops pointing toward center. Set aside.

2. Combine brown sugar, 2 tablespoons rum, lemon juice and butter in microwaveable dish. Heat on high in microwave until butter is melted, about 30 seconds. Brush mixture over pears.

3. Bake, uncovered, until pears are just tender, 20-25 minutes, brushing with pan juices 2 times during baking. Reserve pan juices. (Pears can be baked 1 day ahead, covered and refrigerated; let come to room temperature before reheating.)

4. Melt caramels with 1 teaspoon rum and pan juices in deep microwaveable dish on medium (50% power) in microwave for 1-1½ minutes, stirring twice. Watch carefully to avoid scorching. Stir until smooth.

5. Cut pear halves lengthwise into quarters. Pour sauce evenly over pears. Bake uncovered at 300° until heated through, about 12 minutes. Spoon caramel sauce over pears once during reheating.

6. To serve, arrange 3 pear quarters in individual dessert dishes. Top with scoops of vanilla ice cream. Spoon caramel sauce over ice cream.

Bananas in Paradise

Serves 6-8

½ cup butter
1 cup dark brown sugar
1 cup dark rum
⅛ teaspoon salt
½ cup Curaçao
6 large bananas, ripe but
  firm, thinly sliced
¼ cup cognac, warmed

1 quart vanilla ice cream

1. In a large skillet over low heat, melt butter. Add sugar and stir until smooth, about 1 minute.

2. Add rum, salt and Curaçao. Increase heat and stir constantly until mixture begins to boil.

3. Add bananas. Cook, stirring constantly but gently, until mixture reaches the boiling point and bananas are tender.

4. Pour the warmed cognac over the mixture and ignite. Stir until the flame is almost extinguished. Serve in individual dessert dishes over vanilla ice cream.

Index